EFFECTIVE DISCIPLINE IN THE HOME AND SCHOOL

~ ~ ~ ~

Genevieve Painter, Ed.D.
and
Raymond J. Corsini, Ph.D.

For individual and group study
the companion book is
*An Action Guide for Effective Discipline
in the Home and School*
by Margaret Cater

ACCELERATED DEVELOPMENT INC.
Publishers
Muncie   Indiana

EFFECTIVE DISCIPLINE IN THE HOME AND SCHOOL

Technical Development: Tanya Dalton
                       Delores Kellogg
                       Marguerite Mader
                       Sheila Sheward

Cover Design: April Rutherford

Library of Congress Cataloging-in-Publication Data

Painter, Genevieve.
   Effective discipline in the home and school / Genevieve
Painter and Raymond J. Corsini
        p.   cm.
   Includes bibliographical references.
   ISBN 0-915202-89-1
   1. Discipline of children.   2. School children--Discipline.
I. Corsini, Raymond J.   II. Title
HQ770.4.P35   1989   89-84337
649'.64--dc20   CIP

LCN: 89-84337

ACCELERATED DEVELOPMENT Inc., Publishers
3400 Kilgore Avenue, Muncie, Indiana 47304
Toll Free Order Number 1-800-222-1166

DEDICATION

To Our Teacher, Rudolf Dreikurs

and

Our Families

PREFACE

This is a manual to assist teachers, counselors, and parents in training and retraining children so that the home and school will be happy and efficient, organized but pleasant—with adults who are satisfied with their children and children who are growing up to be respectful, responsible, resourceful, and responsive. We devote many pages to the solution of problems likely to arise between adults and children. We also suggest ways to make the classroom and home, in general, thrive in more harmonious atmospheres.

Too frequently schools criticize parents for sending children to them who are untrained and parents in turn criticize schools for not doing a good job. Negative blamings are not useful in raising children. Cooperation between the home and the school can greatly benefit all concerned. When a partnership exists between teachers and parents and if they use similar successful methods, then children will become happier and better prepared for life.

Too often parents and teachers feel defeated in that their goals and aspirations to have happy homes and schools seem impossible to achieve. Many good teachers leave the profession, defeated, feeling that they cannot cope with the problems of classrooms and many parents can hardly wait for the day that their children will leave the nest.

In place of discouragement, we offer hope that a general philosophy and theory of human relations, based originally on the work of the Austrian psychiatrist, Alfred Adler, which was further developed by our mutual teacher, Rudolf Dreikurs, can help establish effective families and schools in an efficient manner. We wish to encourage adults to experiment and adopt new attitudes changing from authoritarian to democratic child-rearing technology based on the central concept of Mutual Respect.

This philosophy of discipline for home and school has been found effective for tens of thousands of parents and teachers in the past seventy years since Dr. Adler began his method of dealing with discouraged adults and children. We have seen changes for the better in our own families, the families of our colleagues and clients, and in schools that have changed from authoritarian to democratic methods.

This book attempts to be a kind of cookbook, giving specific recipes for dealing with specific problems, but it also attempts to give a certain amount of necessary philosophy and theory. The section on Parenting is taken from our earlier book, *The Practical Parent*. The sections on the Adlerian Classroom and Centering are newly written to offer similar theoretical and practical ideas for schools and to incorporate a cooperative venture between home and school.

We are indebted to many people for assistance we have received in the past for the other editions, and wish to thank them again. We specifically thank Margaret Cater who has worked on materials for presentation of our Adlerian ideas to parents and teachers in study groups and for the preparation of her guide for studying this edition. A complete listing of other people, some of whom have been mentioned in previous editions of this book, is out of the question since in fact we have learned from hundreds of people—our teachers, our clients, our associates, and our friends—that which we are pleased to present to adults who are in need of some sympathetic guidance in the use of effective and efficient methods of dealing with young people.

Genevieve Painter

Genevieve Painter, Ed.D.

Raymond J. Corsini

Raymond J. Corsini, Ph.D.

October, 1989

CONTENTS

LIST OF FIGURES

Part I

EFFECTIVE DISCIPLINE IN THE HOME

A

FUNDAMENTALS OF PRACTICAL PARENTING

1

THE IDEAL FAMILY—
THE IDEAL CHILD

When Grandmother Brown got off the airplane, her husband, Val, met her.

"How are Elinor and the kids?" he asked.

"Fine," she replied, "I had a very nice stay."

"Good," Val said, but he sounded doubtful. Only the year before, their visit with their daughter Elinor, her husband, Allan, and their three children had been a disaster.

"Val, you wouldn't believe how changed those children are. I went there expecting the worst—crying, demanding, disobedient brats. I thought Elinor would be a nervous wreck. I remembered how angry Allan was with the kids. But this time it was a pleasure to be with them. You should have come."

Val Brown looked at his wife carefully. "Is that the truth?"

His wife replied, "It's like a miracle. The children were friendly, polite, affectionate, even respectful. I asked Elinor what on earth had happened.

"She said she had gone to her doctor for ulcer symptoms and she told him how she was run ragged, chasing and fighting those kids all day long. The doctor advised her to go to a Family Education Center. There she learned how to cope. In only one month, she told me—and Allan agreed with her—fighting had practically stopped, the children didn't clutter the house anymore, Dennis wasn't dawdling, Penny no longer sucked her thumb, riding in the car wasn't a horror, Harry was doing better in school—just about *everything* had changed for the better. Then things did start to go bad again, but Elinor and Allan persisted with the program. After about three months, things got straightened out again, and now they've been going well for almost a year.

"Elinor remembers how upset you were at your last visit and how you said you'd come back when the children were all grown up. But you won't have to wait that long—you'll be happy at your next visit. We were discussing it at their family council."

"Family council?" Val asked. "What's that?"

"It's how their family operates. It's a sort of democracy in the home. They have a weekly family meeting, where they discuss things, make decisions, settle problems."

"You say Dennis doesn't dawdle anymore? How on earth did they accomplish that?"

"Oh, it was simple. They stopped waiting for him. At dinner-time, instead of having to stay at the table until he ate everything, Dennis was to serve himself, taking what he wanted. After about twenty minutes, when everyone else had finished eating, they took his plate away."

"They took his food away?"

"Yes, and it worked; he eats well now. If he wasn't ready to go someplace, they just put him in the car in his pajamas and he had to dress in the car. They call it 'logical consequences.'"

Such success stories are common in our experience. Parents *do* learn to change their ways. Children *do* learn to accommodate to new parental strategies. Families do become better organized, more efficient, happier.

Of course, many systematic ways are available for dealing with family relationships and problems. The system we favor was developed by Dr. Alfred Adler, an Austrian psychiatrist who started child guidance centers in Vienna in 1922, the forerunners of the Adlerian parent education centers in the United States. Since 1922, hundreds of such Adlerian centers have been established, and tens of thousands of families have been counseled.

The essence of the Adlerian system of family relationships is respect. Parents must learn to respect themselves; they must also learn to respect their children.

WHAT IS RESPECT?

We all know the meaning of this word in its usual sense. In what sense are we using it with regard to family relations? What is disrespectful parent behavior?

In our judgment, generally, parents are disrespectful when they

> tell children what or how much to eat (except, of course,
>   for poisonous substances),
> do work that the children should do for themselves,
> scold children,
> punish them,
> reward them,
> nag them,
> caution them repeatedly about the same things,
> clean up after them,
> censor their friendships,
> control their money,
> permit them to dawdle,
> interfere in their schoolwork, and/or
> repeat orders.

OUR IDEAL CHILD

Individual Psychology, the school of thought established by Dr. Alfred Adler, stresses human dignity and freedom. Our approach stresses consideration for both children and parents. We believe that functioning as a parent can be the most exciting and rewarding part of life. Alas, only too often parents find that their children cause them a great deal of difficulty. More than any other single factor, quarrels about children disturb marriages—more than problems about money, sex, or in-laws.

Although parents want good children, they usually do not know how to train them. Over the years, in dealing with thousands of parents, we have found that almost all of them agree that the ideal child should have what we call the four R's: respect, responsibility, resourcefulness, and responsiveness.

Respect

Our ideal child is considerate about the feelings of others and treats them fairly. The ideal child does not permit others to mistreat him or her.

Children become respectful when treated respectfully.

Responsibility

Our ideal child contributes to the family well-being and is helpful in the home, does chores without needing reminding, participates willingly in family life, and does not act like a prince or princess who expects service.

Children become responsible by being given responsibility.

Resourcefulness

Our ideal child takes care of self, can entertain self, can meet new people and new situations, is independent, and is self-reliant.

Children become resourceful if permitted
to solve life's problems.

Responsiveness

Our ideal child is friendly, affectionate, and loving; likes adults; and is a pleasure to be near; and is one who enjoys life. As part of the family, he/she receives love and reaches out to give love to others.

*Children become responsive when treated
fairly with love and respect.*

If children are consistently treated in respectful ways as responsible people, if they are required to use their own resources to solve their problems, and if attitudes of parents are friendly and loving, children will achieve the four R's. Angry, rebellious, uncooperative, hostile, or vengeful children are usually the result of a lack of parental know-how. Many parents simply don't know how to handle their jobs. They don't understand the child. They don't understand human behavior. They have incorrect concepts about discipline and training.

2

FUNDAMENTALS OF CHILD DEVELOPMENT

HOW PERSONALITY DEVELOPS

A child inherits certain propensities, lives in a particular environment, observes what goes on about him or her, and interprets those observations accurately or erroneously—*in his or her own unique way.* The child interacts with, and adapts to, members of the family. Through experience the child discovers which actions succeed and which ones fail.

Family Constellation

Children have special positions within the family, and these play a significant part in the growth of their personality. The family begins with a couple. The first child usually receives much attention—gets much and gives little. When the second baby is born, all intra-family relationships change. The "first" baby becomes the old one and must establish self in a new position. The newborn is now the "baby" of the family, but this position differs from that formerly held by the child who entered the family first. And the parents now must deal with *two* children.

With each new baby the family constellation becomes bigger and more complex, with the wider range of interactions and a new position for each child. As the family constellation changes, a place is found in each person's own way. An older child may strive to stay ahead of the baby, or he may give up. A second child may resent the first and may try to surpass the other or may give up. Not all first-born children run to keep ahead of the others, and not all last children remain "babies" always in need of help. Each child tries to gain recognition in some way. If a first child does well academically, a second may cede school to the older child and may become the most charming family member. Or the second child may become the most ambitious child, seeking to surpass all the others.

The child's "life style" is determined by experiences and interpretations of them. "Who am I? What is my place?" The child may conclude: "I have a place only if I am on top—or am always right—or am treated as a prince or princess—or always please others." These responses are basic mistakes because they spring from mistaken attitudes.

Desire for Competence

Babies strive to grasp a spoon. Once they have it, they wave the spoon in great glee. We note a similar "drive for competency" in people who work for years to receive a diploma, promotion, or pension. This drive—to become smarter, more attractive, more competent—is a basic force that pushes people into action. It is an inherent motivation, the urge to move from minus to plus.

Desire to Belong

Most children also want to find a secure place within their family and within society. Children generally have a strong impulse to identify with others. This is a basic urge; to be part of a group, a community—to *belong*.

Conflict of Directions

The desire for competence and the desire for belonging may pull a child in different directions at the same time. The search for competence elicits competitiveness and a desire for superiority—feelings that can corrode a sense of belonging to a group. Some children become power-seekers, wanting always to be first, to be best, to be dominant. Other children show an urgent desire to be liked by being excessively pleasing and charming. Often domineering children make few friends, while children who try always to please may become angry if their efforts go unnoticed or may behave like "martyrs" who feel misunderstood and mistreated.

Social Interest

Adler called the feeling of belonging to others while at the same time feeling good about oneself *social interest.* Children with social interest recognize that their family is devoted to them, likes them, and has confidence in them. They each feel: "These are my people and I feel equal to them." At the same time each feels: "I am an O.K. person; I like myself, and I can do things for myself and for others." These children will work toward the good of the whole family. The same attitudes will later determine their roles and behaviors in adult society.

Parental Guidance

The wise parent understands that children operate to improve their status while at the same time they respond to the needs of others because they wish to belong. The wise parent allows children sufficient latitude to develop without letting them encroach upon the rights of others.

Children's Goals

Parents can be successful guides for their children's development if they understand the goals of child behavior. An encouraged child who has faith in self and in others holds cooperation as a goal of behavior. But a discouraged child who feels unfairly treated, whether because of overindulgence or overrepression and punishment, refuses to cooperate. Instead of pursuing useful goals, he or she may seek useless ones. Dreikurs and Soltz (1964) categorized these useless goals as follows:

1. Excessive **attention**—wanting to keep everyone busy with him or her, requesting special services, clowning, and/or being a nuisance.

2. **Power** through negativism—trying to show everyone that he or she will not do what is asked.

3. **Revenge** through disobedience and other misbehavior, including delinquent behavior.

4. **Inadequacy**—playing the baby, acting as though worthless, incapable, hopeless.

Children's misbehavior may result from pursuit of one or more of these four goals. Usually they are not precisely aware of what they want to achieve. They may be misbehaving to get *attention,* or to demonstrate his/her *power.* Or the behavior may be a *revenge* tactic, which says in effect, "I can hurt you by not doing what you request." Or it may be manifestation of *inadequacy,* which purports to say, "It's not my fault; I just can't stop doing it."

You can tell which goals your children are seeking by their behavior if you will examine your own feelings in reaction to each behavior:

1. If you feel annoyed or smothered by your child's requests, the goal is probably *excessive attention.*

2. If you feel anger or resentment, the goal is likely to be *power.*

3. If you feel hurt and upset by your child's behavior, the goal may well be *revenge.*

4. If you feel helpless when confronted by your child's apparent inabilities, the goal of the behavior is quite probably a defensive, *assumed inadequacy.*

Development of the Will

Good physical development, emotional stability, mental prowess and spiritual enlightenment are not only essential to the child's well-being, but they enable the child to start learning to exercise will—inner motivation for self-discipline and his ability to manifest ideas and visions.

The ability to sit still and complete a task can be learned as part of the development of the will. Children need to feel a sense of order within the family atmosphere in order to develop purpose. You can discourage your baby from flitting from one activity to another by limiting the number of toys available to the baby at one time. Simply say, "Let's finish with this game (or toy) first and then we'll play with the other one." As your child gets older, extend this by encouraging the completion of one task before starting another and to plan the daily sequence of events. The development of the will is what instills the inner motivation for successful living.

3

DEMOCRACY— NOT AUTHORITARIANISM

Many parents try to operate under an authoritarian system—"You do what I say or else!" But in today's environment the child often rebels and will do what the parents wish only under compulsion. Indeed, more and more children refuse to obey arbitrary rules regardless of the severity of punishment. This angers authoritarian parents, and sometimes a result is a "battered child syndrome," in which the child gets beaten with such harshness as to land in the hospital.

What is required is not the assertion of authority but the establishment of mutual respect! Parents must respect children—give them freedom of action, consider their wishes, grant them independence, and no longer regard them as property. Parents also must respect themselves and require respect from their children: *Respect demands respect.*

Although love is the primary bond between parents and children we also must emphasize respect. Love will be even stronger when relationships between parents and children are mutually respectful. A loving parent can damage a child through disrespectful behavior. Because of love, parents often overprotect and shelter a child from valuable experiences. But this cannot happen when respect is the primary bond between them. Respect cannot harm.

DEMOCRACY

We suggest that parent-child relationships should catch up with our political ideals and be based on equality. We advocate that the family become, insofar as feasible, a democracy. In Figure 3.1 is a list of statements that reflect authoritarian and democratic attitudes.

Does this mean that every issue has to be voted on? No: Voting does not work in family affairs because someone loses. Rather than majority rule, what is needed is consensus. Unanimity must be sought on all issues. Reasoning—explanation and discussion—should always be the order of the day.

Does this mean that the parent cannot say "No"? That the parent loses all authority? Again the answer is *no*. Parents *do* have responsibilities, and they do have authority. A parent should take a knife or a bottle of poison away from a child who may be incompetent to judge the danger. Parents have responsibilities to laws, to the rest of the family, to their own conscience, to their financial situation—and they must respect their own rights.

The democratic system of child-rearing advocated by us has these features:

1. Equality of all members of the family, each contributing to the family in proportion to the individual's ability.

2. An orderly way of functioning established democratically through discussions.

3. The inviolability of certain rights of the individual, such as privacy and self-determination in personal areas.

Authoritarian	Democratic
Stop!	Let's think about this and talk it over.
Watch yourself!	I think that's dangerous.
Because I say so!	Let's discuss it.
Come in at once.	We agreed this would be the time to come in.
Take your medicine.	Doctor says you need this medicine.
Go to bed right now!	Let's figure a good time to go to bed.
You do the chores I assigned you or you get a licking.	Let's plan chores together.
Because you are fighting, go to your room.	I'm leaving. I'll come back when you kids stop fighting.
Eat what I put on your plate.	Take what you want.
Wake up right now!	Here's an alarm clock for you.
Wear what I tell you.	I feel uncomfortable when you wear that.
Take a bath; you smell!	When you smell bad, you may not stay near me.
Do your homework!	Your schoolwork is up to you.

Figure 3.1. Statements reflecting attitudes.

4. Straight and honest dealings between family members.

5. No forcing of one person's will upon another.

6. No harsh punishments.

7. No manipulations, such as bribes and blackmail.

8. Family relationships based on logic and reason.

9. Logical and natural consequences as a major training method (see Chapter 5).

10. Mutual respect among parents and children.

11. Parents who are friendly but at the same time firm with their children.

12. A unanimous, harmonious effort for mutual as well as individual goals.

ATTITUDES

We'd like you, the parent, to adopt four attitudes and follow through with related behaviors.

Have Confidence in Children.

Some parents see children as inadequate, weak, dangerous, self-destructive—they think that unless children are constantly watched they will perish. Overfearfulness is harmful to children. The "good mother syndrome" in exaggerated form is decidedly ineffective.

Stop Pampering

A closely related and equally erroneous parental failing is to give children constant attention and service. Spoiling is harmful to children—it gives them an incorrect view of life and makes them dependent and demanding.

Stop Overestimation

Some parents overestimate their children, thinking that they are the smartest, the cutest, the best. Such parents often expect their children to be given preferred treatment. Such overestimation is harmful to them.

Stop Oversupervision

Some parents believe that they should always know what their children are doing—that they should hover over them, watching them constantly. Such parents monitor their friends, check their schoolwork, etc. They attempt virtually total surveillance. Needless to say, such smothering is harmful.

CHECK POINTS

To see where you are at this point, check your reactions to the following:

1. To be a parent is an exciting, wonderful adventure.

2. I will do all I can to help my children grow up to be healthy, efficient, happy.

3. I respect each of my children's individuality and uniqueness.

4. I am willing to give my children as much freedom of choice and action as is consistent with their survival.

5. I will avoid doing things "for their benefit" that may result in their feeling that I am unfair.

6. I view them as my equals; but I know they are immature, and I stand ready to direct and guide them in a friendly manner.

7. I must be tolerant—after all, they are children and will act and think like children.

8. I realize that I do not own them but have only temporary custody of them.

9. I accept that I should become unnecessary to them as soon as possible so that they can go into the world on their own.

OUR CHILDREN, OUR BEST TEACHERS

We generally believe that we are our children's teachers and, of course, we are. But just think of how much our children actually teach us: patience, love, how to play, the need for honesty and integrity—all of which helps us reach our higher potential. In our daily lives our children show us, directly or indirectly, the areas in which we need to improve. For example, when we tell our children to clean their rooms while our own rooms or offices are cluttered, we are inviting them to challenge us. If we demand that they control their temper tantrums although we ourselves yell, they may point out the obvious inconsistency. Rearing children gives us the marvelous opportunity for mutual education and the chance to reach our higher potentials.

If you agree with the statements in this chapter, all you need are some guidelines to implement the attitudes they express. You will, we hope, find these guidelines in this book.

4

REWARDS AND PUNISHMENTS: A MISTAKE

Many people believe the best way to train children is to reward them when they do something they like and punish them when they do something they don't like. And it is unquestionably true that in this way they can "shape" a child's behavior. However, *rewards and punishments can have undesired side effects.* The rewarded or punished child may become dependent and fearful, rebellious and antagonistic, sneaky and untruthful, servile and unsure.

As child-training devices, rewards and punishments have serious flaws. They are incompatible with human dignity. They show lack of respect. They glorify force and power. A reward is often a bribe; punishment is often revenge. They are examples of superior-inferior relationships.

REWARDS

The king gives his vassal a gift. A general gives a private a medal. The father gives his child a dollar. In each case a superior gives to an inferior a bounty for good behavior. The father who says, "I'll take you to the ball game if you get a haircut," is bribing his child. Mother says, "If you make your bed I'll give you a quarter." The next day the child says, "If you give me a quarter, I'll make my bed." The child thus learns to blackmail parents.

PUNISHMENTS

The king demands work from a peasant; if the latter refuses, he or she is punished. If a private goes AWOL, the general court-martials him or her. If a child does not do as ordered the child gets scolded. In each case we have a superior bossing an inferior.

Frequently, punishment is meted out simply because the parent knows no other way of dealing with the child. Punishment comes in many forms: physical abuse (slapping, spanking), verbal abuse (scolding, humiliating), deprivation (being sent to bed without dinner, not being permitted to watch television), isolation (being made to stay in one's room alone for a specific period of time), grounding (not being allowed to go out with friends), etc. A brief against punishment as a child-training method could make these additional points:

1. **Punishment is usually an arbitrary exercise of power by the parent, who alone decides whether, when, and how much to punish.** The parent becomes prosecutor, jury, judge, and warden. "Might is right," the child may conclude—power is what counts.

2. **Punishment often is not logically related to the offense.** If we tell a child that one cannot see television without washing one's hands, no logical relationship exists between the "crime" and the "punishment."

3. **Punishment creates resentments.** The child may think parents are unfair because the punishment was disproportionate to the offense.

4. **Punishment tends to create character defects.** The punished child will tend thereafter to try to avoid detection. The child may begin to be sneaky and lie.

5. **A child may lose respect for orders.** If punished too lightly, a child may try to get away with other offenses—after all, the child may reason, the penalty isn't too bad.

6. **The child may try to get even.** If one feels unfairly punished, one may try to get revenge, by hurting oneself or one's parents, or both. The so-called Samson phenomenon of punishing both oneself and others does sometimes occur with often-punished children. They may become wild, rebellious, and delinquent.

7. **The child may begin to punish also.** By punishing the child, you teach that this is a way to treat others. The child is likely to adopt punitive tactics against animals, other children, and even you, the parent.

8. **Punishment has to be discontinued eventually.** When their child reaches a certain age, parents just have to give up this procedure. An attempt by a parent to punish a big child may result in a situation very ugly for both.

9. **Punishment is not effective for the long-range most important objectives.** At the moment punishment may stop objectionable behavior. But if the child stops only because of fear of punishment the child is likely to refrain from undesirable behavior only while the fear remains. The child is not helped to develop inner control for good behavior. Parents should not merely try to stop particular forms of misbehavior; their primary, over-riding goal should be to help the child become cooperative. The punished child often develops undesirable characteristics—lying, cheating, sneaking, and is not likely to learn to cooperate for the good of all. Punishment not only exacts a heavy toll from the child but seriously disrupts family harmony.

10. **Punishment tends to become more and more severe and at the same time to become less and less a deterrent for bad behavior.** Parents who horribly mistreat their children usually do so as a result of their having ceased to fear punishment. When spanking holds no terrors for them, the parent may resort to whipping, and when this too fails to deter, may in baffled fury go to appalling lengths.

11. **Punishment may actually encourage misbehavior.** Under some circumstances a child may actually misbehave *in order to obtain punishment!* And the more often, the more quickly the parent punishes, the more often the child misbehaves.

EXAMPLES

Son Demands That Father Plays

Father is looking at a newspaper. His five-year-old son tugs at his arm and demands that Father play with him. Father says "No!" several times, but the boy keeps coming back. Finally, Father yells at him, "I swear, you're just asking for a licking!"

The child continues pulling on Father's arm and suddenly, in exasperation, Father slaps him. The child begins to screech with wild fury. Remorsefully, Father looks at his beloved five-year-old, who only wanted to play, and picks him up. "Jimmy! Quiet down. I didn't hurt you that bad. Father *loves* you. Let's play! Here is a quarter. Let's look at your comic book. I'll get on my knees and we'll play horsie."

After a while the boy's sobs slow down, his tears are dried, Father gets on his knees, and Jimmy rides on Father's back, giggling with glee.

Asking for punishment *was* worthwhile!

Does Differently Than Told

Here is an example of a situation that could be handled well or poorly. Ralph and Carol asked their son Chris to please go downstairs and put their name on a blackboard at the tennis club for 8 A.M. He agreed, and came back stating he had done this. Ralph called friends to inform them that they have the tennis court reserved. When the four adults meet the next day to play tennis, their names are not listed for 8 A.M., but for 8 P.M. The parents were furious, the guests disappointed. What to do?

Father's first reaction is to give Chris a piece of his mind; Mother's reaction is the same, although she is willing to concede he meant well, but Father believes this is another example of Chris's playing "dumb" and sabotaging his parents.

Were the parents to vent their feelings against Chris, this would be punishment, and would make him feel more inadequate, more fearful, and less inclined to do things for them. But what should be done in such situations?

Almost anything but punishment is preferable. Saying nothing would be one solution. Telling him in a humorous way what happened would be another way to handle this. What counts is that the child should not feel humiliated, alienated, or hostile. Everyone can make a mistake. The child meant well. To punish him in any manner will simply drive him underground, make him resentful, less cooperative.

Adlerians see problems—and this is an example of a problem—as opportunities. Ralph and Carol can use this situation to actually strengthen relationships—if they are wise enough to deal with it sensibly.

When an act occurs which we consider negative it helps to look for the child's *good purpose* (good intention) so that we can overcome our own anger. If we continue to be angry, the relationship worsens. In this case Chris was trying to be helpful (his *good purpose*); he carried out his parents' wishes but made a mistake. If his parents had realized that Chris was not deliberately sabotaging their tennis game, they would have been able to give up their anger much sooner and to get on with the relationship in a more constructive way. It would then be helpful for the parents to make a win/win statement (one in which each side wins): "I know you were trying to be helpful by making the appointment for us. Putting down 8 P.M., instead of 8 A.M. was only a mistake and we all make mistakes." In this statement both sides win, no one is put down, no one loses. Just think of how much better Chris might feel; he must have felt bad to have made the error. This statement would be encouraging for him and he probably would be more careful in the future.

Neither rewards nor punishments are effective training methods for today's children. The best way for a parent to correct misbehavior and yet maintain good relations is the method called *logical and natural consequences*, discussed in the next chapter.

5

NATURAL
AND LOGICAL
CONSEQUENCES

What should we do if we don't punish or reward? Parents should always try first to obtain voluntary cooperation from their children by encouragement, being cooperative themselves, and by using democratic procedures in the home. If these fail, parents should fall back on the method widely known as *natural and logical consequences. This method is in accord with reality and helps to prepare the child for the ways in which nature and society are going to react to behavior.*

NATURAL CONSEQUENCES

A woman who had been attending one of our child guidance centers summarized natural consequences thus:
"When a child does something wrong, you don't hit or scold; you do nothing. You let the situation get worse and worse until the child becomes uncomfortable or sees that the situation has become ridiculous. Finally, the child makes changes voluntarily." She was quite right: *The essence of natural consequences is to let the child learn from experience.*

Examples

A mother complains that her son is a poor eater and that she has to nag to get him to eat. We regard constant nagging as punishment. We advise her to employ natural consequences, that is, to stop her nagging and to allow him to learn by experience.

The following morning, her son rushes out to play without having eaten his breakfast. Several hours later, he is famished. He is experiencing the natural consequences of not having eaten breakfast. *She does not give him food until lunchtime.*

A toddler is intrigued with the shiny toaster and wants to handle it while Mother is using it. Mother says, "Don't touch it. It's hot." But the young master insists and gets burned. Instead of scolding or preaching, Mother merely puts ointment on the burn. He has experienced the natural consequences of his behavior.

A child insists on wearing a particularly odd article of clothing. Mother says nothing and does not interfere. The child goes out wearing the item, but returns within a few minutes and removes it because other children laughed.

A child straps on his skates incorrectly. Father points out the error, but the son thinks he knows better. When he stands up, his skates fall off.

A child wants to see a late television movie. Mother points out that the child must get up early for school and won't get enough sleep. The child disagrees. Mother lets the child stay up. In the morning the child feels groggy and tired.

A boy teases his companion until the other boy hits him and leaves him.

A child refuses to clean his/her desk. The parents say nothing. Eventually, the top of the desk is completely littered, and the child does homework on the bed. This is uncomfortable, and the child cleans off the desk so it can be used.

Comments About Natural Consequences

In relying upon natural consequences, parents will discover that nature is their best ally. A child who doesn't eat gets hungry; one who plays too hard gets tired; one who forgets to take money for a school lunch goes without; one who cheats at games finds oneself without playmates; one who neglects one's homework discovers that teachers call him/her to account.

Parents must, of course, be alert to nullify any possibility of serious harm to the child. Certainly a child cannot be permitted to fall out of a window or to eat poisonous substances. Natural consequences must be used *with discretion.*

Parents have an obligation to inform this child once of the natural consequences of any specific behavior. If they keep reminding, they are either giving unwarranted service or punishing by nagging. *One such warning in a lifetime is usually enough.*

Parents should not feel that they are cruel when, within reasonable limits, they allow their child to experience the natural but unpleasant consequences of behavior. Parents should not intervene between the child and reality except in emergencies. What more can a parent do for a child than to help the child learn the consequences to be faced when the laws of nature or society are violated. In our tender youth, we came near a swarm of bees. "Don't go near them," Father warned. "They can sting!" And so we learned by sad experience a lesson that after forty years remains: bees do sting!

LOGICAL CONSEQUENCES

Natural consequences alone are not sufficient to train a child. In many cases parents must do something more. The course of action we recommend is called logical consequences. It is more effective than punishment but has none of punishment's drawbacks. It requires an understanding, expressed (preferable) or implied, between a parent and the child as to what is expected from the child and what is to happen if the child does not perform as expected or misbehaves. What happens then must be a logical consequence to the child's conduct.

Examples

Father tells his daughter that he will take her to the movies if ready by three o'clock. The child asks at four o'clock to be taken to the movies. Father simply says "You knew you were to be ready by three. Now it's four. I'm sorry. I will not take you now."

Little Bobby is whooping and hollering in the living room where Father and Mother are reading. Father says, "If you can't be quiet, go to your room." Father now has an understanding with Bobby: *If you are quiet, you may remain; if not, you must go.* Bobby continues making noise and Father says firmly but without anger, "Go to your room. Come back when you can behave yourself."

Illustrative Statements

The child is always given a choice and parents must not show anger. If the parent is angry or doesn't offer a choice, the technique is *not a consequence but is punishment, and it won't work.* The following parental statements illustrate the techniques of logical consequences:

"If you don't behave yourself at the restaurant, I will take you home."
"Unless you agree to act properly at the supermarket, I will not take you there."
"If you lose your money. I will not give you any more."
"If you break the window playing ball, you'll have to pay for a replacement."
"If you don't eat at lunchtime, you cannot eat until supper."

When the understanding is clear and consistently followed, the child cannot feel that his/her parent is being unfair and so harbors no resentment.

TECHNIQUES

Ignoring or Withdrawing

Some parents frequently find-themselves arguing with a child with the hope of stopping unwanted behavior. They do not realize that ignoring or withdrawing from a child's misbehavior is better way to teach than talking.

Let us suppose that you are reading a newspaper, like the father in the example given earlier, and that your child persists in begging you to play. You feel tired, and this is not the time for playing with you. You have already did so, but the child continues to whine. *You leave the room and go somewhere else to finish reading your paper. You withdraw from the behavior. Or suppose you are having breakfast and the children are noisy. You pick up your toast and cup of coffee and finish your breakfast in the living room. You withdraw.*

When we advise parents to withdraw from a child's tyrannical behavior, they often try to equate such withdrawal with defeat, with running away from a situation. They are wrong. Withdrawal here simply means going from a spot where there is trouble to one where there is none. It gives this message: "When I don't like *what you do,* I go away from you." When we use withdrawal as a training technique, we must be careful to indicate that we are not fleeing from the individual but rather from the *behavior.*

Leaving the child can be effective means of discouraging annoying behavior no matter what the goal may be. If the child is acting silly to get attention, if trying to initiate an argument to show power, if pretending disability in order to get you to do things, if having a temper tantrum, often all you need to do is ignore or withdraw. In this simple way you terminate the child's useless behavior and demonstrate that it will not work!

Parents often wonder why withdrawal is so effective. The child's behavior is purposive. If the child wants to get you involved against your will and you resort to punishment, you have become involved. But if you vanish, you do not become involved, and you frustrate the child's attempt to force the goal-oriented behavior on you.

Bathroom Technique

After a season of family counseling, we recently asked the assembled mothers what had impressed them most. One young mother enthusiastically stated: "The bathroom technique! It's the answer I've been seeking for years."

Suggested by Dr. Rudolf Dreikurs, the bathroom technique is almost absurdly simple: when children press you with their demands, withdraw to the one room in every household in which a person can barricade oneself—the bathroom! We recommend this technique to Mothers harassed by demanding younger children. The mother who wants to escape the tyranny of her child's demands enters the bathroom and locks the door. While there, she does not respond in any way to the child—even if the child whines, cries, screams, or hits the door. If the child continues, she turns on the radio, and the child still persists, she takes a bath! She concentrates on composing herself, but at the same time she is training her child. When all is calm, she comes out with a smile. But if the child reasserts demands or exhibits other undesired behavior, back she goes to the bathroom!

If there is only one bathroom in the house, the clever child may suddenly scream, "Wee-wee!" What should Mother do now? *She should remain in the bathroom.* The child is being trained. The message that Mother is getting across is that she will no longer take any nonsense. If the enraged child begins to hammer on the door or to break furniture, Mother should still stay in the bathroom! The event may have a powerful effect on the child; it may be a crisis that profoundly changes the perception of Mother. If Mother is foolish enough to come out when the child threatens, she loses a very effective training device. Once she has entered the bathroom, she should leave only when she is ready, not when the child wants her to. She should not come out until she is calm and relaxed. The most helpful thing for her to think about her stay inside is that her child is being taught to improve behavior.

Withdraw without Rejection

It is important not to reject children when we withdraw from them. We must explain that we are withdrawing only from the behavior and not from them. Mother could say, "From now on when you misbehave at the dinner table, I am going to leave and eat in my room because I can't enjoy my food when people are noisy or run around. However, when you are ready to behave you can come and get me and I'll be glad to rejoin you." Mother would then leave if the children misbehaved and return to the table when they told her that they were ready to behave well. If after she returned they began to misbehave again, she would then silently leave the table, go to her room, and not come out until she had finished her meal.

The key to not rejecting children is always to let them know that they are in control of their behavior and that when they behave well, they have access to you.

Discussion

In the following part of our book where we discuss specific problems, we will suggest a wide variety of logical consequences. We have never yet been confronted with any situation that calls for a child's punishment. All misbehavior by children can be handled best by the method of natural and logical consequences.

Parents who begin to think logically rather than punitively will begin to treat their children with respect and will be on the way to a happier family life.

6

ENCOURAGING
THE CHILD

Encouragement is the nourishment of the soul just as food is the nourishment of the body. Any uncooperative child is likely to be a discouraged one.

PITFALLS OF DISCOURAGEMENT

A discouraged person is usually convinced that he or she is not as adequate as others; often gives up without even trying.

Unwittingly, parents frequently discourage this child. Indeed, in their very attempts to encourage, they often achieve just the opposite result.

Discouraging Statements

The following are typical discouraging statements made prior to behavior:

> Don't get dirty.
> Watch yourself.
> You aren't old enough.

Be careful.
Let me do it for you.
Let me show you how.
I know you can't do it.
If younger children can do it, so can you.
Look at how well your cousin does it.

The following are typical discouraging statements made after behavior:

No, that's not right.
I should not have trusted you.
You could have done better.
You should have watched me.
I've told you a thousand times.
When will you become responsible?
You did it again.
Oh, when will you learn?
I am so ashamed of you.
Haven't you any self-respect?
I'll tell your father when he gets home.
If you'd only listen to me.
If only you weren't so lazy.
You'll be sorry when I'm dead.

Normal parents who love their children frequently talk this way. They want their remarks to make them try harder. And in the immediate situation this may happen: to get the parents' approval, the child may make a special effort. However, negative parental remarks do not work in the long run. If this steady diet of such discouraging remarks continues, the child eventually feels: What's the use? I can't do things. I can't win. I can never satisfy them. Everyone does better than I do. *I won't try anymore.* The child usually feels this way unconsciously—without awareness.

ENCOURAGEMENT

Encouragement implies your faith in the child—communicates your belief in the child's strength and ability.

Parents easily see their child's weak points; they should look hard to find the strong points. No matter how trivial those may seem, it is wise to let children know they are appreciated. Sometimes we hear a parent say something such as this: "I can't see anything good about Billy; he irritates me all the time." When parents are irritated, they often have difficulty seeing the child's good qualities. At such a time, the parent needs to rise above the irritation and to say positive rather than negative things to the child. Always at least some small points exist upon which the parent can focus an encouraging remark. "You made a good try at getting your newspapers delivered on time," one mother said to her son, whom she had usually criticized for late deliveries on his paper route. The boy was faster the next day.

Dangers of Praise

Praise may or may not be encouraging. Lavish praise usually seems insincere. The child may feel unworthy of it. Praise may actually discourage a child if he or she fears that next time the child may not be able to live up to it.

One praises when a job is well done. However, when a child does poorly the child needs encouragement much more than when doing well.

For assistance on how to distinguish between praise and encouragement see Figure 6.1.

Encouragement Procedures

1. **Build on the child's strong points.** Look for good things, including efforts.

2. **Do not emphasize liabilities.** Do not criticize, nag, or complain about what should have been done.

3. **Show your appreciation.** "I do enjoy hearing the songs you sing," "I appreciate your setting the table and making the salad; it makes my dinner preparation so much easier."

4. **Be friendly.** A friend shares and listens: "You seem troubled; want to talk?" "I met Jerry's mother at the grocery today." Just sitting nearby is friendly.

5. **Show your affection.** A kiss, a hug, or an arm around the shoulder causes the child to feel that you like him or her.

6. **Suggest small steps in doing a task.** The entire job may seem too much. Give small portions of food to a finicky eater; it will be encouraging to ask for seconds.

7. **Spend time in play with the child.** Through play you can build a good relationship.

8. **Use humor.** A wiggled nose, a wink, as pun, or a laugh at oneself can warm the relationship. Always laugh *with*, never at, the child.

9. **Notice an attempt to do a job.** Recognize the effort even if the job is not well done.

10. **Become fully aware of the interaction between yourself and your child.** The child will at times provoke your anger by testing you to the limits of your endurance. At such times it is best not to show anger but just to walk away and stay away until you cool off. When both are calm, you may explain that such behavior angers you.

11. **Discipline the child in silence.** Angry words are extremely discouraging. After disciplining, resume talking or you will appear unfriendly.

12. **Mind your own business.** Learn to depend upon the method called natural consequences. Allow the child to solve problems alone. Don't be on the child's back at all times; give the child the widest latitude possible in attending to concerns and interests.

13. **Don't use rewards or punishment.** They do not encourage.

14. **Accept the child as is.** The more emphatically you do so, the more emphatically you say "I like you."

15. **Be understanding.** Try to see the world from the child's point of view. And don't forget that you can sometimes be wrong.

16. **Have faith in your child.** Who knows what your child may become? The kid who isn't doing homework, who gets into your things, who does not want to go to bed on time, who messes up the room, who fights with brothers and sisters—who knows but what that child may become a fine success someday. Author? Minister? Doctor? United States senator? President?

17. **Be an optimistic person yourself.** Children often pick up the attitudes of their parents. If you are gloomy and dissatisfied, your child may adopt your outlook. Instead of thinking: It won't work, think: Maybe it will work.

18. **Do not feel sorry for the child.** Feeling sorry for the child shows that we do not have faith in the child's ability to do things or to cope. Use the many suggestions for encouragement and the child will very soon stop being self-pitying.

Praise	Encouragement
1. Praise is given to the *doer:* "You are a good boy for drawing such a nice picture for me."	1. Encouragement is given for the *deed:* "That is a pretty picture" or "I'm sure you enjoyed drawing your picture."
2. Praise is given for work well done: What good grades you have brought home!"	2. Encouragement is also given when work is done poorly: "So what—we all make mistakes; I'm sure you'll do better next time."
3. Praise implies a demand for continued high performance.	3. Encouragement makes no demands.
4. Praise often seems phony.	4. Encouragement is sincere.
5. Praise may not increase self-esteem.	5. Encouragement fosters self-esteem.

Figure 6.1. Differences between praise and encouragement.

7

GENERAL RULES FOR CHILD TRAINING

In this chapter we give parents general rules and principles for implementing the specific recommendations we make in the chapters that follow. Here we are concerned with HOW the parent acts. In the rest of the book we are concerned primarily with WHAT the parent does. Success depends just as much on *how* you deal with children as *what* you do.

Father and Mother should read this chapter carefully and come to complete agreement about its contents. They might well read this chapter aloud, stopping to discuss each point.

FOUR FUNDAMENTAL RULES FOR DISCIPLINING A CHILD

1. **Understand** exactly what you are supposed to do. Do not tackle a problem until you really grasp the *how* and the *why* of the advice.

2. **Inform** the child, explaining clearly what you intend to do about the problem. Listen to the child's point of view and answer questions.

3. **Act** rather than talk. Silence is necessary during the disciplining. Warnings, reminders, discussions, threats about the problem are unwise.

4. **Be consistent** during the disciplining. Avoid variations and exceptions. do not let others sway you. Do not feel sorry for the child; pity will not help.

These four rules are applicable to practically every problem in nonpunitive child discipline. So, without yelling, nagging, preaching, punishing, or threatening, do exactly what you have told the child you will do, and do it consistently. Any variation is likely to necessitate a lengthening of the disciplining and may even make the training procedure fail!

Never start to discipline the child unless you are prepared to stick to the recommended procedure. You should show no anger when you explain what you are going to do or when you are doing it. The child may return your anger, and you will probably fail to effect the change you desire.

GENERAL PRINCIPLES

Of course, no substitute will do for parental common sense. The following principles are not a substitute for sound judgment, but they should be helpful if kept in mind:

When you don't know what to do, do nothing.
Treat the child with the respect that you expect.
Don't do things routinely for a child that the child can do alone.
Learn to mind your own business.
In training a child, *act* rather than talk.

WHEN PARENTS DISAGREE

"My spouse won't cooperate!"

We often hear this complaint. Most frequently the complainant is a woman who informs us that her husband is sure that he knows all the answers for family problems and that if only she will listen to him everything will be fine. Sometimes a male client informs us that his wife believes love is enough and that if he would only stop interfering things would straighten out.

WHAT TO DO IF YOUR MATE
WILL NOT GO ALONG WITH YOU

Even if your spouse does not agree with the methods we advocate, he or she may not object to your following them. If they work, your spouse will see the success you are having and is likely to adopt an approach similar to yours.

After learning our ways of operating, Milly informed her husband. He pooh-poohed them but told her that she could deal with the children in those crazy ways if she wanted to. The major problem was the children's fighting. Milly began to use our methods systematically. Gradually the children stopped their fighting when Mother was around. When Father was around, they continued fighting. Eventually Father noticed the difference. He too began to use the methods Mother was using; and, sure enough, the children stopped their bickering in his presence.

If the parents are not in a power contest with each other, if each will give the other freedom to do what the other thinks best, the family problem becomes a kind of experiment—and the better method will surface.

The better procedure, of course, is for both parents to take the same approach from the beginning. We suggest that parents read this book together, discuss its suggestions, get to understand the Adlerian theory and methods of family relationships, and then see if they can find areas of agreement so that they can as nearly as possible present a common front.

If this cannot be done but if one parent will at least permit the other to handle the children by our methods without any interference, progress will occur, though not as rapidly. But if the different approach causes dissension and if a power contest occurs between the parents that cannot be resolved peacefully, they should seek other ways to achieve family harmony. Such families need more help than a book can provide. A family counselor may be necessary.

UNEXPECTED BENEFITS

You may be wonderfully surprised to find that when you solve one problem, some other problems have automatically been solved too. When, for instance, you help your child learn to get up in the morning or to keep clean, you are taking the child and yourself into a new and better way of life where respect and reason rule. As this new regime takes over, the old negative games involving you and your children—senseless bickerings, punishments, harassments, and conflicts—will disappear. New and better family relationships will result. The home will become harmonious and orderly, with children who are cooperative and parents who are satisfied because they are successfully training their children for respect, responsibility, resourcefulness, and responsiveness.

IMPORTANT NOTICE

This is a do-it-yourself manual. Please pay special attention to the following points before going on to the next section, in which we deal with many specific problems involving children in routine family life.

VALIDITY AND PRACTICALITY

Every suggestion we make has been tested and found practical and effective over and over again in many, many families in actual life.

CONSISTENCY

For successful child-training, consistency is vital. If you decide to use our techniques, give them a chance to work; follow them all the way through, with firm, undeviating, absolute consistency.

STARTING

Do not start any procedure we recommend until you understand the theory and principles on which it is based.

COMMUNICATION

Trickery has no place in our system. You can let the children know exactly what you are reading; indeed, you should make this book available to them if it may interest them. You should tell them your objectives in training them. You also should tell them what you intend to do.

ATTITUDE

You must be firm and friendly at the same time. You respect your children and control your own temper—no nagging, no punishment, no violence!

FAILURE

If, using our methods, you fail in one problem, you should *not* tackle another one. Our methods have worked for thousands of families. If you really understood our theory, faithfully followed our instructions, and yet failed, our suggestion is that you drop this book and find a qualified family counselor.

FOLLOW THROUGH

If you do solve a problem, don't think it is settled for good. That problem is likely to recur, since children often "test" parents. We call that "the second offensive." Don't be dismayed. All is not lost. Use exactly the same tactics that worked the first time—in silence, of course (you do not have to explain again). The technique will work anew! Sometimes there may be a third occurrence—again, use the same techniques. A fourth offensive is very rare, practically unheard of. If a third or fourth offensive occurs, check your feelings. If you are acting in anger these techniques become punishment and punishment will not work.

B

PROBLEMS
OF
ROUTINE
LIVING

PRELIMINARY NOTE

We have already presented a considerable amount of material intended to help you understand the general approach to child-rearing that we recommend. Now you are ready to begin the process of actually retraining your children.

In this section, "Problems of Routine Living," we discuss six common problems: (1) getting up, (2) getting dressed, (3) eating, (4) cleanliness, (5) home-school relationships, and (6) bedtime.

So common are these problems that some parents think that every family must have them. It actually surprises some parents, for example, that bedtime need not be difficult, and that in some families an argument never occurs about eating or dressing. What a shame that so many families are never free from tension because of constant conflict in these everyday situations!

Besides their being so prevalent, why is the solving of these six problems so important? First, if you can solve any one of them, you can solve every other! Second, if you solve one, other problems may solve themselves. Third, success in handling one of these will give you self-confidence as a parent.

A final preliminary word: Pick only one problem of routine living, and work on this alone. When it is solved, and only then, begin on a second problem. Good luck!

8

GETTING UP

THE PROBLEM

"**D**id you call Harry and Ellen?" Father asked.

"Twice already," Mother replied testily as she turned over a pancake.

"It's seven-thirty. You'd better go wake them. I have to leave by eight. If they want to ride with me, they'd better get up."

"Please, *you* do it. I have my hands full. You'd think a boy of eleven and a girl of eight would be able to get up by themselves. Kids are just so spoiled nowadays!"

Father got up and climbed the stairs. he knocked at Harry's door and then opened it. The boy was sleeping, as usual face down. Father shook Harry, who opened his eyes slowly as he turned around.

"What time?" he asked sleepily.

"Almost a quarter to eight. You have to hurry." While Harry was rubbing his eyes, Father rushed to Ellen's room to repeat the same performance. He then went down to the kitchen.

"Every day we go through the same damn routine. This morning I'm leaving at 8 A.M., rain or shine, kids or no kids."

"But they can't leave without a good hot breakfast," Mother said, "and they can't walk to school today. It looks like rain."

Father sighed deeply. "I just don't know. When I was a kid, I used to walk a mile and a quarter to school. *Half* a mile is too much for *these* kids. One of these days I'll lose my job on account of being late so often."

Instead of answering, Mother went to the foot of the stairs and in a shrill voice yelled, "Hurry up, you kids! Breakfast is ready."

She then sat down to finish her breakfast with her husband, commenting grimly, "I wish I knew how some families manage to get their kids up without so much trouble every morning."

DISCUSSION

In many families such morning difficulties occur almost every day. Fathers and Mothers are tense and upset, having called their children a number of times, knocked on doors, pleaded with them to get ready, helped them to dress, argued with them that it really is time to get up, and so on. Some parents give children a great deal of service and are almost angelic in their servitude; other parents get angry and even violent. But still other parents just do not have this trouble at all. Their kids get up on their own, take care of themselves, and leave the house without difficulty.

What is the secret? Is it a matter of temperament or physiology? Is it that the children do not get enough sleep, having worked too late on homework or watched television too long? Actually, it is none of these.

Children will learn to get up on time and take care of themselves if they must face the natural consequences of being late. This means that parents must realize that getting up is the child's business—and that they must keep out of the whole matter. The child, not his or her parents, must experience the consequences of being late.

SOLUTION

We suggest the following:

1. If you think your child is old enough to use an alarm clock (usually children at five are old enough), get one and teach its use.

2. If you prefer not to use an alarm, tell your child you will call only one time in the morning.

3. Discuss the best time to be awakened, your object being to help set an awakening time that will allow just enough time to do the morning routine, dress, get breakfast, and take off for school.

4. If children sleep in separate rooms, you may want a separate alarm (or a separate call) for each room.

5. From then on, just keep out of the way. Say nothing more about getting up and see what happens, allowing the children to experience the natural consequences of oversleeping.

APPLICATION TO HARRY AND ELLEN'S PROBLEM

The parents had a discussion with their children.

"From now on, getting up in the morning will be *your* problem. Your mother and I will no longer assume responsibility for it," Father said.

"But we may be late for school," Harry objected.

Father's answer surprised him: "Then you'll just have to take that up with your teachers."

Ellen spoke with an air of adult concern: "But if I get up late, I won't have time to have a hot, nourishing breakfast and I may get a vitamin deficiency."

Mother's reply shook her a bit: "That's too bad. I do want us all to be healthy, but if you want your breakfast, you'll have to get up on time."

"You won't wake us up?" asked Harry. "You said I'm such a heavy sleeper. How will I know when to get up?"

Father answered, "We'll give each of you an alarm clock and show you how to set it. If you oversleep, you'll just have to explain things to your teachers. Furthermore, from now on I am leaving at exactly eight o'clock in the morning. If you're ready, then I'll be happy to give you a ride. But if you're not ready, I'll go without you."

"How will we get there?" Ellen asked, apparently rather intrigued. "What if we miss a ride with you and it's raining?"

Smiling, Mother said, "Then you'll go with a raincoat, an umbrella, and rubbers."

The parents put this procedure into effect. The first two days, the children got up with their alarm clocks, but on the third day, Harry overslept. He was not awakened by his alarm clock because he had failed to set it. Father went to school with Ellen. When Harry awoke, he was already late for school. Mother refused to let him stay home. He took off for school and got there three-quarters of an hour late.

At school his teacher asked him why he was late. When he said he had overslept, she told him he would have to stay after school for three-quarters of an hour. That night he was careful to set his alarm.

Several days later, Ellen came flying down from her room just as Father was about to start the car.

"Just a minute, Daddy. Please wait till I eat my breakfast. Please."

Father looked out of the car window and said, "I'll wait exactly one minute. I am leaving at eight."

Ellen dashed back into the house. While she was still gulping her breakfast, Father started the car and drove off. She ran out of the house, but Father had left at exactly eight o'clock. She wiped her mouth and began to walk to school. Her mother looked on in silence, realizing that Ellen was learning the hard way, through experiencing the consequences of her behavior; if she overslept, she would have to walk.

Within two weeks both children were arising promptly at the sound of their alarm clocks and were ready to leave the house at eight sharp. Even Harry, who had merited his reputation of being a "heavy sleeper," seemed transformed. The parents were no longer in the service of their children as human alarm clocks.

FURTHER EXAMPLES

Being Late to School

The Pryor family also faced morning battles. The parents purchased an alarm clock for each child, but the kids did not use them. The parents said absolutely nothing about the matter. The children were late for school every day for a week. Eventually, the school counselor called. The conversation went as follows:

"Mrs. Pryor, are you aware that both Gail and Eve have been late every morning this week?"

"Yes, I am."

"Don't you think you can do something about it? Why don't you get them out of bed earlier?"

"Mrs. Locke, I have been studying a new way of getting along with my children and am trying to help them become more responsible for their behavior."

"Don't you think it's your responsibility to get them up on time?"

"I used to think that but I am now realizing that when I take the responsibility for them they never seem to learn things for themselves. I realize how difficult it is for you to deal with my children. However, I would like to ask you if you would perhaps be willing to try something else which may be more effective, since it would give the children the responsibility."

"What's that? We've warned them over and over again not to be late. We don't know what more we can do."

"Okay, then my suggestion would be that you require them to make up any time that they lose by being late. For example, you might request that they stay in at recess or lunch or after school as a consequence of being late. I want to assure you that I will be completely supportive of you in your handling the situation in these ways."

"I think you have an unusual approach, Mrs. Pryor, but I am willing to give it a try."

As the days passed, Mrs. Pryor noticed that the children were getting up earlier and leaving home to get to school on time. She said nothing about it, being wise enough to know that when children do what they are supposed to do, parents should not make a comment of any kind.

Several months later the counselor and Mother met at a PTA meeting. The counselor said, "Mrs. Pryor, the girls are on time now. What a change! Quite frankly, at first I thought you didn't care but now I realize you care a lot and wanted the girls to experience the consequences of being late. They are more responsible now."

Alarm Clock and an Agreed Time

Mornings were not the happiest time of the day at the Kosak household. After talking with a family counselor, the parents held a family council with their children.

"We think you kids are old enough to get up by yourselves," Mother told Harold, Linda, and Birdie, "I am going to get you an alarm clock to keep in your room. I'll show you how to use it. What do you think of that?"

The kids were excited.

Nine-year-old Harold, the oldest, said "Can I set it?"

Mother smiled. "It will belong to all of you. What time do you think you ought to get up?"

Linda shouted, "Six o'clock!"

"That's too early," Birdie the youngest, age six, yelled. "Seven o'clock, when Mama wakes us."

"I won't be waking you anymore," Mother said. "The alarm clock will do it, but you will all have to decide on the right time to set it."

At first the alarm was set to ring at six. The kids didn't have to leave until eight. After a week, it was set at six-thirty. Then after several days, it was set by agreement at seven and finally, after several more days, at seven-thirty.

Thus by trial and error the children arrived at the time that was best for everyone. They were able to work this out on their own because Mother and Father did not interfere.

One Alarm Clock—Two Boys

Eight-year-old Barry and ten-year-old Ron were given an alarm clock to share after Mother read the suggestion in a book. Without her knowing it, Ron would get up at the ring of the clock but Barry would stay in bed until Ron shook him. Mother found out when she walked by their room one morning.

She said, "Ron, you shouldn't shake your brother; he's supposed to get up by himself when he hears the alarm."

"Aw, he'll just sleep all day; he can't hear it, Mom."

Mother explained, "But if you keep this up, he'll never learn to respond to the alarm."

"He'll be late for school."

"That's the way he'll learn. Will you help him grow up?"

"O.K., but I don't think it will work."

That evening Mother told Barry that Ron had agreed with her that Barry was old enough to be responsible for his own awakening and that Ron would no longer shake him if he did not hear the clock. Barry warned them that he would not hear the alarm because he was such a sound sleeper. Neither Mother nor Ron said more.

Barry was late for school two mornings in a row, and his teacher asked him in front of the other children to give the reason for his tardiness. Barry heard the alarm the third morning and thereafter.

Setting a Time and Following Through

The Boel family had a problem in getting up that was somewhat different, since both parents had to leave their house at 8 A.M. to get to work by 9. En route they would drop off their child at school, which started at 8:30. The family routine in the morning was ridiculous, with many reminders and much nagging.

The counselor made a suggestion to the parents: call Elmer at 7:40, which was about the time he usually got up; then leave at 8 A.M., taking him along whether he was dressed or not, whether he had eaten breakfast or not. The parents were told to keep a set of clothes in the car, so Elmer could dress as they took him to school.

The parents didn't like this suggestion too well but nevertheless decided to try it. They had a talk with Elmer, who didn't like the idea either. However, the plan was put into effect, and the first morning it worked well—Elmer was ready at eight. But the next day, after Mother called Elmer, he answered sleepily, "I'm getting up," and then went back to sleep. At five to eight he was awakened by his father, who said, "We are leaving with you in five minutes." five minutes later, unwashed, unfed, but dressed, Elmer was in the car.

A week later, Elmer again did not get up when he was awakened and at eight o'clock was still asleep. Mother awoke him and carried him to the car; and all three took off, with Elmer, unfed, in his pajamas. En route, Elmer dressed himself.

In the succeeding year there were perhaps two slip-ups, but the pattern was established: his parents knocked on his door at seven-forty, he sprang up, and was completely ready to go in twenty minutes, dressed, washed, and fed. The nonsense that all three had suffered so long was over.

Doctor's Orders

A simple solution worked beautifully in a family where the mother was a worrier. She had slipped into a morning routine in which she called and called her three kids, became involved in their dressing, checked whether they had enough lunch money, supervised their eating, made sure they had their schoolbooks, etc. When the children finally left for school, she had been working for almost two hours, and was exhausted. The solution was elegantly simple: she just wasn't to get out of bed until eight-thirty—doctor's orders!

Mother fought the counselor's suggestion, but it made good sense to the father—and reluctantly she agreed. She explained to the children, "When I do too much work, I get exhausted and need some rest. I'm going back to bed. It would help me if you took care of your own responsibilities." Within two weeks the kids had worked out a routine in which, on their own, they got up, dressed, prepared and ate breakfast, and managed to get to school on time, with their lunch money and schoolbooks. True, before they accepted the fact that Mother meant it, they did a lot of crying and complaining. But after all, it was doctor's orders—strict orders—for her not to be out of bed before eight-thirty.

SUMMARY

An important aspect of children's lives is for them to be responsible for their own behavior. Parents agree on this point in theory but often find it difficult to train their children to become responsible because they continue to give them unnecessary service and to overprotect them. Even a nursery school child can learn to set an alarm clock, listen for it, and get up without help from parents. This is one of the simplest ways to teach responsible behavior at a very early age.

Caution: You must have and show faith in the child's ability to heed the alarm; and you must not feel sorry for the child should he or she experience the natural consequences of being late. That is the best way to learn—through experience.

9

DRESSING

THE PROBLEM

Mrs. Hayward shook her head as she watched Kevin, her four-year-old, attempt to get into his undershorts. First he put one leg in, and then he tried to put the other leg in the same hole. Both feet in, he then tried to pull the shorts up, but fell over. Mother released him and patiently said, "Try again." This time he did get each leg in separately, but when he pulled them up, the pants were on backward. He took them off and refused to try again. "When will you ever learn?" Mother asked as she began to dress him.

DISCUSSION

Dressing can be a major problem. In many homes, children expect parents to dress them, refuse to learn, can't find the right clothes, and thus are late for school.

A child should become independent as soon as possible. Parents should not do for a child what the child can do alone.

Many children like to keep parents occupied by expecting or even demanding service. Our general training procedure is simply to withdraw from giving undue service to a child so that the child will learn to be independent. The child probably will make many mistakes—but will learn from them. A problem can be an opportunity for learning.

SOLUTION APPLIED TO KEVIN

Mrs. Hayward, after being counseled, talked with her husband, who agreed to the suggested solution; simply to refuse to dress Kevin. The next day, he came into their bedroom in his pajamas and asked to be dressed. "Sorry, Kevin," Mother said. "From now on you have to dress yourself." He immediately indulged in a temper tantrum. Father went to the kitchen. Mother ran to the bathroom and locked herself in while Kevin pounded on the door. She turned on the radio. His pounding and screaming continued. She began to fill the tub full force, put in crystals for a bubble bath and prepared for a long soaking (see bathroom techniques in Chapter 5). Eventually, Kevin stopped his pounding and screaming. When Mother finally finished her bath and came out, Kevin was naked. And so he remained for two days! Father would not dress him, Mother would not dress him. Whenever a visitor showed up, Kevin hid, coming out after the visitor left.

On the third day of his nakedness, Mother, upset by his constant whining and complaining, crossed the yard to her neighbor's to get away. This was the first time Kevin had ever been left alone. "I wonder," she said to the sympathetic neighbor, "whether he can really dress himself? I used to think that at least he was trying hard. But when the counselor heard that Kevin always put on his shorts backward, he said Kevin must know how to put them on properly; otherwise he would manage to get them right about fifty percent of the time!"

At that point they heard a knock on the side door. The neighbor opened the door and there stood kevin, completely dressed.

FURTHER EXAMPLES

Clothes Not Placed in Hamper

Mike, ten, had been told "a million times" to put his clothes in the hamper when they were dirty, but Mother kept looking in his room and picking up things, putting them in the hamper herself on the day she did laundry. Finally, she decided that she would do no more picking up and from now on would wash for him only what he put in the hamper—and so informed Mike. This information went in one ear and out the other. And Mike's shirts, shorts, socks, and pants remained on the floor of his room.

"Ma, I got nothing to wear," he said one Monday morning, coming to her in the kitchen, still wearing his pajamas.

"You have lots of things to wear."

"Nothing clean," he said patiently.

"Well, wear something dirty," she replied.

"Everything is too dirty to wear," he told her.

"Why don't you wear some of my clothes?" Father said. (Father weighed about two hundred pounds.)

"Too big for me," Mike answered.

"I'm sorry," said Mother.

"I'm sorry too," said Father.

"What should I do?" Mike asked.

"Search me," said Father.

"I don't know," said Mother as she continued with her cooking.

Mike pouted and thought about making a scene or having a temper tantrum. Instead, however, he went back into his room, pawed through the dirty clothes on the floor, and, taking the least soiled items, dressed himself. Then he put his other clothes in the hamper, filling it with almost two weeks' accumulation of dirty clothes. Later he went to the kitchen to have breakfast.

"When are you washing?" he asked Mother while eating.

"My usual day," Mother said. "Thursday."

"Could you do some today?" Mike asked.

"No," said Mother, gently but firmly. "You have decided that I should not do your laundry since you did not give it to me."

Mike got up, not finishing his breakfast, and went off to school.

Mother refused to wash his clothes before Thursday because she didn't want to give him special treatment; she wanted him to experience the logical consequences of his behavior. That night Mike washed his own socks—a rather messy procedure. The next day he went to school with a stained shirt. Mother was tempted to keep him home. She even thought of purchasing a new shirt for him but decided to let him learn and said nothing. When Thursday came, both Mother and Mike were practically in a state of exhaustion.

Thereafter Mother never found Mike's hamper empty on a Thursday morning.

Bad Weather and Choosing Clothes

One morning, as usual, Mrs. Goss and Evelyn, eight, got into a battle. "Evelyn, you'll catch cold and be sick if you don't wear your coat, hat, scarf, and boots; it's twenty degrees out there." Evelyn was strongly against wearing them, but at the end of the hassle she went off to school with all the clothes on her that Mother thought she needed.

Father thought this kind of battle was a nuisance, and he said to his wife, "Evelyn ought to know how she feels; maybe she just doesn't feel the cold as much as you do." But Mother knew best.

Next morning, as the daily battle was raging, the family doctor came to see Grandmother Goss, who was not well. Dr. Brown heard Mother stressing the need to wear heavy coats and bundle up if one wanted to avoid colds and not die of pneumonia. As he was leaving, Dr. Brown mentioned that he had heard the argument about clothes and added that colds do not come from cold weather but from viruses. Thus, in a few words, he demolished one of Mother's most cherished theories of health—a theory that still persists in folklore.

After the doctor had left, Mr. Goss put his foot down. He told Mother that she should not interfere with Evelyn's state of dress since Evelyn was an intelligent child, that perhaps she did not need as much clothing as others, and that in any case she should find out for herself what suited her best. And so Evelyn was allowed to choose her own clothes. She proceeded to go out in zero weather without her heavy coat. She returned from school blue and shivering, and Mother fully expected her to come down with a bad cold. But Evelyn did not get a cold all winter. After one more day of going coatless, she decided, without pressure from anyone, to dress appropriately for the weather. In fact, she started wearing just about the kind of clothing Mother thought she needed. Now, though, she was doing it *on her own.*

Special Occasions and Choosing Clothes

Every Sunday morning, almost without exception, a battle occurred at the Slackman home. Whereas the other children dressed appropriately for church, little Susan insisted that she be allowed to wear jeans and a T-shirt. Sometimes Mother would forcibly dress Susan, who then yelled and cried; when they finally got to church, the whole family was feeling upset.

Mother was advised to let Susan wear whatever she wished, and the counselor suggested that Easter, which was coming soon, might be a good time to try this approach. Mother agreed reluctantly.

Easter morning, Mother told Susan, "You can wear what you want: your new white dress or your jeans and T-shirt." Surprised, Susan dressed in her everyday clothes, and the family drove off. Her brothers, Michael and Noah, were practically stiff in their brand-new clothes. At the church the parents got out of the car, then the children. When Susan saw how nicely all the other children were dressed, she climbed back into the car. The parents nodded at each other and went in to the service. The brothers went to the Sunday school. Susan stayed in the car. When the services were over, her parents said nothing about her dress or her behavior.

From then on, Susan was permitted to wear what she wanted—and she usually wanted to wear something appropriate to the occasion.

SUMMARY

In most cases, nagging about clothing is unnecessary. If at all feasible, let children wear what they select. They will quickly learn what is and what is not appropriate. By refusing to wash or clean clothes except on scheduled wash days, by refusing to purchase new clothes to replace clothes that have been mistreated, by wearing appropriate clothes yourself, you are doing your part. If a child dresses inappropriately, give your opinion—but go no further. Let the child learn to take responsibility for choosing what is worn. You show respect for children when you let them dress their bodies with their own selection. However, you do not have to go out with them if you would feel uncomfortable at being seen with them because they are dressed so badly. You can always say, "You can dress this way, but if you do, I feel ashamed of your appearance and will not be seen with you." Do not say this, however, unless the appearance is such that you really would be mortified.

10

EATING

THE PROBLEM

"Hurry," Mother said to Peter. "Breakfast is getting cold." Reluctantly he came to the kitchen. She asked gaily, "How do you want your eggs?"

Peter frowned. "I don't want eggs."

"Now," Mother said wearily, "you know you need eggs; you need protein. And how about some Jumbies?" This was a reference to the popular cereal he had demanded a week ago.

"No," Peter answered, "I want Quickie Dickies." He knew she didn't have that cereal.

"How about Mumbo Tumbos or some Juicy Deucies?" the harried Mother asked.

After several minutes of discussion and negotiation—he wanted pineapple juice and French toast—she finally managed to get a breakfast that appealed to him. The entire process took fifteen minutes of talk, fifteen of preparation, five for eating.

DISCUSSION

Dr. Dreikurs often said, "There is only one creature on earth that does not want to eat—the American child." The reasons are varied; one is the misconception, widespread among Mothers, that a fat baby is a healthy one. This causes them to push food on their young child, trying, for instance, to get the child to take "another bite for Mother" and then "another bite for Daddy." This is one of many games used to stuff a child. Mothers generally fear that their children will not take in each day the amounts and kinds of food that are best for them. Some even fear that their children may die from some kind of dietary deficiency.

In 1928, C.M. Davis reported an experiment now considered a classic ("Self-Selection of Diet of Newly Weaned Infants," *American Journal of Disease of Children*, 1928, pp. 36, 651-79). It involved letting an experimental group of young children eat whatever they wanted. A matched comparison group of children were given dietetically selected foods. The results were interesting: the children who had been permitted to eat whatever they wished were taller, heavier, and healthier than their control mates. An examination of what these children had chosen to eat revealed some unusual feeding patterns. Some went on "fads" and for several meals would eat just one or two foods, perhaps cottage cheese, chocolate, milk, or chopped meat. Then they would go off this fad and perhaps not eat a previously favored food for a month. Some ate very little one day and three times as much the next day. But when their intakes were totaled, it was found that every child, even though any single meal may have been unbalanced, had achieved a balanced diet every week!

Meal times should be happy times. Parents have a right to enjoy their meals. Young children need some help, but parent should not give them too much service. Mother can so easily slip into the habit of doing just that: to pour juice for the kids, to fill all the plates, and to run and get what family members request from the refrigerator or cabinet. She is then reduced virtually to the status of a servant, forever at the beck and call of her children. She must disengage herself from giving her children unnecessary service and must teach them to become self-sufficient as soon as possible.

SOLUTION

Parents can usually correct feeding problems rather quickly. They should keep these points in mind:

1. Feeding time should be pleasant.

2. Children should decide for themselves how much, if any, they are to eat of the foods Mother has prepared (if the demand for any dish exceeds the supply, the child must, of course, be limited to a fair share). They should be permitted to serve their own plate from serving dishes; when necessary, a parent may help. The selection and the amount of food on the plate should be determined by the child without any comment from others.

3. Given enough time and freedom of choice, children will develop a taste for many foods. They start life eating only one thing—milk; at five they may like to eat two dozen things; at ten they may eat a hundred. An adult, of course, may like several hundred, including snails and eels. But children, especially younger ones, are usually traditionalists. One must expect them to be reluctant to try new things.

4. A child should not be expected to eat the same amount at each feeding. At one meal Charlie may eat four ounces and at the next, twelve.

5. Dessert should never be a reward. It may be placed in a small plate at each place setting at the beginning of the meal. If a child eats only dessert, that is all right. Since it is a small portion, the child will soon be hungry.

6. Eating should be the child's business. Parents do not necessarily know best. The less parents worry about eating, the better for everyone.

7. When the family, except the problem eater, is through eating, all plates should be removed from the table. If the child is not given between-meal snacks, the child will be hungry at the next meal.

8. A very stubborn child may choose not to eat for several meals or even for several days. Meals should be served with the other family members. No mention should be made of eating or failing to eat. The plate should be removed when the rest of the family have finished. The child should not be allowed snacks. If parents stick to this procedure, the child will eat eventually. No one can go very long without food.

SOLUTION APPLIED TO PETER

Peter's mother was in an Adlerian study group with other mothers. She learned our approach to feeding problems and discussed it with her husband and children. She then established the following routine: she rang a bell ten minutes before mealtime and again when the meal was to be served; everyone was then to come to the table. For this meal there was to be only this serving for everyone! Peter balked at the first breakfast served in this manner. After he went hungry for a few mornings, he then ate what Mother had prepared.

FURTHER EXAMPLES

Planning Breakfast

The Smiths and their four children—eight, seven, four, and two—went to visit Mrs. Smith's parents, the Riggs, in a distant city. William, the four-year-old, told his grandmother upon arrival, "Nana, I only eat cereal," and proceeded to look through kitchen cabinets until he found a box of dry cereal. This he placed on the dinner table. During dinner the Smiths continuously argued with William, saying that he should eat the meat and vegetables. William continued to eat his cereal. Everyone was upset by the arguing.

The next morning Mrs. Smith was helping her mother fix breakfast. She started by asking each child what he wanted to eat. Grandmother Rigg was surprised but said nothing as her daughter prepared a different meal for each child.

To give the young couple a vacation from the children, the grandparents offered to baby-sit; and the pair left for a four-day visit with friends in a nearby town. Grandfather Rigg called the children and Grandmother together to plan the next few days. Each of the children was given an opportunity to suggest a fun activity. Grandmother said, "I need a little help so that I can have time to join the fun. I would like everyone to help me plan a breakfast menu." The children agreed to help her do it. William suggested cereal for the next morning; Grandmother wrote that on her list for Monday, the first day; she then asked John and Dick what they wished and listed their requests for the next two days. The baby made no requests; in fact, she did not seem to understand what was going on. Grandmother explained that on Monday she would fix cereal and everyone would eat that. On Tuesday she would serve bacon and eggs as John requested and on Wednesday pancakes and bacon as Dick wanted.

Monday's breakfast went well. Tuesday, William looked at the bacon and egg on his plate and started to complain, but no one paid attention to him and he ate no breakfast. On Wednesday, he stared at the pancakes and bacon on his plate for a while, then heaved a sigh and started to eat slowly. He quietly said to himself, "Pancakes aren't so bad," and cleaned his plate. From then on he ate all the meals Grandmother prepared.

No Meat Eaten

Mother and Father complained to a family counselor that their three boys, eight, ten, and twelve, would not eat meat. (This incident was recounted to us by Dr. Dreikurs.) A pediatrician had assured them that the kids were physically normal. The counselor asked why such a fuss was made over eating. Mother explained that the proteins in meat were better than those in cheese and beans and that, anyway, kids should eat everything.

The counselor suggested that the parents tell the children once and only *once* that from now on they could eat or not eat meat as they pleased and that the parents would respect their decision. The parents did so, and all three boys said they chose not to eat meat.

The usual hassle at table, with Mother and Father pleading and cajoling the children to eat meat, stopped. Mother prepared meat for herself and her husband and only vegetable dishes for the children. Peace descended on the family.

Several weeks later, Mother bought five chickens, fried them, and arranged the pieces on a tray to serve to company. Just before the first guests were due to arrive, she glanced at the tray and something looked wrong. She counted chicken legs—sure enough, one was missing. She immediately called her husband and began a tirade: "Why couldn't you wait? Sneaking a leg! That isn't right. . . ." The startled husband proclaimed his innocence. It took only a few seconds for them to figure out the answer: one of the children had stolen a chicken leg! Husband and wife hugged each other and began laughing.

That was the end of the meat-eating problem. From that time on they noticed that meat was disappearing from the refrigerator—a slice of packaged ham or a hamburger that had been put away. And slowly the children began "testing" meat at the table. The parents were smart enough to say nothing, and within a month all three children were eating meat.

SUMMARY

If parents would treat eating as natural, they would not reinforce the poor eating habits of their children by nagging and scolding. Parents are often overconcerned about their children's getting the correct kind and amount of nutrients. Forcing food upon a child usually brings on a counterattack— not eating. Quite strangely most people admire trim and slim adults but prefer young children to be chubby. Good eating habits can be easily learned when meals are planned to give a balanced diet and children are allowed to eat what they wish from what is placed before them. Snacks should not be given to children who are problem eaters, but may be offered to children who eat their meals.

We believe that the best procedure is to have an open kitchen: any child can eat whatever and whenever, going to the refrigerator at any time and taking out anything except things clearly forbidden, such as bottled soda or desserts. The meal table then has to compete with the refrigerator and the pantry. If a child wants to eat catch-as-catch-can, there is no cause for alarm. Very soon the child, especially if required to clean up and put dishes and utensils away, will realize that cooked meals regularly served are better than hastily executed peanut butter and jelly sandwiches. Kids learn by experience the value of home cooking.

We think these general rules make sense about food:

1. Parents should buy and prepare food that suits their budget and is convenient for them, with consideration for children's preferences, if feasible.

2. Children should serve themselves.

3. Children should decide for themselves, without discussion, how much to take from serving dishes. If one child avoids onions and another asparagus and a third pineapple—fine.

4. A child should usually be expected to finish what he takes. if not, the parent can dish out a reasonable amount for the child for a day or two, until the child learns to take only what will be eaten.

5. Dessert is not a reward. It may be eaten first or last.

6. During a meal no comment should be made or discussion held about the child's eating.

11

KEEPING CLEAN

THE PROBLEM

"Jeff, did you take your shower?" Mother shouted.

"No."

"Hurry, they'll be coming soon to get you. You know you can't go till you've had your shower."

Father put down his paper and said to Mother in exasperation, "Harriet, why do you have to fight with Jeff every day about showering?"

"I don't know. He's certainly not like Frances. I guess girls are naturally clean and neat. Jeff is so thoughtless; if I didn't remind him, he would never bathe or wash his face."

"Well, he's eleven. When will he ever learn?"

"I have no idea. Jeff! I don't hear that shower running!"

"Darn it!" Father said in disgust. "It's so unpleasant when you shout at him. You're after him all the time."

"Well, why don't *you* come up with the answer? I'm positive that if I didn't keep after him all the time, he'd just be black as pitch. And during the summer when he runs around a lot and sweats a lot and gets so dirty, he just has to have a daily bath or he will smell."

"Maybe it would be better if we let him reach that state," Father said wearily. "At least maybe that way we would have some peace."

DISCUSSION

Problems involving the bathroom—washing one's face, brushing teeth, flushing the toilet, taking a bath, drying off properly, and so on—arise in many families, and few parents know what to do. Usually parents talk, talk, talk. But it does little good. Most parents give up after a while; but some are more determined, and keep on investigating and asking questions. They check the toothbrushes after the children have left the bathroom, to see if they are wet. Some parents go so far as to check the contents of the toilet bowl: they have to examine urine and feces for color and shape; they feel negligent if they do not check *everything.*

SOLUTION

1. You, the parents, should have good toilet habits yourselves.

2. Instruct the children as to just what they should do (instruction may be by parents' example).

3. Check occasionally but do not conduct an FBI-type investigation.

4. The child should experience the natural or logical consequence of behavior.

5. Tooth-brushing should be an issue between the child and the dentist and not between the child and the parents.

6. Meals should not be served to a child who has not washed hands and face.

7. If the child does not bathe and smells bad, you can ask the child to remove the plate and eat the meal away from you—in the kitchen, for instance, if you eat in the dining room. The child should not make your meal unpleasant. However, if he or she is in a power contest with you, it is wiser for you and your spouse to remove your plates and eat elsewhere when the child smells bad or looks dirty. You could say, "I feel uncomfortable when I smell something unpleasant, so I'll leave."

APPLICATION TO JEFF'S PROBLEM

"Let the child decide," the family counselor said to the parents. "In this case, tell Jeff that from now on it will be his own decision whether or not to bathe."

The mother immediately disagreed. "I know my son. He just will not wash himself *ever*. Who knows what will happen?"

"What could happen?" the counselor asked.

"He would smell bad or something."

"So much the better," the counselor stated. "That may get him washing himself on his own. If he smells bad enough, others will tell him. This would be a natural consequence. From this he would learn."

The parents discussed the advice and decided to take it. They talked to their two children and part of the conversation went as follows:

"From now on, it is up to you to take a bath when you want. We'll no longer keep after you."

Both kids jumped up and down for joy. "I'll never take another bath again," Jeff said excitedly but firmly.

And it seemed he meant it because a week later, he still had not taken a bath. His skin was dirty and he definitely smelled bad. Mother tightened her fists and held herself back. Ten days later, she heard Jeff crying, and she went into his room. "What is it?" In answer he raised his left arm, and she saw along his body a line of small white pimples. "It hurts," he complained. "We'll go to the doctor," she said. "Get dressed." She was just about to tell him to take a bath before dressing to go to the doctor but decided instead to phone the counselor. His advice as to having Jeff wash was: "Don't."

"That is a condition that afflicts dirty people. You haven't taken any baths. Why? Is there a shortage of water?" asked the doctor later at his office.

"No, I asked our family counselor, and I was told to let him suffer the consequences if he didn't take a bath, and this is what happened."

"Well, young fellow, if you don't keep clean, you get this impetigo type of sore. No, there is no medication. Just keep yourself clean. That's all."

And from that day on, there was no trouble with Jeff about showering, except that every once in a while he would be in the shower too long and use too much hot water.

FURTHER EXAMPLES

Washing Hair

Mrs. Johnson and her daughter Nancy would fight periodically about Nancy's not washing her hair. Finally the mother gave up the battle and said, "It's your hair." Nancy let her hair go. It got very oily and then began to smell. When other kids mentioned this, Nancy began to wash her hair.

Playing in The Bathroom

Almost every night when the twins were told to wash, Mother or Father felt it necessary to come into the bathroom to urge them to hurry, stop playing, finish their bath, and go to bed. Sometimes Mother or Father washed them. The parents were told by the counselor to let the kids play as long as they wanted, to see what would happen. The parents agreed to go along with this. The first week the children were in the bathroom an average of forty minutes every night. The second week they averaged about twenty. The third week they averaged five.

The children had played excessively and dragged out their bath because the parents interfered. Once they had freedom to play, it was no longer as much fun, and so they cut down the time.

Avoiding Bathing

Dan did not take a bath for quite a while and began to smell bad. When his parents mentioned it, he got very angry. They felt uncomfortable eating with that odor, but they knew that Dan would be furious and would not leave on his own if told to eat in the kitchen—he would have to be dragged there, and he was a heavy eleven-year-old. The parents took their plates to their own room. There, for several days, they ate their meals. One evening, another family called to ask if Dan's family would join them in eating at a pizza place. Dan was left at home after the parents explained to him that they did not wish to inflict his odor on the friends or on others in the restaurant. They told him this only once, in a quiet, friendly way. Dan decided that very night to take baths—he really wanted to be with the family.

Brushing Teeth

Mrs. Cleworth really had a thing going with her son, Paul. She was keeping after him to brush his teeth. Practically every night she would harangue him about the importance of properly cleaning his teeth, how cavities would occur, and so forth. His younger brother, Sam, always brushed his teeth carefully. However, whenever they went to the dentist, it was Sam, the tooth-brusher, who usually had cavities, while Paul never had any. Paul used this fact as an argument against his Mother's prodding.

And so Mrs. Cleworth consulted the dentist. He told her that no one really knew what caused cavities and that some researchers wondered whether tooth-brushing might not actually help bring them on. He himself believed that children *should* brush teeth but felt that gum massage was even more important. He informed her that there were people in their late seventies who had never had a toothache and had never brushed their teeth. "It's probably a matter of heredity, for the most part," he told her. "In any case, why make your child suffer about tooth-brushing? Let him get a cavity—that might make him brush his teeth. But I still think it is more heredity than anything else."

With that Mrs. Cleworth gave up, thinking: After all, they're *his* teeth. Let him experience the consequences. Unfortunately, perhaps, he never did get any cavities. Anyhow, the battles were over—and that, the husband said, was a blessing.

SUMMARY

The bathroom should be the child's domain when in it. Constant supervision or battling is ineffective in training the child about cleaning up. These matters are the child's business. Parents have an obligation to be good examples—to keep themselves clean—and to instruct children in good toileting procedures; nagging and making a big issue about them is unnecessary and unwise. The best general rule is to let the child experience the natural consequences of behavior. Bit by bit the child will learn. One toothache can be a lifetime lesson.

12

SCHOOL DIFFICULTIES AT HOME

THE PROBLEM*

This day has really been something, Mrs. Thompson reflected as she waited for her husband to come home; some day indeed. About 9 A.M., the school clerk had called to say that Timmy, thirteen, had not yet arrived. When he and his sister Debra came home that afternoon, they brought their report cards. Timmy had two C's, two D's, and two F's. He had been late twenty-eight times and absent four times (as far as Mrs. Thompson could remember, he had been absent—for illness— only two days). Debra, ten, brought home one B, four C's, and one D. Attached to her report card was a note asking Mrs. Thompson to make sure that Debra would in the future come to school with her homework completed, and to please check her homework because Debra usually brought work to school

*This incident was recounted to us by Mrs. Bronia Grunwald.

that looked as though she had given it only about ten minutes' attention. And then, to cap everything, Mrs. Thompson found a note in the mail about her youngest child, Ted, five, still in kindergarten, asking Mrs. Thompson if she would please take him to a doctor because he might require medical attention since he found it so difficult to sit still and to follow directions.

What a situation! Mrs. Thompson reflected. How will my husband react?

DISCUSSION

Similar school-related situations occur in millions of American families and are generally considered by the parents to be matters of the utmost importance. Most parents are eager to do anything in their power that they think will help their child's schooling. Indeed, many seem to consider themselves and the home to be virtually an extension of the school system. They check to make sure that the child does the homework, and then they double-check to make sure it is done correctly. Great concern exists over report cards, and children are gravely warned about not being able to go to college if they have low grades.

What should parents do—and *not do*—at home to help their child at school?

SOLUTION

Our answer to this question is in two parts: one deals with improving the attitude of the child; the other with improving the attitude of the parent.

Parents should motivate the child to study and to enjoy learning. Lecturing is generally useless, such as saying that school is necessary for success or happiness, or making comparisons with other people's children, or recounting all the mistakes you, the parent, made in your own education. Other, more effective things can be done by you.

At table, talk about interesting intellectual subjects, such as religion, politics, history, science, art, music. Search newspapers and magazines and "bone up" on topics for discussions. If the children venture opinions, encourage them to talk by listening to them.

Take courses yourself, whether it be in basket-weaving at the local YMCA or in the history of philosophy at the nearest university extension department. Do your homework in plain sight, and discuss your courses.

Subscribe to magazines that are intellectual and interesting to children as well as to adults, such as *National Geographic* or *Scientific American.* Hang really good art around the house rather than calendar-type art; get good music on records and tapes, and play them.

Invite people over, and try to lead the discussion away from topics such as what's on television or who committed the latest local nuisance.

Have at hand books, encyclopedias, atlases, almanacs, and other reference matter.

A good globe of the earth is helpful. A telescope for searching the heavens at night and a microscope for examining water, leaves, and insects will stimulate interest in the world of nature. Toys of an educational and scientific nature, such as chemistry sets, can be quite worthwhile.

Educational play can be started in infancy. For more information see the book, *Teach Your Baby* by Genevieve Painter, published by Cornerstone Library/Simon & Schuster, New York, 1982. Games such as Scrabble are of value in alerting children to the use of vocabulary.

Take them to plays and operas.

Encourage them in every way you can to enter the world of the intellect.

In short, if you want your children to become interested in learning, the best way is to lead them, not to direct or force them. By forcing you will make them hate school, but by leading it is possible that you may awaken interest in education. If a child has already established other interests, or has low intellectual potential, even these steps may fail. In any case, don't forget this: the sure way to fail to make children want to do something is to try to force them.

What attitude should the parent take about school?

1. To the very limit that is feasible, let school be the child's business. The child is not going to school for your sake.

2. To the very limit that is feasible, let the school handle the child's schooling—let the specialists teach and guide. Except in very exceptional circumstances, your interference is more likely to harm than to help.

3. Do not do the school's work even if school personnel ask you to. Gently refuse to involve yourself in conflicts between the child and the school. Refuse to check the child's homework, or to urge that it be done by a certain time.

4. Do not do the child's work, but do help if you are asked to quiz on spelling, multiplication tables, and the like. Direct the child to reference sources, rather than serving as an information agency. "How do you spell 'quickly'?" the child asks. Mother should suggest looking up the word in the dictionary.

5. Do not reward or punish the child for schoolwork. For good grades, do not go into raptures; for poor grades, do not criticize.

6. Do, however, show interest in the child's schoolwork. Ask questions about what is being learned, and be ready to see demonstrations—such as getting a square root.

7. Join and be active in your Parent-Teacher Association. Be concerned about the kind of school you have.

SOLUTION APPLIED TO THE
THOMPSONS' PROBLEM

After a session with a counselor, Mrs. Thompson had a talk with the children.

"From now on, school is your business. I will not get involved anymore with your schoolwork. If you have homework, it is up to you to do it—I'll not remind you to do it, nor will I check it. I repeat: *school is your business from now on.* Do you understand?"

"Will you help me when I can't do my homework?" Debra asked.

"No," said Mother. "Homework will be your problem, not mine. If you pay attention in school you will learn what to do. I want you to get a good education, but I will not do your work for you."

Mother had a talk with the teacher too, when she called to say that Debra was not doing her homework.

"I'm sorry," Mrs. Thompson said. "Debra should, of course, do her homework. She must start being more responsible so I'm no longer going to supervise her homework. She seems to think I should do most of it for her and she blames me if it isn't okay. I have consulted a counselor who is giving me some new ideas about training the children for responsible behavior."

"But, Mrs. Thompson," Miss Fujiwara complained. "She just doesn't do her homework, and you *should* check it."

"I do not think she will become responsible that way. I actually think she knows how to do it but she waits for me to help, then I do more than I should and we get into fights about it. Would you please take care of it when she does not do her work? Perhaps you can keep her in at recess, or after school, or give her poor grades. I will totally support you and your decision in the way you want to handle it. Truly, the more I interfere, the worse it is for her."

Mrs. Thompson also spoke to little Ted's teacher; "I'm sorry, Miss Redwin, that my Ted doesn't behave himself in kindergarten. I do not want to take him to the doctor to get drugs. I would like Ted to become responsible. I can't help him sit still in school, but I am learning to train him in better ways at home. I have been told by the counselor I'm consulting that I have to allow Ted to become responsible for his own body and actions. I would like to ask you if you would be willing to train him in school. It may be that the thing I train him for at home will help him learn to sit still and work at school."

Mrs. Thompson told her husband: "From now on, as far as I'm concerned, school is the kids' problem. I'll just make sure they have the supplies they need, like books, pencils, and paper. I'll make sure they don't stay home when they should be in school. I won't bug them about homework or make a big fuss about their grades. When report cards are brought home, I'll sign them without comments, unless the children ask for them. I'll go to PTA meetings and see if I can't change things about so that instead of excessive concern with things like buying equipment for the football team there will be some attention to the kind of schooling the children are receiving.

As a result of Mrs. Thompson's new attitude, the kids began to get better grades and to behave better in school. Mrs. Thompson found that she now had more time to do other things, and she started some formal learning of her own—with a Great Books study group—and increased her pleasure in intellectual discussions.

FURTHER EXAMPLES

Disinterested in School

A mother called a counselor after her sixteen-year-old son had struck his father and run away. The dispute had been about school. When the parents came to the counselor for an interview, the father raged about his son, saying that the boy was interested only in playing, did not study, did not do schoolwork, brought home poor grades, would not be able to enter a good college, etc.

The counselor interviewed Father and son together on a subsequent date. The father repeated his complaints; the son expressed disinterest in school and showed great resentment of his father for many years of harassment about school.

The counselor advised that from now on the father should completely disregard the son's schooling, and leave it up to the boy. The son was delighted with the advice, and the father finally agreed reluctantly to take it.

The boy stopped attending school, got a job, and worked for a year. He then took examinations for entering college but made very low scores. He enrolled at night school, worked hard on his academic deficiencies, took the examinations again, and passed them. He then went to college and now is doing well there.

When the counselor interviewed the youth again, he said, "I think now that my father was right, but I just wouldn't listen to him. That year I worked showed me that education is important. But—I had to find out for myself."

Not Attentive in School

Mrs. Richman was a very good mother. Every night she helped her son with his schoolwork. She was most concerned that he do well in school. He was quite docile and learned quickly. Yet his teacher kept reporting that he was uncooperative and inattentive. Mrs. Richman finally said to the teacher, "I can't understand why he pays attention to me but not to you."

The teacher replied, "If you didn't try to do my job, if you would stop tutoring him, perhaps he'd pay more attention to me."

That possibility had never occurred to Mrs. Richman, but the suggestion seemed to make sense. So she stopped helping her son and told him that school was the place for him to look for assistance in his schoolwork. Sure enough, in a short time her son began to pay attention in school. Why would he pay attention in school as long as he had a private tutor at home?

Promise Unkept

Irving's father was sick of his son's poor grades and said to Irving, "I'll give you a hundred dollars for every A you bring home." Two months later, the son brought to his father a report card with five A's.

"Where's my five hundred dollars?" the boy asked, for he had a minibike all picked out.

"Here is five bucks," the father said. "I was kidding about giving you one hundred dollars. I just wanted to see whether you could get an A if you really tried. And now I know you can if you want to."

"Well, next report I'll have all F's. I'll show you."

And that is exactly what happened. Do not make promises you cannot carry out.

Irving quit school at fifteen, in his first year of high school, to work for his father on the farm. At seventeen he volunteered for the army, and there he served for six years. At twenty-three, he passed the GED examination. He went through college in three years and medical school in four, and at thirty was an M.D.

SUMMARY

One of the most serious and common errors by parents is interference in their children's schooling. Parents should try to motivate them indirectly by creating an intellectual atmosphere in the home rather than directly by lecturing and criticizing, by punishing and praising.

School is, and should be, the child's business. Do not help, do not supervise, do not criticize. Depend on the child's natural desire to improve. And remember: higher education is not a must for everyone.

13

BEDTIME

THE PROBLEM

A young couple named Schuetz had two children: a seven-year-old boy and a five-year-old girl. The parents were teachers in an elementary school in a residential area. The Schuetzes lived on the school ground in a large dwelling with three other families. An overriding concern of the Schuetz couple was to not disturb the others in the dwelling. They lived there rent-free and intended to save enough money eventually to buy a home of their own.

The big problem was bedtime. Because of their concern that the children's crying would disturb others and also because of their faulty concepts about sleep, a typical schedule from about 7 P.M. to 7 A.M. ran as follows:

7:00 P.M.—Mother would ask the children to put on their pajamas and get ready for bed. There would be squabbling.

7:30—Mother would take the kids to the bathroom, wash them one at a time, and supervise their tooth-brushing.

8:00—The parents would don pajamas. Father would go into the son's bedroom and read to him for a half hour. Mother would do the same with the daughter.

8:30—Father would leave the son and re-dress himself. Mother would lie on the bed with the daughter and stay there for about a half hour until the child fell asleep. Mother would then re-dress herself.

10:30—The parents themselves would go to bed.

1:00 A.M.—The daughter would get up and awaken Mother, who would then take the girl to the bathroom, wait while she urinated, take her back to her bed, and lie down with her until the girl fell asleep again.

2:00—The boy would come to the parents' room and wake up the father, who would take the boy to the bathroom and then tuck him in bed.

4:00—The daughter would get up and go to the parents' room and get into bed with them.

5:00—The son would enter the parents' bed, and the father would get up and go to finish his sleep in the son's bed.

7:00—The parents would get up.

DISCUSSION

While the preceding situation is highly unusual, bedtime problems are quite common—and usually completely unnecessary. Frequently, problems arise from misconceptions. Many parents do not realize that no one knows how much sleep is needed by anyone.

Instead of "bedtime" a better term is to call it "roomtime," since you cannot make children sleep no matter how hard you try, but you can establish a time for them to go to their room. Children can have the light on or off, can read or play with toys until they get tired. The child who is used to parents insisting on being in bed and trying to fall asleep may at first stay out of bed and play for a long time—or may fall asleep on the floor. This does not matter. Within a few days the child will be in bed and sleeping regularly. Each individual must find, by experience, how much sleep is needed. Jim, ten, may need ten hours of sleep while his twin sister, Susie, gets along fine with eight.

SOLUTION

Our suggestions for solving bedtime problems should work within a week—if you, the parent, follow them consistently.

1. By discussion with the children, find the time they think they should go to bed. Usually children are more reasonable on this point than the parent might expect. They may say eight-thirty if bed time has previously been eight. If they decide that they want to stay up so late that you and your spouse would have no time to be alone together, you can tell them that they must be *in their room* by an appointed hour, because you would enjoy some time to yourselves.

2. Explain that they must stay in their room, that they may have the light either on or off, and that they may go to sleep whenever they wish. You should not lie down with a child to "help" the child fall asleep.

3. After they are in their room, they may call you to read a story or simply to tuck them in. Then they may sleep or stay awake, but they must stay in their room.

4. If the child comes out of the room take him or her back, in silence. If the child comes out again, simply go to your room in silence; have a pleasant look on your face so that the child does not think that you are angry.

5. See that the child gets up at a regular time. If the child is tired, so much the better. Children should not be allowed to sleep late if they have stayed up too late the night before.

6. If a child has to go to the bathroom during the night, do not accompany the child. Keep a very weak light on in the hall and bathroom.

7. Do not allow a child to get into your bed except when you want. For example, you may invite your child to come into your bed any weekend morning by leaving your bedroom door open. If from the start you do not allow sleeping in your bed, the child will go along with that. If the child has already trained you to accept him or her in your bed, say—but only once—that it disturbs your sleep and that you will no longer allow it. If, after being told the child does disturb your sleep, lock your bedroom door. You will not have to lock the door more than once or twice.

8. If a child has a bad dream or is afraid of the dark, do not pay a lot of attention to it. See Chapter 27, in which we discuss this in detail.

9. Do not make a big fuss over sleep, for that may cause the child to develop undesirable sleep habits that persist into adulthood.

SOLUTION APPLIED TO
THE SCHUETZ FAMILY

Following their counselor's instructions, the Schuetzes went to their adult neighbors and explained what they were going to do to solve their problem. The neighbors applauded them for seeking professional advice and assured them that if the children cried for a time it would not annoy them. Armed with this assurance, the Schuetzes had a talk with the kids. They said that they would like to help them become independent since they were growing up. They would have to be in their bedroom by eight-thirty but that if they wished, Father and Mother would come in for a few minutes to say good night or read a story. From now on they were to go to the bathroom by themselves. The daughter announced that if Mother didn't sleep with her she would cry. Mother, who had been forewarned about children's tendencies to blackmail, merely said, "Well, go ahead and cry if you want."

That night, at precisely eight-thirty, both kids were taken to their rooms. To the surprise of their parents, neither cried. About nine, the son called for Father to tell him a story; this the father did gladly. The little girl did not ask for a story. Eventually the kids went to sleep, and the parents retired. About one o'clock, as per her usual schedule, the girl appeared at Mother's side of the bed, but the Mother refused to get up. The girl began to cry. Mother, following the counselor's instructions, got out of bed, took the child out of the bedroom, and closed the door (but didn't lock it). The girl cried for about five minutes, then went to bed. About two o'clock, the boy showed up at his father's side and just waited there, saying nothing. Father did not get up. Eventually, the son went back to his room. At 4 A.M., the girl tried to get in bed on Mother's side, and Mother wouldn't allow it. She then tried to get in on Father's side, and he wouldn't allow it. She then crawled in at the foot of the bed. Father picked her up—all this in silence—and gently put her out of the room, closing the door. Again she cried, but she went to her room. The boy did not show up for his usual 5 A.M. visit.

Within two more days the problem was completely solved. On Sunday, having been reminded by the parents the night before, both kids were welcomed into the parents' bed by 7 A.M.

FURTHER EXAMPLES

Refusing Roomtime

Larry, two and a half, stubbornly sat down on the kitchen floor when his divorced mother said it was roomtime. But Mother had learned about logical consequences from a counselor: she went into her own bedroom, closed the door, and read until she fell asleep. The next morning she found Larry asleep on the kitchen floor. She said nothing to him about the incident. Thereafter Larry went to bed at the proper time since he realized he would not get a payoff (attention or a fight) for refusing to go to bed.

Greg Refusing to Go to Bed

Four-year-old Greg and his mother came to our Family Education Center. Mother told the counselor that Greg would not go to bed on time, that they had a fight on this matter every night. The counselor talked with Greg while Mother was out of the room.

Counselor: Mother says that you don't want to go to bed at night.

Greg: That's right.

C: How late would you like to stay up?

G: Late.

C: As late as the news on TV?

G: Yes.

C: As late as when TV goes off the air?

G: Yes.

C: How many nights?

G: Three.

C: O.K. You may stay up for three nights. You are not to get into your bed, but you may use the couch in the living room.

G: O.K.

Mother was told to allow Greg to stay up and to tell Father about the plan.

A few days later, she called the counselor to report: Greg had slipped into his bed during each of the three nights. They had no more problems with Greg about bedtime. He had learned that sleep is a necessity.

Nap Time

A similar procedure should be used for young children's naps. Many parents decide that a child no longer needs a nap if it is resisted. Most children four years old and younger actually do need a rest time in the middle of the day, usually after lunch. Simply tell the child that it is rest time or roomtime. If resistance occurs, ask, "Would you like to go to your room on your own or would you like some help? If the child wants help or just does not go the room, carry the child gently but firmly to the room. The child does not have to fall asleep. He or she can play with toys or look at books. Generally, when allowed to quiet down a child does fall asleep.

If the child does not sleep set a timer to ring in forty-five minutes. This keeps the child from asking you whether he or she can leave the room yet.

SUMMARY

Many parents do not trust their children to act intelligently; this in effect shows that they lack respect for them. If given the chance, a normal child will be watchful, wary, and sensible. a child is quite capable of learning by experience how much sleep is needed and of seeing to it that he or she gets it. By so doing, the child learns to take responsibility.

C

PROBLEMS
OF
ORDER AND
COOPERATION

PRELIMINARY NOTE

For a family to be happy, cooperation is necessary. If one does less than one's share, one puts a burden on the others. If one does more, one is letting the others take advantage. In some families, one member is virtually a slave, while another lolls about not doing a fair share.

How can one get a child to cooperate? How can one get a child to do chores if the child absolutely refuses? If a child wants to be sloppy, how can one get the child to help keep the house fairly straight and clean? What about that especially difficult area, the child's own room? Is there a way, without screaming at children, without threats or spankings, to get them to do a share of keeping the house in order?

By using natural and logical consequences rather than punishment, you will improve your relationship with your children and they will be more likely to cooperate. Even if your children never do chores, you can succeed in training them to cooperate by the consistent use of consequences and thereby improve your relationship with them. Lessen your anger, use encouragement instead of criticism, have a special playtime with each child daily.

14

COOPERATION

THE PROBLEM

Mrs. Fisher was having a cup of coffee in her living room with her neighbor Mrs. Kozuma. Suddenly, hearing a slight noise, Mrs. Fisher jumped up and ran into the kitchen. A moment later, the neighbor heard Mrs. Fisher shouting, "No, no, no!" Then came the sounds of a slap and a loud wailing. Mrs. Fisher came from the kitchen leading her two-year-old, Linda, by the wrist while the little darling screamed bloody murder. "You keep out of the kitchen," Mrs. Fisher said sternly to Linda, "and keep out of the cabinet!" After this admonition, she kissed her squalling child and pushed her out into the yard.

"What was all that about?" Mrs. Kozuma asked.

"I just can't make that child obey. I don't want her to go into the kitchen."

"Why not? What's wrong with the kitchen?"

"Linda always opens my cleaning cabinet. I have all kinds of dangerous things in it: ammonia, soap powders, bleaches, cleaners. I must have told her a thousand times to keep out of it, but she's so stubborn. Really! I have never known a child quite like her. How do you make a child understand that you mean it when you say 'No'?"

"I don't know. I guess every child is different. Mine went through disobedient stages, but Harry was the most difficult," said the older woman.

Mrs. Fisher went on, "My husband says that I should slap her hard every time, that I don't hit her hard enough, but you can't go around slapping a two-year-old. She just doesn't understand. I don't want her to hate me."

"And you can't really reason with a two-year-old. I guess you just have to always be alert and know where they are at all times to keep them out of mischief," the neighbor replied.

DISCUSSION

To get children to cooperate for their own good and that of the entire family may seem difficult or even impossible. The children's rebellious attitudes indicate that the parents as well as the children are in a power struggle and neither side wishes to give in to the other.

We *can* scare a child into obedience; we *can* punish a child into compliance. But would you really want your children to become blindly obedient and not to think for themselves? How can parents inspire their children to be concerned for the good of the family, and to be cooperative with parents and siblings as well as self-confident and resourceful?

SOLUTION

1. **Minimize the necessity for orders.** The best procedure, if possible, is to arrange matters so that the parent does not have to give orders. You should, so to speak, "child-proof" your house. If you put away expensive, fragile things, you avoid many unnecessary problems with young, exploring children.

2. **Discuss and plan with the children** the rules and procedures all family members should follow. (See Chapter 33, "The Family Council.") parents as well as children must keep their agreements. We cannot expect the children to put away their things, to help with the dishes and other chores if either parent refuses to cooperate. Since children want the desired circumstances, they will soon learn that they will be allowed them only if they comply with the requirements or limitations as agreed upon by all. Parents make the rules and procedures for children under three years of age.

3. **When feasible, make a request instead of giving an order.** An order must be obeyed; a request gives the child a choice.

4. **Make unmistakably clear to all family members what each is expected to do or not do.** Never should doubt or misunderstanding occur as to the requirements or limitations regarding rules and procedures.

5. **Work out with the children the consequences for not choosing to cooperate.** For example: If the child does not help with the dinner dishes or is not ready to leave for school in the morning, ask: "What do you think we should do about it? What would be a good consequence?" You as well as the child can help decide what the consequence should be.

6. **Obtain each person's agreement** to the requirements or limitations of the rules and procedures. If a family member violates an agreement, the consequences should follow immediately. A second chance may be given if the child is again willing to make the same agreement. Ask the child if he or she thinks that he or she is not old enough to follow through.

7. **If the child violates the agreement a second time,** the child again experiences the consequences and must wait a longer time for another chance.

8. **Since children want the desired circumstances** they will soon learn that they will be allowed them only if they keep their agreements with the requirements or limitations as defined by themselves and other family members.

The child learns by this method to choose desirable behavior instead of misbehavior. One learns to make good decisions and will become a more responsible adolescent and adult. The parents also have an opportunity to observe and refine their commitment to keeping their own agreements.

APPLICATION TO THE
KITCHEN CABINET INCIDENT

Let us now return to Mrs. Fisher. She went to an Adlerian family counselor and explained her problem with the kitchen cabinet and two-year-old Linda.

Counselor: You are in effect rewarding Linda when she opens that cabinet. She gets you involved with her. If she is lonely, or bored, or wants your attention, she knows just what to do—she opens the cabinet, and you drop everything to "play with her."

Mrs. Fisher: Play with her? I do just the opposite!

C: But is that how she sees it? We have to see matters from the child's point of view. Your behavior is reinforcing her behavior even though your intention is just the opposite.

F: You mean I cause her to misbehave by giving her attention? How else can I get her to stop opening that kitchen cabinet and rummaging in it?

C: I'll tell you exactly what to do. This method usually works quickly with very young children. We assume that the child wants attention from you and that you give it to her when you talk to her, telling her not to do it again, spanking her, and so on. True, the attention you give is unpleasant, but perhaps she would rather have that than get no attention at all.

F: Do you think that I should give her attention in other ways—that if she gets favorable attention for other things she may stop misbehaving?

C: While I do recommend attention for useful behavior, that in itself will not stop poor behavior. I suggest you make a contract with her: "If you behave yourself in the kitchen, you can go into it; but if you don't behave, you can't."

F: How do I enforce that?

C: Get a gate, perhaps one of the type that opens up like scissors, and put it on the door of the kitchen. Then, when you are in the kitchen, if she opens the cabinet you can put her on the other side of the gate, telling her she has to stay out until she is old enough not to go into the cabinet.

F: I see. I am to take her out of the kitchen and close the gate behind her.

C: Right. But this is important: you must remove her *pleasantly and in absolute silence.* And one more thing: *do it as soon as she does something you don't want her to do.*

F: O.K. I can do that.

C: Do you know why I emphasize silence and speed?

F: No, not really.

C: First, *speed.* She should learn that misbehavior brings immediate unpleasant results: exile! Second, *silence.* She is likely to think you do not like her if you yell at her or even just speak disapprovingly to her, and she may begin to not like you. Let her learn that your behavior when she does undesirable things is rapid and friendly. In this way she will learn that it is her misbehavior (not Mother's anger) that leads to the undesirable results for her: the logical consequences.

F: Suppose, after she's taken out, she asks to come in and promises not to do it again?

C: We communicate with children only when we and the child are calm. If she is crying and sobbing and saying that she won't do it again, don't answer her; just go about your work. After she stops crying, you can talk with her and ask her in a quiet voice, "Do you want to come into the kitchen? Do you think you are old enough not to go into the cabinet?" And if she says "Yes," you say "O.K., come into the kitchen. I am glad to hear that you are a big girl." Then let her in. If she opens the cabinet, even one-eighth of an inch—out she goes again, rapidly and in silence. If you do not let yourself get upset but faithfully and consistently follow the procedure I have outlined, it is practically sure to work.

A week later, the counselor and Mrs. Fisher met again.

C: How did it go?

F: Fine. She no longer goes into the cabinet. I followed your suggestion. I told her once: "From now on, Linda, you may be in the kitchen only if you are old enough to stay out of the cabinet. If you open it, you must stay out of the kitchen until you grow old enough to stay out of the cabinet." She looked at me kind of oddly, because I wasn't angry when I said it. And she didn't touch it at all for two days. Usually she's at it five or ten times a day. She certainly understands more than I'd thought. The third day, she just started to open the cabinet and I immediately put her out of the kitchen, behind a chair I used as a barrier. She cried. When she quieted down, I asked her if she was old enough now. She said "Yes," so I let her into the kitchen. She tried again at the cabinet about fifteen minutes later. so I put her out again. Then I didn't let her back into the kitchen for the rest of the day. Finally, the next day she decided she was old enough, and she hasn't bothered with that cabinet since. I think I've licked the problem.

C: Congratulations, but you may be wrong. She may test you again. Usually, when you use Adlerian training techniques, they work right away but after a week or two the child may mount a second offensive—so there may be another flare-up of this problem. And you must do exactly the same thing the moment she starts again—if she does. Rapidly, silently, no anger, etc.

F: I think I understand, and what's more, I can see how I might apply this theory to other things. Thank you.

FURTHER EXAMPLES

Crossing a Busy Street

The client was a heavy-set, gray-haired woman, and she told her problem to the Adlerian psychologist in a weary, discouraged way.

"My husband and I have four children. The oldest is twenty-two and is married. We have a daughter, twenty-one, who goes to college and a nineteen-year-old son, who lives with us. Our fourth is only five. He was a change-of-life baby; we did not plan to have him. We love him, of course, but he's so different from my other three. He's driving my husband and me up the wall. You see, we bought this house we live in soon after we were married, almost twenty-five years ago. Since then the city has grown and now a highway runs right in front of our house. A lot of families have moved away, but we really don't want to move. Still, we may have to move because of Donald—our five-year-old."

"What is the problem?"

"He likes to run across the street. It's like a game. No sooner is he out of the house than he darts into the street; since it has heavy traffic, this is extremely dangerous. My husband, my other son, and I have tried everything we can to stop him— we've talked to him, we've tried to bribe him, we've punished him, we've kept him in the house for days—but he's like a little maniac; his one aim in life seems to be to cross that street. He's just a little fellow but he has a will of iron. We keep the whole house locked up all the time. We have snap locks on every door, we keep the windows locked, the screens screwed in. If a door is every left open, he sneaks out. We just can't trust him."

"This is certainly serious. Let me give you a complete program for training him.

"Step One: Talk to Donald. Take him out of the house and show him the exact limits within which he is permitted to move: how far he can go west—up to the curb; how for north, south, and east. Make sure that he understands these limits. Question him to make sure he knows how far he can go.

"Step Two: Ask him if he wants to play outside.

"Step Three: If he says 'Yes,' ask him if he feels he is old enough to stay within the allowed areas. If he says 'Yes' to that, ask him to tell you what is the farthest he will go in every direction—and only if he tells you or shows you the limits are you to let him out. Do not let him out unless he assures you he will not cross what ever boundaries you and he have established. If he refuses to make the agreement, don't let him out. When he does agree, let him out and watch him carefully, preferably from a place where he cannot see you—perhaps through a window. Have on your sneakers.

"Step Four: If he crosses any boundary, run out and get him as quickly as you can and in *complete silence* bring him into the house. You can grab him by the wrist or the shoulder but say nothing at all. Don't look angry or upset. You want him to blame his misbehavior, not your anger, for the unpleasantness that is happening to him.

"Step Five: Once in the house, he may ask you why you brought him in; he may deny crossing the boundary; he may have a temper tantrum—but you are not to respond in any way. When he is calm, say to him that he may go out if he wants to, and then once again go over the boundaries with him. Then tell him—and please use these exact words if you can remember them—'If you don't stay where you should, I will bring you in again and you can't go out again today. We'll have to wait until you are older and can act like a big boy.' Then give him his second chance. When he goes outside, again you look out the window. If he stays within the boundaries, fine; if not, take him in immediately in silence, and he stays in for the rest of the day. The next day, go through the same routine, but this time give him only one chance."

The mother followed this program exactly as suggested. In three days the little boy was playing outside the house and not crossing the street. In the next two weeks, however, he did try twice to cross it, and each time he was brought in for the rest of the day. He then stopped trying to cross it. He knew that he could not go out if he did.

This procedure has worked with hundreds of little children who had had trouble staying where parents wanted them to stay.

Noisy Children

Mrs. Jones was a divorcee with two children, Mark, six, and Beth, eight. Her problem was unusual: twice she had to give up an apartment because of the noise her children made. She informed us that after losing the second apartment she had to send her children to her mother because she could not get suitable housing. While with Grandmother, the children were extremely upset and bitterly regretted the misbehavior that had caused the loss of their own place. After six months in which they constantly pleaded to be allowed to go back, their mother did succeed in getting an apartment, and she and the children were reunited. Sadly she informed us that her new landlord had the other day come to see her to tell her that he would file a dispossess notice if she did not keep the children quiet—that all the neighbors were complaining about their noise.

Whenever the mother in any way opposed the will of either of the children, either or both would back up against a wall and hammer on it with their elbows or bang a chair against the floor. This, of course, was blackmail, pure and simple: they knew their poor mother would do almost anything not to have the neighbors disturbed. She was at the mercy of tyrant children. If she attacked one, the other banged, and if she went after the banger, the other would make noise until she promised them whatever they wanted.

The mother explained to us that she felt torn between sorrow for her children because they had no father and desire to send them away. She felt completely defeated by them.

We suggested the bathroom technique (see Chapter 5 for explanations), but it did not work—the children made such a racket while Mother was in the bathroom that she came flying out to give in to whatever they wanted. We then advised her to tell the children that henceforth she would act as follows: if they started banging *she would run out of the house*, regardless of time, weather, or her condition of dress. [For a similar solution to an adult problem see R.J. Corsini, *Roleplaying in Psychotherapy* (Chicago: Aldine Publishing Co., 1966) pp. 17-20.]

And this she did the very day she was given the advice. At dinner the kids started banging because she had no dessert for them. She got up from the table and away she went—down the stairs, into the street. The two kids followed her, crying, telling her that they wouldn't make any more noise; but she kept on going. This infuriated the children so that they banged on cars, walls of houses, etc. She walked and walked until both she and the children had calmed down, and then they all returned home. That same evening, when she was about to go to bed, the kids started banging again. She grabbed a dressing gown, threw it over her pajamas, and ran down the stairs, again followed by her kids. And again she led them on a very long walk that lasted for hours, refusing to listen to them, just walking, walking, walking. The three finally got home about midnight, with the two kids exhausted. For several days there was no banging, but one evening they started doing it again. As it happened, a near-hurricane was blowing that night. Out went Mother, without raincoat or umbrella, but this time the kids did not follow her. She walked in the rain to a cafe, where she had several cups of coffee and a long, long conversation with a friend. She returned home several hours after she had left. And this was the last time she had any problem with her children about noise-making.

No Response to Call

The mother of a retarded boy, seven, reported that he never did what he was told. To prove this, she called her son; he didn't even look up. "You see," she said, "he just doesn't pay attention to me." She said she worried that someday there might be a dangerous situation and that he wouldn't listen to her call and would get hurt.

The counselor advised the mother to do as follows: She was to call the child *in a low voice* and then, if he did not *immediately* come to her, she was to *run* to him and take him to where she had been—and each time she did this, she was to do it with increasing firmness. The first six times she called him, she had to drag him to her chair, but the seventh time he got up and came over. During the next hour, the mother called the boy several more times. Each time he came quickly. Mother was told that from now on she must never call the boy unless she really wanted him. If he should disobey, she should make him mind by proper action; and if she could not think of any proper action, not to give him an order in the first place. But she was never to repeat an order!

The mother was almost in tears at this point. She called her son again and, when he came over, stroked his head and said, "I can hardly stand it. For the first time in his life he listens to me and comes when I call."

SUMMARY

At times to have a child obey promptly, without question, is necessary. Children will do that only if demands on them are few and if they trust the parent, knowing that the latter will give a sudden command only for sufficient reason, such as impending danger. In general. the wise procedure is to make very few demands, and, when possible, to make a request rather than to give an order. Remember that we do not want to make robots who jump to any command. However, when parents do feel the necessity to give orders, the general advice given here should work with children below the age of twelve. *With teenagers this method usually will not work.*

15

CHORES

THE PROBLEM

The Vernon family—parents and five boys, six to fourteen—came to be interviewed at a Family Education Center. The parents, it soon became clear, had no control over their children. They awakened the boys in the morning and then fought with them throughout the day—to make them eat properly, do chores, do homework, stop fighting, share the television, get off the telephone, clean their rooms, use their toothbrushes, take baths, go to bed on time. The parents ranted and raved; the kids didn't even pay attention.

During the children's interview, they elbowed each other, went into paroxysms of laughter, tickled and batted each other around like five mad clowns. The counselor was unable to talk to them since any attempt to get their attention led to further clowning, so they were asked to leave.

Everyone felt sympathetic toward the parents. They were asked what single change would be most helpful.

Father: Cooperation, just plain cooperation. These kids don't do a thing to help out.

Counselor: What have you done to try to get them to cooperate?

Father: Everything we can think of. My wife and I work. We leave at 6 A.M. and we come home at 6 P.M. We do the shopping. My wife does the cooking and I do the cleaning. They just don't do anything—except laughing and giggling. If I hit one of them, they all cry like mad, jumping up and down, the whole lot of them. We tried a policy of no work—no food, but they would just snack before we came home. Nothing works!

DISCUSSION

In many families, some members take life easy, getting a great deal of service from other members, who work like slaves. Such a situation is unfair not only to those who work but to those who shirk. Part of the obligation of parents is to train their children to cooperate with the members of their group—to carry their share of the effort necessary for the group to function.

Before going further, let us make clear what we mean by "chores." Making one's bed is not a chore, nor is cleaning up one's room. Homework and putting away one's toys *are not chores!* A chore is a recurring activity that serves the whole family. If a child wipes up milk spilled on the floor, the child is not performing a chore—only cleaning up the child's own mess. but if a child regularly puts milk in a dish for the family cat, this is a chore, since the cat is the family pet and someone in the family has to feed the animal. A chore benefits everyone— taking out the garbage, cooking meals, washing the dishes, driving the car to the store, buying the groceries, taking in the mail, and so forth.

Chores are not paid for. One does chores simply because one belongs to the family; it is fair to contribute to the general good since one obtains the benefits of the work of other members. No connection should be made between allowances and chores. A child should get an allowance whether or not the child does chores, and should do the chores whether or not an allowance is made.

In a loving family in which good relations exist, use of the method we call *logical consequences* is not likely to be necessary with regard to chores. Discussions in the family council should settle readily the question of who is to do what, and the children should be quite willing to do their parts.

SOLUTION

The family should discuss the necessity and fairness of sharing the chores. It should be pointed out that Father goes to work for all and that Mother cooks, cleans, and shops for all. The discussion should include how much time and effort each of the children should put in. Decisions on this point should be based on such factors as the child's age and other activities, including school, baseball practice, piano practice, etc. A general formula such as this may be acceptable: to require chores at three or four and at that age to expect about five minutes a day; at six, ten minutes; at seven, fifteen; and so on up to age thirteen, when the time could be about an hour a day.

For nonperformance, the method of logical consequences should be followed:

1. no one else should do the chore, so that it remains undone;

2. the person who wants to eat or sleep must first do the chore;

3. in extreme situations, a work stoppage on the part of the parents may be advisable (this should rarely be done); and

4. parents should not remind or nag.

SOLUTION APPLIED TO THE VERNON FAMILY

The counselor suggested a *parental strike* and told Mr. and Mrs. Vernon how to do it. Here is how it worked.

The parents did not do any shopping for several days but made no mention of this to the children. The family's supply of milk, bread, cereals, cookies, and other easily consumed foods diminished rapidly. Then one night the parents called a family meeting. Their kids paid attention to them because of their unusual gravity.

"You kids don't help around the house. We're tired of doing everything ourselves, so from now on we'll not cook or clean for you. We'll start cooperating again with you—doing things for you—when you decide to cooperate with us." Father's voice was friendly and caring.

The kids began to cheer, giggle, poke each other, and laugh. It was the biggest joke. Whoopee!

And so began the strike.

The following morning the parents left the house to have breakfast elsewhere. When they came home that night and saw no chores done, they turned around and went out to dinner, then to a movie. At about ten o'clock they came home, and the kids were watching television. Ordinarily the parents would have had a fit, demanding that the kids go to bed, brush their teeth, say their prayers, etc.; but instead the parents now just went to bed. And the next day they went through practically the same procedure. On Saturday, Mother did only her own and her husband's laundry, and then the two took off for the beach.

Except for the parents' bedroom and bathroom, which they kept spotless, the house was becoming more and more littered. When they noticed that the family dog wasn't getting fed, they took him away and left him with friends. The garbage from cans that the kids had opened was overflowing.

As recommended, Mr. and Mrs. Vernon had informed their neighbors, friends, and family of their parental strike and asked them not to feed the children; the couple also asked the neighborhood grocer not to give them food. The two continued to spend as much time as possible away from home, eating their meals out and visiting friends frequently. They were not impolite to their children. They were loving toward them, but maintained a strict do-nothing policy. This state of affairs dragged on for six days.

On the evening of the seventh day, when Mr. and Mrs. Vernon came home to check on things, ready to go out for dinner together again if chores were not done, they found the kids lined up ready to discuss matters. The parents sat down with them. The problem was food. The conversation went somewhat as follows:

Son 1: We get nothing to eat.

Father: There is food in the house.

Son 1: You have to provide us with food we like.

Father: Who says so?

Son 2: It's the law.

Father: Then call the police and have us arrested.

Son 1: You ought to provide good food for us, not just canned food.

Father: You ought to do chores. We told you that if you cooperate with us, we'll cooperate with you.

Son 3: I want my dog back.

Father: If you had fed him, you would have him.

Son 4: I'm hungry. I want hamburgers.

Mother: I'm willing to cook but only if you kids cooperate with us.

Son 1: I'll cooperate.

Father: What do you mean?

Son 1: I'll do my chores.

Father: How about you others?

(All kids except Henry, age ten, agree to do their chores.)

Father: It isn't good enough. All of you have to agree. (Parents leave the house.)

Two days later, when the parents came home, the house was in good order: the huge pile of dishes had been washed, the garbage taken out, and almost everything was done except for certain chores that had been assigned to Henry, including raking leaves in the yard and sweeping the porch. As the parents looked around, the children followed them, a ragtag, dirty group.

Son 1: Well, we did our chores. Will you now feed us, right?

Father: Only when all the chores are done.

Son 1: Only Henry didn't do his chores.

Father: Only when all the chores are done!

Son 2: It isn't fair. Why don't you feed us and not him?

Father: We'll cooperate with you when all of you cooperate with us.

Son 1: Henry, you jerk, we're going to kill you if you don't pitch in and do your work. (Henry runs out of house.)

Father: When all the chores are done and when all you kids agree to cooperate, we'll cooperate with you. (The children look disconsolate. Gone is their rowdiness. The parents leave again.)

On the next day, the ninth day of parental strike, the parents found the whole house, inside and out, in spic-and-span order. Once again all five kids were present and another discussion ensued.

Son 1: Everything is O.K. now. Our rooms are clean. All the chores are done. Now will you stay home like you are supposed to?

Father: We will only if you all agree to cooperate the way you are supposed to.

Son 1: It's just him (pointing to Henry) who won't cooperate. We had to do his chores for him.

Father: I told you yesterday, and I'll tell you again, unless all of you kids agree to do your chores, and do them, we aren't going to do ours.

Son 2: Why should we be punished for Henry?

Father: Mother and I are treating all you kids alike. We are not going to deal with you individually. We found that when we tried to talk to one of you, or to discipline one of you, the rest of you began to act up.

Mother: Only when all of you agree will we agree to do our part.

Two days later—eleven days after the parental strike had started—almost the same scene was repeated.

The kids were wearing dirty clothes and smelled bad.

Son 1: Aren't you coming back home, like you used to do?

Father: If you kids aren't cooperative, we aren't going to play your game.

Son 1: We all agree to cooperate.

Father: Everyone? (All nod.) Well, then, since you all agree to cooperate—who will go with me to the store for shopping, to push the wagon? Mother will start the wash. (All the kids volunteer to go along with Dad, and he rolls out with five kids in the car, all of them happy.)

FURTHER EXAMPLES

Garbage Emptying

Dade had agreed at a family council to take out the garbage. According to the rules for assigning chores, the parents had seen to it that all necessary elements were clearly understood:

Who—Dade

What—Take out garbage

Where—From kitchen to the trash can

When—By bedtime

How—Without spilling anything

Why—Fair for him to do some of the family work

The item most frequently overlooked is *When*. We strongly recommend that all *Whens* be established in terms of "by such and such time"—and that this time be either just before a meal or just before bedtime.

Dade remembered the first and second nights, but the third night he forgot. Before going to bed, his mother checked under the sink and, sure enough, there was the garbage. She started to take it out, but her husband stopped her.

"Better leave it there."

"Insects will come."

"Spray it with bug killer."

Mother did just that, and left the garbage. The next day the can was overfull, and Mother had to put the sack with garbage on the floor. That night Dade remembered and, when he looked under the sink, saw that there was garbage all around. "Gee, I forgot," he said. "Well, just make sure you clean up the floor nicely," his mother said. He remembered for four more days, and then forgot for three. Mother kept using bug spray rather than saying anything, but finally she told her husband, "We just have to tell him. He sees nothing."

"Yes. I'll talk with him."

A few minutes later, Father had a talk with his son.

"Here's the story, Dade," Father said. "We know that people forget things from time to time, and we wonder what we can do about helping you to do your chore about the garbage."

"Oh, darn it—I forgot about it again. I'll take it away right now," the boy said hurriedly.

"Well, let's wait a bit. What I'm wondering is how can we help you to remember? First, maybe you don't want to take out garbage. What do you think? Maybe you want a different chore."

Dade considered. "No," he said finally. "That's all right."

"Do you want to remember?"

"Yes."

"We'll remind you then if you forget. Is that O.K.?"

"Sure, O.K."

"The best way to help you to remember is for us to remind you at times before you do something—for example, before you eat or sleep. If you really want us to help you remember, you have to give us permission not to serve your dinner, or let you go to sleep until you take out the garbage. When do you want to take it out?"

"How about before dinner?"

"All right. So, if you come to the dinner table and the garbage is still under the sink we'll remind you."

"Oh, O.K. I'll try to remember."

After this discussion, Dade remembered to do his chores for several days, but one night he forgot. When he came to the table, Father said, "You're not ready for dinner. You forgot something."

"Oh yeah, the garbage." Dade threw it out. He needed only two more reminders in the next two weeks and then remembered on his own.

Caring for the Dog

Nick wanted a dog badly. Father didn't like pets but finally agreed to get one only after Nick solemnly promised to take care of him. Nick promised to feed him, make sure he had water at all times, brush and comb his coat weekly, change a flea collar every three months, and pick up his droppings from the enclosed yard. Father was doubtful that Nick, who was ten years old, would keep his end of the contract, and he had the boy write a list of what he was to do and when he would do it. Nick was ecstatic and he kept meticulously to his agreement for exactly eight days. Then Mother noted that no water was in the dog's pan. She reported Nick's misattention to Father. The parents had a conference with Nick. All he would say for himself was that he "forgot." Father suggested that if Nick couldn't take care of the dog, perhaps the family should sell it. Nick became quite upset and promised strongly to "remember" in the future. However, a week later, another conference was held because again Nick had "forgotten."

Mother came up with a suggestion acceptable to all: Nick was not to eat until he had done everything he had promised to do for the dog. Nick readily agreed to this, and this procedure solved the problem. The parents would wait until Nick was seated and just about to eat, and then they would ask him whether Pluto had been cared for. If he had not, Nick would jump up and attend to his chores. But for Nick to "forget" and have to leave the table became a very rare occurrence indeed.

SUMMARY

Every member of a family needs to contribute to the family well-being. The size of this contribution is best determined by unanimous agreement among all the family members, including the contributor—all should agree that the arrangement is *fair.* For one member to do less than "fair share" of family chores is morally wrong. Equally wrong is for one family member to do *more* than a share of those chores—no member should be, in effect, the others' servant.

Chores should be treated as a kind of contract in return for the benefits of a family membership—shelter, food, clothing, allowances, etc.—children should contribute through chores. In working out a list of chores, the questions who, what, where, when, how, and why should be discussed and answered by unanimous agreement. Perhaps the most important, as a practical matter, is when. Parents and children should also discuss and reach agreement on what is to be done if a chore is "forgotten." Our suggestion is logical consequences affecting eating and sleeping: one doesn't eat until one does one's chores; one doesn't sleep until one does one's chores. But the child must freely agree to accept the consequence—otherwise it would be punishment.

The method of logical consequences for chores usually does not work with rebellious teenagers but usually works quite well indeed with sub-teen-agers.

16

CLUTTER—
MESSINESS

THE PROBLEM

Mrs. Rosenberg looked at the clock; five thirty-five. She then looked around her living room. A mess! Books, papers, toys strewn all around. Playing under the table were Tom and Tod, seven and eight. "Now hurry and clean up. Put all your things away. Dad will be home soon and you know he doesn't like to see things messy." Then she heard the hiss of boiling water overrunning the kettle and she ran to the kitchen. A minute later, Mother shouted, *"Did you put your things away?"* Her shrill voice energized them to get up and look around. Tod picked up a special toy, took it to his room, and tossed it on his bed, where a dozen other items already lay. The floor of his room was littered with toys and other paraphernalia dear to the hearts of children. Mother yelled again, and Tom picked up an item belonging to Tod. When Tod saw Tom with one of his toys, they got into a fight. At this point Father came home. When he saw the littered kitchen and living room, he blew up. "How is it that every time I come home the place looks like a pigpen?" he asked as his wife came to greet him. Her nerves snapped. "I wish you were here to do better!" she said as she flounced off.

Father set his teeth and didn't reply. He went to the TV and turned it off. The kids looked up in surprise. "Come on, scouts," Father said with forced gaiety. "It'll be time to eat soon. Let's clean up." Reluctantly, they began to pick up their things, with Father helping them. How long will it be before they learn to take care of their things and be reasonably neat? Father thought.

DISCUSSION

About neatness, two kinds of people make others uncomfortable: the compulsive neatniks and the compulsive slopniks. Some people get upset if anything is out of place; others just don't seem to care and leave a trail of misplaced objects behind them. Sloppiness, fighting, and "laziness" are the big three of family conflicts. Most children are not neat. (Indeed, a very neat child is probably not really happy—the child may be trying to act overly good.)

How should parents train children to be reasonably neat and orderly?

SOLUTION

As is usual when we use a new technique with children, we should discuss it with them beforehand: what we expect from them and why, and what we will do if they do not comply with the rules. They should not only understand the new approach but should agree to its adoption. Communication can be effective only if it occurs in a low voice, when all are really listening. For this reason the family council (see Chapter 33) is the best place for introducing changes. But the parents must not suggest a new procedure unless they have thought it through and are determined to follow it with calm, firm, undeviating consistency.

So let us now assume that the parents are tired of a sloppy house—they want to teach their children general habits of neatness and are willing to put in the necessary time and effort.

1. The parents should ask the children, "Do you like it better when the house is neat and you can find your things, or when everything is messy?" Most children, unless they are in strong rebellion against their parents, will say that they would rather have a neat house. Establish with the children what you expect regarding each area of the house. For example: (a) You can do what you want in your own room; (b) You cannot play in our room and make it messy; (c) If you mess up the living room, kitchen, and yard, you must clean them up.

2. The parents should thoroughly discuss the new system with the children and get their agreement, including what the logical consequences would be should they "forget." Explain that you do not want constantly to remind them and that they would learn to remember for themselves if they were reminded once a day. Give them a choice of being reminded before they eat breakfast, dinner, or before they go to bed at night.

3. Once they have chosen the time, explain to the children that they will not eat or sleep until they clean up the mess.

Parents must be careful not to let the children return to their earlier habits. At times children may try a second offensive to see whether they can get away with it. That is the time to be strong and not become discouraged. Simply remind them not to sleep or eat until the mess is taken care of. Of course, you must not leave your own things around, and you must not show anger during the training.

If your children are in very strong rebellion, you must first improve your relationship with them *before* attempting this training: Lessen your own anger, use encouragement instead of criticism, have a special playtime with each child daily, show much love. When the relationship has improved, then start the training.

APPLICATION TO TOM AND TOD

After having decided what they wanted to do to handle the problem of clutter in the home, the parents called their boys in for a discussion.

Father: Mother and I have been talking about keeping the house clean. Do you like it better when the house is neat and you can find your things or when it is messy?

Tom: I like it neat.

Tod: I don't care.

Father: I understand that you don't care, but which way does it seem nicer?

Tod: When it's neat.

Father: We want to be fair with you and say that we think you can keep your own rooms just as you like them—either messy or neat.

Tod and Tom: Great! Wow!

Father: And we want you to not go into our room to play; we want to keep it just like we like it. Is that fair?

Tom and Tod: Yeah.

Father: Now, what should we do about the rest of the house: the kitchen, bathrooms, living room, and porch? You both said that the rooms look nicer when they are neat. How about all of us picking up our things just before dinner or just before breakfast or just before bedtime? Which would you prefer?

Tod: I have to hurry in the morning to get ready for school.

Tom: Before dinner or bedtime would be better.

Father: Well, if you forget it would be good to teach you how to remember. You would learn to remember better if we picked up every day at the same time.

Mother: I think before dinner might be good because we would have more time then.

Tod: I am sleepy before bedtime. Before dinner is better for me.

Tod: Before dinner is okay with me.

Mother: It would only take about five minutes if Dad and I picked up our things if we left them around and you picked up your things every day before dinner. Then I could quickly check before I serve dinner. If anyone leaves something on the floor or where it doesn't belong I'll say when you come to the table, "When you're ready." That will mean that something is still not in its place. Is it okay if we use, "When you're ready," as a signal?

Tod: Okay.

Tom: That's all right.

Father: Mom and I have to keep things in the right place, too.

The plan worked well for three days and then on the fourth day, Mother and Father were sitting at the table when the boys came in.

Mother: When you're ready.

Tod: I didn't leave anything.

Tom: What's out of place?

Mother: When you're ready.

Tod: Tell us what room.

Mother remained silent.

The boys left to look and came back.

Tod: Tom was playing with the boat in the sink.

Tom: But it's his boat.

Tod: But I let you play with it. You left it there.

Mother served Father and herself and the boys were astounded.

Tod: Aren't you going to let me eat? I didn't play with the boat and leave it in the bathroom.

Tom: It's your boat and not mine.

Mother: You can work that out by yourselves. (She and Father continued to eat.)

The boys left the room and came back quickly.

Tod: I put it away. It's my boat and Tom played with it last.

Mother smiled and served dinner to the boys. The system worked for a long time and everyone was pleased about the way the house looked.

In this incident we have introduced a new element—"putting the children in the same boat"—treating them alike when only one of them didn't do what should have been done and the parents do not know which one it is. It may seem unfair that neither child should eat if only one of them refused to put away his things, but this system works better than attempting to deal with each child separately. Let's see why:

Mother: Tod, when you put away the boat, you can eat.

Tod: Tom borrowed it and played with it. He took it without permission. You should tell him to put it away.

Mother: What do you say about that, Tom?

Tom: I didn't play with it. Tod and his friend Bruce were playing with it last!

Tod: That isn't true! I found the boat on the couch. Tom had used some Magic Markers on it. So Bruce and I cleaned it up.

Mother: Why didn't you return it after you cleaned it?

Tod: He should have returned it. He took it out of the room.

Tom: That's a lie! I found the boat on the couch. I think Tod put it there. I painted it just for fun.

Mother: You shouldn't have done that.

Tom: He should look after his things better.

. . .and on and on and on.

Now, let's look at what happens if Mother puts then in the same boat.

Mother: When you're ready.

Tod: Tom took it out of the bedroom.

Mother remains silent.

Tom: I did not.

Mother remains silent and doesn't serve either of the children until the boat is put away. She looks pleasant and refuses to get entangled in arguments regarding whose boat it is, who took it, who is responsible. She is friendly when they return to the table and during the meal.

FURTHER EXAMPLES

Leaving Dirty Dishes

Martin was described by his mother as an agreeable eleven-year-old who left his snack dishes all over the kitchen and TV room and the counters a sticky mess. Every day his parents either cleaned up themselves or told him to do so. He would clean the mess good-naturedly and promise to continue to do so from now on, but he would never do it on his own. The parents were frustrated and talked to a family counselor. This is the way they carried out her suggestions:

They told Martin they would not remind him again and that they would be able to cook dinner only after he straightened up. The next day his parents came home from work, found a mess in the kitchen, and went into the living room. When Martin came to ask when dinner would be ready, his parents just kept on reading the evening paper and remained silent. Martin quickly cleaned up the mess and Mother then cooked dinner. This continued for two more days. Thereafter, Martin cleaned up by himself before his parents came home and he continued to do so since he wanted his dinner.

Messy Children

A mother at a Family Education Center said that her husband and their four children, twelve, nine, six, and three, were inconsiderate and never put anything away. [This incident, in an expanded form, was reported in *The Individual Psychologist*, 7 (1970): 47-51.] They didn't put dirty clothes in the hampers, they didn't hang up their clothes, they left everything everywhere—and the house was a mess. A social worker who made a home visit reported that the house was filthy and stank. The mother talked, talked, talked—but no one in the family listened to her. She felt desperate. Her husband was physically handicapped and was no help with the children.

A plan was suggested to the mother, to be put into effect only if her husband agreed. He did so. And so—

One night, after supper, Mother asked the children which they would prefer: (1) that she continue nagging them to put their things away or (2) that she start acting like the rest of the family, never tidying up but just letting things lie or kicking them out of sight, etc. They liked plan 2.

So Mother stopped her nagging and let everything pile up. She kept her own room clean. Within a week, she reported, things everywhere in the house were piled high, and the children had no clean clothes. This didn't seem to bother them at all. But Mother was quite upset: what would the teachers think if the kids came in smelling and wearing dirty clothes? The counselor advised Mother to continue the program. A week later, when she reported again, Mother was practically desperate. The kids now were really filthy, and the house was like a junkshop. She was advised to continue in her new way without deviation.

At this point her children were interviewed. They were dirty but happy and smiling and didn't think that there was any real problem.

Three weeks later, when seen again by the counselor, Mother was even more upset. Some of the children were complaining that they wanted new clothes—but the hamper was empty. She reported that one child, her nine-year-old daughter, was starting to hang up some of her things. Mother had even complimented the girl. "Stop it," Mother was told. "No compliment should be paid to a child for doing what she is supposed to do." Mother was asked to continue in the same way—to let the situation get worse.

Four weeks after the initial conference, Mother came back again and informed us that on the prior Saturday the four kids had gone on a cleaning bee: they had kept the washing machine going for almost twelve hours straight, and they had put everything away. For the first time in many years, the house was neat.

And she reported something else: the three younger children had been bed-wetters. She had never mentioned this to the counselor because she was ashamed to say it. After first being counseled, she had decided, on her own but in harmony with the advice the counselor had given her, not to do any more cleaning up after them. She hadn't done their sheets for four weeks. The middle two children had stopped wetting the bed, and the three-year-old was skipping every once in a while! Thus she had hit upon the right way to stop the bed-wetting (see Chapter 29). She had helped the children conquer this problem by her refusal to continue being their servant.

Her previous efforts to change the kids by helping them and nagging them had been useless, but her new procedure of giving them responsibility had worked. Within a matter of weeks, the family had become reasonably happy, with a house that was relatively neat and three younger children who no longer wet the bed.

SUMMARY

Talk the problem over with your children, come to an agreement with them, and then *never again discuss the matter*—just carry out the agreed procedure without anger. Keep to that procedure without fail.

We have found that the two methods suggested here work well: in one, food and sleep are tied to neatness; in the other, things are allowed to go to pot. In general, the first method is far preferable and only in more resistant situations should the second be attempted. Before you begin, resolve that you will be totally consistent while doing the training. Obtain the children's agreement and carry through completely. We strongly recommended that you do not do this training if your children are in powerful rebellion. First, improve the relationship, then start the training.

It goes without saying that parents who want their kids to be neat should themselves be good examples.

OWN ROOM

THE PROBLEM

"Do you remember the lecture you gave Harold last week about keeping his room clean?" Mrs. James asked her husband. "Well come and see it."

In the large, well-lit room was a desk, two chests of drawers, and a bunk bed. A chair, a bookcase, and a large toy chest completed the furnishings. On the top bunk were various items of clothing that Mrs. James had washed and pressed. On the desk, chair, and floor were soiled clothing: socks, undershirts, a pair of pants, a jacket, and a coat. Piled on top of the desk were papers, magazines, and books. The floor was littered with toys, sports equipment, and other possessions dear to eleven-year-old boys.

"Looks like a junkshop," Father said. "How can we teach that boy to be neat? We've tried everything."

"I'm ashamed to let anyone see this room. It really is a disgrace," Mrs. James said.

"I suppose we just have to keep after him," said her husband.

"But we've been after him for years, telling him to clean up, refusing to give him his allowance if it wasn't clean, calling him in from play to clean it up, telling him he's inconsiderate. I feel we've failed completely. How on earth can we ever get him to be neat?"

"Maybe there is no way," Father stated. "Maybe boys are just naturally sloppy."

DISCUSSION

Criticizing, advising, preaching, bribing, withdrawing privileges, taking away allowances, and other forms of reward and punishment usually work—but not for long. Yet a solution does exist. We have seen hundreds of children learn to keep their rooms neat and tidy. Unfortunately, a solution usually takes a long time. Most of the procedures that we suggest in this book for particular problems work satisfactorily within a week or so; the procedure we are about to explain can take up to a year. But remember: it usually works.

SOLUTION

The parents agree with Mike that he has a right to keep his own quarters just as he wishes—that his room is his business. In effect, they make a contract with him as follows: "We will supply the room for you if you promise to take care of it one hundred percent. We'll not pick on you for its condition. You are free to keep it just as you wish. It is *your* place."

The parents' hope is that the room will soon get so untidy and so uncomfortable that the child will realize, on his own, the necessity for cleaning and making it orderly. They should realize that some children may never become as neat as parents would like them to be.

One of the great advantages of this procedure is that the parents no longer get angry about the room. And they should not let themselves become upset by the opinions of members of the family or visitors.

The parents must disregard the room once the contract is made. They must act as if the room doesn't exist, and say nothing about it. If cockroaches, mice, or other undesirable vermin come into it, they can disinfect the area outside the room. A mechanical door closer may be used to keep the child's door shut if the sight of the room is upsetting to the parents. However, they should not install this gadget unless they have the child's permission.

If the room is kept fairly neat from the beginning, be happy; but if it is kept completely dirty and disorganized, be even happier—your child will come to realize fully the value of cleanliness and order even sooner.

Is this method fair and feasible when two or more children share a room? Yes. The general principle to follow is this; *kids settle any problems about the room themselves.* It is a basic error for parents to try to enforce justice between children—to try to judge the fairness of their relationships with each other. We urge: *Don't.* The child who seems weakest is often strong enough to manage if given a chance. When parents intervene, the usual result is greater rather than less friction between the children.

Our method works best when applied strictly as we have outlined it. If that is not feasible, parents may, of course, make necessary modifications. However, they should be very careful not to introduce variations that weaken or dilute the method to such an extent that it cannot develop responsibility in the child. Here are some possible variations:

1. American children frequently have three times as many clothes and toys as they need. This makes it difficult to keep the room neat. Ask your child to go through things with you so that some can be thrown out or given away. Others could be stored in a closet, to be brought out again in a month. This prevents the child from being

overwhelmed by too many things with which to deal at once.

2. For the younger child, two-and-a-half to three years, devise a pick-up game at meals and bedtime. Help make the room neat before mealtime or before bedtime. Also, allow the child to assist you with a weekly room cleaning. As the child gets older you can become less involved, and by age six to eight the child can entirely take care of the room. Be prepared for some disorder until the child learns the value of order in being able to find things when needed.

3. The parents agree to help with a periodic cleanup. This may take place, say, once a month: beds are made, room is washed and vacuumed, etc.

We suggest that every fourth Saturday morning be agreed upon for the cleanup and that Mother work rather slowly but methodically. The child will then want to work quickly to get it over with and go out and play. The date should be written on a piece of paper kept in the child's room as a reminder of the engagement. As the date approaches, the child may begin to keep the room in better order so that he will not be kept in too long.

We caution that no nagging or complaining or advising be done. Let this cleanup period be a pleasant one. Mother should elicit directions from the child, saying, "Now, where do you want me to put this?" rather than "Please put your skates in the toy box!"

SOLUTION APPLIED TO HAROLD

"Harold, Father and I have been talking about your room," Mrs. James began.

"Oh, I'll keep it clean from now on," Harold began, expecting a lecture.

"No, we want to discuss something else," Mrs. James went on. "We want to give you the room."

"Huh?" said Harold suspiciously.

"If you agree to take complete charge of it, we will agree never to say a single word about it. It will be yours to do with as you wish."

"As a matter of fact, Harold," Father added, "you can keep it as neat or as dirty as you want, and we'll not say a word."

Harold looked at his parents. "You mean. . .you won't pick on me anymore?"

"Exactly. The room is yours, keep it just as you want. But you have to agree to take care of it. I'll no longer vacuum it or dust it or anything. As a matter of fact, Father and I will agree not even to enter your room without permission, unless some emergency occurs. Now, will you accept the room?"

"O.K. And I can keep it just as I want?"

"It will be your room. I'll show you how to make the bed and how to vacuum it," said Mother.

Father added, "There is just one thing I want to ask you to do."

"What's that?" asked Harold, his suspicions flaring.

"The one thing is that you keep your door closed so that if Mother and I happen to pass by we can't see how you keep it."

"I promise," said Harold.

"Good!" said Mother. "I think you are old enough to become responsible."

After that no more discussion was held about Harold's room. Once a week, when Harold was not in the house, the parents looked in his room.

First week. The room is immaculate. Everything is put away neatly. It looks like a room at West Point.

Second week. There are five or six items on the floor and about a dozen scattered elsewhere about the room.

Third week. There are now about a dozen items on the floor and two dozen scattered about. The bed has not been made since the end of the first week. The sheets are now a bit gray.

Fourth to sixth week. The bed linens have not been changed yet. There are about one hundred items on the floor; newspapers and books, clothing, toys, tools, pencils. There are many items cluttering the tops of the bureaus, desk, and bed. At the foot of the bed is a pile of dirty clothes. The top bunk is covered with clean clothing which Mother had originally deposited outside Harold's door.

Seventh to twelfth week. Bed still not made. The sheets are now dark gray. The pillowcase is almost black where Harold's hair hits it. The floor, bed, and desk are now about four inches deep in things: coats, shirts, shorts, socks, hats, toys. Mother wants to take a tranquilizer when she looks in the room.

Thirteenth week. Inexplicably the room is neat. Everything is in place. Linen has been changed. Parents, amazed, say nothing.

Thereafter, at the end of one week there might be nothing out of place, at the end of another there might be fifty items. The condition of the room varied—*but every two or three weeks it would be cleaned.* One day Mother heard Harold vacuuming the room, and a little later on she noticed he had some friends visiting him. She realized that he had finally learned the lesson. And from that point on, although the room wasn't always too presentable, it was at least usually fairly comfortable and neat.

FURTHER EXAMPLES

Brothers and Dirty Room

We will never forget one of our first cases. Mother was confined to a wheelchair. Father did all the cooking, washing, cleaning, and shopping. Their boys, eight and nine, did their chores reluctantly. The parents expected the children to clean their room, but it was a shambles. Father, in anger, stated that he had tried "everything" to get the kids to clean up. He had cried, telling them how hard he worked and how crippled their mother was. Then he had lost his temper and whipped them severely. He had taken them to the parish priest. Nothing worked. When we advised him that he should give the children the room and that they would eventually clean it, he stated emphatically that this would not work—that he had tried this system. We asked how long he had tried it. "For several weeks," he replied sadly. "Not long enough," we told him. "You must try longer." "How much longer?" "For about ten more years," he was told.

Finally, both parents agreed to give this procedure a real try.

Periodically, they reported by telephone. The usual message went something like this: "I don't know how they can live in such dirt. My God, you should see the place. It's filthy. There's stuff in one corner piled three feet high. The room stinks. I don't know how long I can take it."

One afternoon Mother called. She cried hysterically that her children were fighting. "They really mean it this time. They're really battling. They're locked in their room and I can't get in it to stop them!"

"What is the fight all about?"

"I have no idea."

"Please call me when you know."

Next morning Father called.

He had looked in the children's room and, to his surprise, everything was in order, with nothing on the floor, the beds made, and the junk all put away. He and his wife looked at the room in wonder—and they noticed a chalk line across the floor. This line ran up the wall and continued across the ceiling, cutting the bedroom in two parts!

Later they discovered that the older boy had beaten the younger one because he had let another boy into the bedroom. This visitor had told other kids about the filthiness of the room, and all of them had made fun of the brothers because of it. After this battle they decided to divide the room, with each to clean up half.

Embarrassed to Have Friends See Room

We once visited a family we had counseled and, on coming in, were asked to look at their eight-year-old son's room. It was a typical disaster, with everything strewn around in complete disorder. Our hostess said, "I'm doing what you said. Isn't that room awful?" "Well, it sure looks messy. How do you feel about it?" we asked in return. "At first it drove me up the wall to see it, but now I have calmed down and I"m curious to learn how long it will take him to begin to clean it up. It has been more or less like this for the past month, and we started the program about two months ago. I'm beginning to think he will never clean it up."

We went on to meet some of the other guests and have dinner. When it was time to go home, our hostess once again suggested we look at the room. We wondered why she asked us. She opened the door to her son's room and we looked in. The room seemed in perfect order! "What happened?" we whispered. She whispered back, "See, on the top bunk? Jimmy has a new friend staying with him. About eight o'clock he asked me if this friend could stay overnight, and I said that he could. Between eight o'clock and nine-fifteen, when this boy arrived, Jimmy managed to clean that room. I would have thought that it would take him three hours to do it. I suppose all the stuff is just pushed out of sight into closets and drawers. But what really surprised me was to learn that he is even aware of the condition of the room!"

SUMMARY

As soon as they are old enough to be able to do it, children should clean their room and make their bed. They will take pride in their own room if they are in charge of it.

Children are not naturally neat. However, if parents keep the rest of the house neat and clean and if they allow children to experience the natural consequences of a messy room, they will eventually learn that living in a mess is unpleasant and unnecessary.

18

MONEY AND PROPERTY

THE PROBLEM

"Daddy, can I have a dollar?"

"What for?"

"Something I want."

"What?"

"A water pistol."

"A water pistol?"

"Yes."

"Why?"

"Alfred has one."

"Ask him to let you borrow his,"

"He won't let me have it."

"Well, Walter, wait until he is through, then lend him something of yours."

"I want it *now*."

"Well, you can't have it now. Besides, I'm mad at you. You left my hammer out on the porch. Now it's rusty."

"I forgot."

"Well, you're not getting a water gun."

"Daddy, I *want* the water gun. Just give me a dollar!"

"Absolutely not!"

DISCUSSION

Conflicts about money and property are extremely common in families. The only problems more troublesome are disagreements about raising children.

SOLUTION

Here are some general suggestions:

1. Children receive money in three forms: (a) *allowance,* which includes expense money (for school lunch, bus fare, etc.), and spending money (for snacks, toys); (b) *gifts* (Grandmother sends five dollars for a birthday); and (c) *earned money* (thirty-five cents for shining Father's shoes, or fifty cents for washing a window.

2. All children old enough to understand the concept of money should have money of their own which they may use without having to account for it.

3. Children should not be made to beg for money. Allowance should be a right, not a privilege, and should be used to teach the child how to manage money.

4. Children should be given opportunities to earn money at fair rates.

5. Money should not be used for reward or punishment.

6. Children should be taught to respect other people's property.

7. Parents should give the allowance at an appointed time, weekly—they should not lend money with expectations of repayment from next week's allowance. They also should be willing to negotiate increases in the allowance as the child gets older.

8. Children have the right to decide how they will spend their allowance, they may make a mistake and squander the money, in which case they will learn not to squander it, providing you do not feel sorry for them and give them money to "make them happy."

9. Children should be encouraged to save part of their allowance. Start a bank account for them when they are old enough to understand the concept of numbers and of saving. They will enjoy seeing the account grow over the years and it will be a very practical asset later on. Children especially like to use the automatic savings machine.

10. Decisions regarding what to do with gifts of money must be decided with the child's cooperation. You might suggest that, if Grandmother sends one hundred dollars for Christmas or a birthday, the child spend only a portion (say, five to ten dollars) on a toy or something special, and put the remainder in the bank.

11. Parents have a right to expect that their things be respected. They should discuss rules for borrowing and what happens when property is mistreated.

12. Dangerous things such as weapons or power tools should be hidden, locked up, or made inoperable. Dangerous drugs should be kept under lock and key and made inaccessible to children.

13. Parents and children should enter an agreement so that if the children are permitted to handle equipment, tools, or other items for their own use and "forget" to return them to their proper places, parents may remind them to return them. Reminding is most effective if tied to eating and sleeping as suggested in Chapter 16. Explain to children that they will learn to remember on their own if reminded before dinner or bedtime. Ask the children to choose the time. If they use a saw and come in for dinner without returning it to its proper place, quietly say, "There is something you didn't do," or, "When you are ready." Do not serve the meal until the saw is returned and do not get into a fight about it. Remaining silent prevents fights. When the relationship improves, you can again allow the use of tools and use the simple reminding technique.

14. If the child misuses equipment, the parent has the right to make that equipment "off limits" for a definite period (this should be a short time).

15. If a piece of equipment is misused and it is impossible to determine which child misused it, it can be made off limits to all children in the family. This is an application of *putting them all in the same boat* (see Chapter 16).

16. If one child uses another's equipment or toys and a ruckus ensues, we recommend that parents keep out of it—that they do not try to arbitrate. Solutions to such problems can come: (a) through the family council (see Chapter 33), in which the children can settle the issue with the help of parents, or (b) through letting the kids settle these issues between themselves.

APPLICATION TO THE WATER PISTOL INCIDENT

Two problems are discussed: (1) the child's begging for money and (2) the child's having used tools he did not return. Let us show how the two problems can be settled through the family council:

Father: Walter asked yesterday for a dollar to buy a water pistol.

Walter: Alfred has one. Why can't I have one too?

Mother: Alfred used the money that Grandma sent him.

Walter: Well, she didn't send me any.

Mother: It was his birthday and she sent him a dollar. He asked me to get him the gun, and I did. When your birthday comes, you can buy what you want with money Grandma sends you.

Walter: But I want a water gun now. We can play together.

Mother (to Father): I think we ought to give both Walter and Alfred some spending money that they can use for whatever they want.

Father: Shouldn't they earn their money?

Mother: I would think so except that, being only four and six, they are too young. I think it would be nice if they had some money regularly.

Father: O.K. How much would you boys want?

Alfred: I don't know.

Walter: A dollar.

Father: A dollar! What would you do with so much money?

Walter: Spend it.

Father: A dollar a day? A dollar a week?

Walter: I don't know.

Mother: I asked some of the other mothers around here, and they give their kids about a quarter or fifty cents a week.

Walter: I'm bigger that Alfred, and I should get more.

Mother: How about thirty cents for Alfred and fifty cents for you?

Walter: O.K.

Alfred: How many dimes in thirty cents?

Mother: Three dimes.

Alfred: Can I have it now?

Father: Yes, you can. We'll give Alfred thirty cents every week and Walter fifty cents. It will be your money, and you can spend it any way you want. Payday will be every Saturday morning. O.K.?

Walter and Alfred: O.K.

Mother: Now there is something else I want to bring up, and that has to do with borrowing things and not putting them away. Somebody borrowed my good scissors yesterday, the ones I use for cutting material when I'm sewing. A lot of paper was all around the floor, and my scissors were on the floor too. From now on, I don't want you to use my good scissors. You have your own scissors, and you should use them.

Walter: It wasn't me.

Father: The same with my tools. If you use them, please put them away. You used my hammer last week, and you left it out on the porch and it got all rusty.

Walter: I forgot.

Father: It would help you to remember on your own if we remind you for a while before dinner or before bedtime. Which time is better for you?

Walter: Before dinner.

Alfred: Yeah.

Father: Okay. We'll remind you then, before you eat dinner.

FURTHER EXAMPLES

Weekly Allowance

The Cater family—parents and four children, two to six—were being counseled regarding family problems. On their third visit they reported that at their family council they established an allowance of fifty-eight cents a week per child. The money was distributed during the meeting, and the children put their money in small purses which they then hung on four hooks in a hallway. Grocery shopping was done on Saturday afternoon as a family outing, and each child took his or her purse along. "But why fifty-eight cents?" asked the counselor. Mother replied, "that gives each of them a quarter, two dimes, two nickels and three pennies. They could spend each amount separately or combined and have a few pennies for tax." She added, "They each bought a candy bar, so Father and I bought a candy bar too. But that was our only candy for that whole week." "Sounds good," said the counselor.

Putting Them in the Same Boat

Mr. Hilliard, an accountant, had an office in his house, which was near a beach. He kept his typewriter covered because the damp air was bad for it. He had two children, Laura and Benny, eleven and twelve. One day Benny asked whether he could use the typewriter. The father said to both kids:

"I don't mind your using my typewriter if you will do two things. One: straighten up after you use the machine—don't leave any papers around; two: put the cover back on. If I find one of you has failed to do these things, that person can't use the typewriter anymore until I give permission."

Both kids agreed, and everything went well for about a week. One day Father found the typewriter cover on the floor. He asked the children, but each denied having used the typewriter. Father found in a wastebasket a sheet with typing that made him suspect it was Benny who had used the machine. Besides, Laura's outcries of innocence were much stronger than Benny's. However, instead of accusing Benny and depriving him of the typewriter, Mr. Hilliard deprived *both children* of it for a week.

"But," cried angry Laura, "he used it, not I. Why can't I use it now?"

"I did *not* use the typewriter," Benny stated with unconvincing force.

"I can't tell who did it and I don't know how to find out. I do not want either of you to use it until you become more responsible. So, please do not use the typewriter for the rest of the week.

Several days later, Benny "confessed" he was the guilty one. Father again had a conference with the children, and this time only Benny was not to use the machine. But if Benny had not made this confession, Father's first decision would have stood. Father was putting them in the same boat. This must be distinguished from mass punishment. If the father had, say, spanked both children or deprived both of dessert or fined both, that would have been punishment—and it would have been unfair. But to protect his property by saying, "Since I don't know who did it, I won't let either of you use my machine," is perfectly fair, even if an innocent child receives the consequence.

"Giving In" to Unwise Choice

Paul, nine, received a five-hundred-dollar inheritance and asked if with it he could buy anything he wanted. His father and mother told him that it was his money and that he could buy anything he wanted within reason. What did he want?

A motorcycle!

The parent argued against it but to no avail. Finally, after considerable discussion, they agreed to let him buy a motorcycle. Saturday morning, they went with their son to a motorcycle dealer, who, when he saw the child, said he was too young. The boy insisted, and the dealer gave him a wild test ride. A badly frightened boy got off the machine—and changed his mind. He decided he wanted a ten-speed bicycle, and the family went home with one.

Had the boy succeeded in purchasing a motorcycle, the parents would then have taken him to the police station to have him try to get a license, knowing full well that none would be issued to him.

Instead of fighting with the boy, the parents were wise enough to appear to give in—to let the child learn by experience. If the boy *had* succeeded in buying a motorcycle, it would have been a constant reminder to him of his bull-headedness, because he could not ride it until he was older.

Buying Expensive Items

"Hey, Dad, can I have an electric guitar?" asked Mike, fourteen.

Later that night, Mike's parents discussed his request at length. Next day, they priced the outfit Mike wanted—it cost over five hundred dollars. That night they had a talk with Mike.

"About the guitar—we found that it costs over five hundred dollars."

"I know it."

"We asked a music teacher and he thinks you ought to first learn to play a regular guitar, and after you know how, we can discuss whether we should buy such an expensive instrument."

"I don't want to learn on a regular guitar. I want an electric one."

The matter was dropped at this point.

The parents had another discussion without Mike's presence.

"He'll be intrigued with the guitar for a week, and then he won't play it and we'll be stuck with a five-hundred-dollar gadget," Father said.

"Well, we can't condemn him in advance," Mother replied.

The next day, after the parents had made further inquiries, they had another talk with Mike.

"Mike, if you'll make the down payment on the guitar, we'll pay the rest of it."

"Huh?"

"Do you want the guitar?"

"I told you I did."

"Well, here's what we propose: you make the down payment on the guitar; there'll be monthly payments after that—we'll pay those."

"What does that mean?"

"If we buy it on the installment plan, it'll cost not five hundred but six hundred. You make the down payment—the first eighty dollars. Then we will pay all of the remaining five hundred and twenty. I'll write it out for you."

	Mike	Parents	Total
Down payment	$80		
Payments		$520	
Total	$80	$520	$600

"We'll pay more than six times what you pay, but the guitar will be yours."

"You know I don't have any money."

"Oh—don't you have some savings?"

"Just what's in the bank. Twenty-five dollars from my Christmas money."

"Well, if you'll work and earn another fifty-five dollars, that will make eighty dollars."

"It'll take me a year to earn that much."

"No, I'm willing to pay you to do some work around the house, and you could ask some of the neighbors for work such as yard-mowing, baby-sitting, etc. You could have that money within a month."

The ending of the story? It could be almost anything. Perhaps Mike insisted that the guitar be a gift and refused to work. Or maybe Mike did work, but then spent his money on something else. Or perhaps Mike did work and make a down payment and then after a week or so lost interest in the guitar. Or maybe Mike became a real guitarist and started a career in music.

The important thing from our point of view is that the parents were wise enough to insist on Mike making a preliminary contribution. They were too smart to fall into the trap that catches many parents—buying expensive items that the children later do not use. Encyclopedias are perhaps the most common traps for parents. A clever salesman intrigues the children with the books, the parents pay several hundred dollars, the kids are wild about the books for three days. Some years later, they are put in a box for the Salvation Army—only about one percent of their contents having ever been used.

Lending Money to Children

Bert needed money to buy a skateboard and asked his father for a loan of three dollars. He promised to pay his father back at the rate of fifty cents a week, using twenty-five cents from his fifty-cent allowance and twenty-five cents that he would earn by doing odd jobs. The arrangement worked—for two weeks. Then bickering and quarreling began. Mother got into the act, saying that Father should never have entered a financial deal with his son.

We agree! Never get into financial deals with *any* relative. It is especially bad to enter them with your children. Such deals produce nothing but trouble. Give if you will, but do not lend!

Use with Supervision

Mr. Stern caught his eleven-year-old, Buck, using the electric saber saw, which he had told Buck never to use. Father disconnected the saw and put a lock on the plug. The next time Buck went for the saber saw, he could not use it. When he asked about it, Father said, "Fine—you can use the saber saw, but you can use it only under my supervision."

Agreement Broken, Property Removed

When Mr. Tyler came home, he saw Joe's bicycle on its side on the grass rather than in the place where Joe had promised to keep it. They had already agreed that should Joe forget to put the bike in its proper place, he could not use it for a week. Father took the bike into the garage and tied a rope around it to remind Joe that he was not to use it for a week. Sure enough, when Joe saw the rope he knew what it meant. A week later, the father removed the rope. Thereafter Joe remembered to put the bike away when not in use.

Dismantling Own Property

Dan had been given a rather complicated toy car with batteries and lights. His father found him working on it—that is, taking it apart. Instead of saying anything, he just looked on. When the car was disassembled, Dan began to attempt to put it together. At a glance, Father could see that this was hopeless. Dan asked Father to help. After examining the car, Father calmly told Dan that it was broken and could not be fixed. Instead of criticizing his son for breaking an expensive toy, Father had let him do as he wanted with something that was his property. Dan profited by the experience. He learned to take better care of his things.

SUMMARY

In dealing with their children about money and property, parents should follow the same principles as in dealing with anyone else. A child's money is his or her own.

Before parents spend a lot for an educational item for children such as an encyclopedia or a musical instrument, they should get them to make some outlay for it, even if it is necessarily only a very modest one. Thus they are less likely to end up with something expensive that the children don't use.

The parent should avoid any deal with children that involves money, especially loans. The parent should not become the third party in money matters involving the child.

Parents should give the child a regular allowance. The amount should be determined by the child's needs, in light of the economic condition of the family and community standards. We recommend that the parents be generous, so that the child can learn to save.

The interval between allowance payments should not be too short. With children under five, perhaps a dime or quarter on a specified day twice a week will be fine. We recommend that when children start school, their allowances be paid once a week. The children should be given enough to pay for school lunches during the whole week and to have left over, say, fifty cents for spending money. As they get older, dues for scouts and other inexpensive activities may be included. We recommend that at age ten, the first of the month should become the payday (however, for a while before starting monthly payments, you may want to try payday once every two weeks). The number of school days should be counted for the forthcoming month, and the amount should cover lunch, bus fare, and the like during the month, plus spending money. As the intervals between allowance payments get longer, the child learns to budget expenditures.

Each parent should have a list of "jobs" for which the child will get paid. These jobs should be work such as shining shoes, filing cards, cleaning out the car, mowing the lawn, etc.—jobs that ordinarily the parents would either do themselves or hire someone to do.

We especially recommend that the parents do not try to drive sharp bargains. Pay the child a normal rate. If, say, a garage is to be painted, get an estimate of what a regular painter would charge and then pay exactly that amount to your child. Expect the same quality of work (or as nearly the same as may reasonably be expected. Allow a specified time in which to finish the job. If the child does poor work, quits before the job is done, or doesn't finish on time, don't pay anything or pay only part—do what would be fair if you were dealing with a regular painter. Incidentally, on this point and on all the others we have mentioned, it is most important that you and the child reach agreement *before the job is started.*

In matters of money and property, common sense is what is most needed in dealing with your child. Do not make children beggars; do not get into deals; make no loans to them; let them handle their own money and property as they wish. If the child is wasteful or destructive, do not replace items which were not cared for.

D

INTERACTION
PROBLEMS

PRELIMINARY NOTE

Problems concerning interactions in the family tend to be extremely upsetting. An angry child or parent can keep the family in a constant turmoil. Too many families live in an unhappy relationship. This is a tragedy, especially since it is relatively simple to change the relationship from tension and despair to happiness and satisfaction.

Many parents believe it is natural for children to fight and that it is necessary to attempt constant control over the children. Fortunately, better ways exist of handling fighting. A related and dangerous problem is fighting in the family automobile. And what can be more distressing to parents than children who misbehave in public? Parents have an obligation not to inflict their untrained children on others.

Training unpleasant children to become pleasant is well worth the time and effort. What greater pleasure can there be for parents than to see their children turn into friendly, cooperative, and likeable people?

19

FIGHTING IN THE HOME

THE PROBLEM

Mr. Alper had a difficult day at the office. When he got home, he took off his shoes and stretched out on the sofa. He had just closed his eyes when the quiet was shattered by a piercing scream. With a start, Mr. Alper opened his eyes. In the dining room they were at it again: Ron and Marilyn trading blows, screeching at each other. He reclosed his eyes, hoping that the children would stop, but they didn't. In a sudden burst of anger, he scrambled to his feet and shouted, "Shut up, damn it! Both of you—*right now*—go to your rooms!" Marilyn began to complain loudly about what Ron had done to her, but Mr. Alper would have none of that. He advanced on Marilyn, his hand ready to slap. Her face contorted with anger, she retreated. Ron had disappeared into his room.

When Mr. Alper turned, his wife, who had seen what went on, said to him, "It was really Ron's fault. Marilyn was playing quietly with her doll when he came up behind her and deliberately stepped on the doll. Now Marilyn is angry with you because she thinks you were unfair." "Oh, nuts!" the father replied. "All I want is a bit of peace and quiet. Those two kids fight, fight, fight all day long. Why do they do it? Do all kids fight? I don't remember doing it with my brothers . . ."

DISCUSSION

We have found that the most common and most annoying problem for parents is their children's fighting. Yet fighting between children is an easy problem to handle!

Why do children fight? Both they and their parents usually believe that the fight is really over the issue that the children appear to be fighting about. Thus, in the incident just reported, Mrs. Alper thought that the reason for the fight was that Ron had stepped on Marilyn's doll. However, we believe that underneath this apparent cause there is a much more fundamental one—what one might call the real reason. *Children usually fight to keep their parents busy and involved with them.* They themselves are rarely aware of this, nevertheless we believe it to be the case: *their basic purpose in fighting is usually to get their parents' attention.*

To end fighting, parents must simply keep the children from achieving this fundamental purpose.

Incidentally, we must make clear that we do not disapprove of fighting per se. Children, in our view, have a right to fight. However, they have no right, in fighting, to disturb others who are not disturbing them. Certainly Marilyn had a right to fight with Ron because he deliberately stepped on her doll. But she had no right to bother her father.

SOLUTION

We offer three ways to deal with children's fights. We suggest that you routinely use the first method to the limit that, for you, is supportable or seems advisable. When that method is inapplicable or proves ineffective, use the second or, if that seems unsuitable or proves ineffective, the third.

Bear It

Remember: they are only kids; they are trying to learn how to deal with life; their bickerings and quarrelings are their way of learning to solve their problems. Just be quiet, let the kids have their fight, and say nothing. Sooner or later, they will stop.

Beat It

Don't be an audience. Go into the bathroom or some other room. When the quarrel is over, you simply come back in silence.

"Boot" Them Out

Put all offenders out the door into the yard or street. However, you must do this precisely in this manner:

1. Say to them: "If you are going to fight, you must go outside. When you are through, come back in." Don't say it again.

2. If they do not go outside, put them out in complete silence!

3. From then on if you use the third method, do it in complete silence!

SOLUTION APPLIED TO THE ALPERS

When the Alpers were told of these methods, both were skeptical. Father shook his head. "You don't know how hostile these kids are," he said. However, both agreed to try our suggestions. Their first step was to talk to the kids. Marilyn and Ron listened carefully. Within fifteen minutes there was an uproar. Both parents looked on and said nothing. The bickering continued for several minutes and then Marilyn ran over to her mother. "Ron has my shoe box and he won't give it to me."

Mother was about to ask Ron to give Marilyn back her shoe box but reflected: I'll get into a fight with him too if I ask him. So she said nothing and just looked at her angry daughter. "Did you hear me, Mother? Make him give me back *my* shoe box!" Marilyn demanded.

Mrs. Alper didn't know what to do. It was uncomfortable just looking and saying nothing. Then she had an inspiration.

"I couldn't find one of my earrings this morning," she said.

Her seven-year-old daughter looked at her contemptuously.

"I said Ron has my shoe box."

"And I said I couldn't find my earring," Mother said clearly. Both father and brother were listening to this weird conversation.

"And I don't care about your old earring," Marilyn said, "I want back my shoe box."

"I'm sorry you don't care about my earring; it means a lot to me," Mother persisted.

Her daughter turned her back to mother and went to her room. Peace followed for an hour, an almost unprecedented event in this family. Then both children got into another hassle. Almost as one, the two parents rose and walked out of the house into the front yard. As soon as the door was closed, the battle ended. The parents talked a bit, and Father commented that it was certainly interesting that the fight, whatever it was about, had ended when they, the parents, left.

FURTHER EXAMPLES

Fear of One Child Hurting Another

Mr. and Mrs. Williams complained that they had to have a babysitter when they left the house because their fourteen-year-old son was brutal to his ten-year-old sister; the parents were afraid to leave the two alone. The parents were advised to use our methods and to leave the kids alone without a baby-sitter.

When the parents discussed this with their children, Mollie said, "He'll kill me!"

Mother replied, "I'm sure he will not hurt you if you don't bother him."

That very night, for the first time, the parents left the children alone. When they came back, both kids were watching television.

Older Child Hurts the Younger

A mother complained that her four-year-old son, Jimmy, so "hated" his baby brother, Billy, that he was always deliberately hurting him. "I'm afraid he's a sadist," Mother said. She was advised to "ignore it," but she stated she couldn't stand her four-year-old's "torturing the four-month-old. She was advised nevertheless to "beat it" (i.e., leave them alone) and see what happened. It was recommended to her that she have a playtime with Jimmy and then give him much positive attention and encouragement.

She reported the next day that when Jimmy pinched the sleeping Billy, the baby awoke and screamed so loudly that Jimmy got frightened and ran to Mother. Mother said nothing to Jimmy. Jimmy asked why Billy cried. Although Mother knew Jimmy had pinched his brother, she answered, "Maybe he's hungry. Should we feed him?"

A week later, she reported that Jimmy no longer was pinching Billy. Then she told the following horror story:

"For several days, Jimmy kept annoying Billy. Each time Billy would cry and Jimmy would get scared, so I realized that the baby could take care of himself. And so I didn't interfere, realizing that if I did, I'd be giving Jimmy attention for his misbehavior and encouraging him to be worse. After four days he stopped annoying Billy. But the next day I saw him with a knife. It's only a toy plastic knife, but it could hurt. Jimmy had it in his hand, and he walked stealthily over to where Billy was sleeping in his crib. He put the hand with the knife inside the crib bars, and then he raised his hand as though to bring the knife down on his sleeping brother. I don't know what kept me from dashing over and grabbing Jimmy, but I just looked on. And Jimmy brought the toy knife down on Billy—but he did it so slowly and touched Billy so lightly that Billy didn't even wake up.

"I heaved a sigh of relief and realized that *he had been doing all this just for my benefit.* From now on I am not going to worry about Jimmy hurting Billy."

SUMMARY

We don't like fights; but if children want to fight, we let them do it, *provided* they do it in a place where it doesn't bother other people. Our experience has been that fighting almost always stops or diminishes rapidly if our methods are used. We have had no serious difficulties with children hurting one another. As a matter of fact, the methods of intervention used by most parents are much more likely to lead to bloody noses and scratched faces than are our methods.

If you have fighting children, use our methods consistently: Bear it, beat it, or "boot" them out. If you give them attention because of their fighting, you are giving them what they are fighting for. Stop lecturing, punishing, sending children to their room, or otherwise "rewarding" children for fighting!

20

FIGHTING IN THE CAR

THE PROBLEM

On their vacation, Mr. and Mrs. Rawl were speeding along a freeway at the legal limit. Suddenly Jon and Roberta, in the back seat, began to quarrel, hitting at each other. Mr. Rawl's temper was short due to the heat and the tension of driving. "Stop it!" he shouted. The fighting abated for a moment, and then it erupted again. Mr. Rawl turned around, holding the wheel with his left hand, his right hand seeking someone to slap. As he hit one of the children, his left hand pulled the wheel and the car swerved. Mrs. Rawl screamed and grabbed the wheel. The car nearly went out of control; it was indeed fortunate that a serious accident did not occur. The entire family, shaken by the experience, quieted down for a while. The parents wondered if they should ever drive again with the kids.

DISCUSSION

Some fifty thousand people are killed annually in the United States in automobile accidents. The number caused by fighting children is, of course, unknown. But we can be sure that auto deaths due to this problem do occur.

Parents' reaction usually is to yell at the children. This generally works for only a little while. Some parents stop the car and spank the children. This frequently makes them even wilder and leads to a still bigger blowup the next time. Making them promise to behave, having some up front and some in the back—these are makeshift measures that do not really solve the problem.

SOLUTION

1. Talk with the children at a time when everyone is calm, perhaps just before the auto trip. Explain what you intend to do should they make a fuss and start quarreling in the car: you will stop the car until they calm down. Having explained this so that they understand, do not repeat it later. From now on you are going to act and not talk.

2. Should a disturbance occur while driving, pull to the side of the road as soon as convenient, and wait in silence until they calm down. If they start bothering you with comments or complaints while you are waiting, get out of the car, and return only when they have subsided. When all is calm—this may take as little as two minutes or as long as several hours—without saying anything, start again.

3. Once you have started, should they again begin to fight, stop—and this time allow calmness to prevail a while before driving off again. They may miss doctors' appointments or be late to school; the more inconvenient the wait for all concerned, the more it will impress the children that their car behavior must be changed. You may, if it seems advisable, return home at this point.

4. Do not discuss the incident at all while driving or afterwards.

5. Should still another outburst of fighting occur, stop as soon as possible and wait as long as necessary for the calming down.

SOLUTION APPLIED TO THE RAWL FAMILY

After learning our solution for fighting in the car, Mr. and Mrs. Rawl talked to their children, explaining what would happen should they fight in the car on their next excursion. The children did not pay much attention to their parents' words and, during the next car ride, they started fighting. Mr. Rawl silently pulled over to the side of the road and waited. The startled children asked, "Why are we sitting here?" Father did not answer. When they were quiet and he felt calm, he started driving again. The children were quiet for a while but soon started up again. Father turned back toward home, ending the planned family outing.

The following weekend, parents and children decided it would be nice to visit the grandparents, who lived about twenty-five miles away. The family got into the car without anything being said about fighting. The children kept themselves amused. Jon counting all the green cars and Roberta counting all the red cars. It was a very pleasant drive.

FURTHER EXAMPLES

Back Seat Fighting

Mr. Thomas and his fiancee, Mrs. Russell, were driving. In the back seat were Mrs. Russell's children, Will and Anne, two battlers. (Mrs. Russell, a divorcee, was at the moment a very fearful woman. One of her former husband's tendencies had been to get very excited if the kids began fighting. He would harangue them while driving, thereby upsetting her.) Suddenly the children began to hit each other and scream. Mr. Thomas pulled to the side of the road. With the fighting still going on, he opened his door and got out of the car, motioning to his fiancee to come too. They walked down the block and entered a store. About five minutes later, Anne showed up, and five minutes after that, Will did too. Nothing was said. All four got into the car and continued. After several such incidents, fighting in the car finally stopped.

Fighting in Car While on Vacation

On vacation, Mr. and Mrs. Miller and their eight-and eleven-year-old children had a discussion regarding the dangers of fighting in the car and what they should do about it. They agreed that the driver would leave the freeway for a side road as soon as possible and stop the car until the battle stopped. The next morning they got an early start, hoping to cover many miles during the day. Within fifteen minutes the children began hitting each other. Father was upset but said nothing. He took the first exit off the freeway and pulled to the curb. The fighting stopped immediately. "Why did you stop?" Phil asked. Father remained silent. They waited for ten minutes and then Mary said, "Let's go." Father started the car, driving along on the side road, looking for a freeway entrance. Within a few minutes the battle resumed, so he again pulled over to the curb. Father got out of the car and walked away. Mother joined him.

"This nonsense has to stop," Father said "I think we ought to stay away from the car for a while to teach them a good lesson." Mother agreed. About fifteen minutes later they returned to the car. The children were silent. Father started the car. Within a block the fight resumed. Father pulled over to the curb, took out the keys, and both parents left the car, staying away for two hours. When they returned they found one child stretched out on the grassy patch near the sidewalk, the other stretched out on the back seat. They all took their places and drove away.

That was the very last car fight they ever had.

Some of the Children Fight, Not All

The King family had four children, ages five to eleven. Fighting in the car was one of their most frustrating problems. After consulting a family counselor, they had a talk with the children about the dangers of car fighting and got their agreement on what to do.

One Saturday the family piled into their station wagon to go to the circus. The children had been looking forward to this event for a long time. About a quarter of the way there, a fight started between the younger, Margaret, and Tony. Father stopped the car and after five minutes of quiet turned on the ignition. Within minutes the two were again battling. Father turned around to go home. "Why?" wailed eleven-year-old Ron, "We didn't start it. They did. Why should all of us have to go back home?"

The parents did not answer. They parked the car and went into the house. All four children were crying bitterly. Margaret and Tony were each blaming the other, and the other two were complaining that they were innocent and didn't deserve this treatment. The parents remained silent. After this experience, the children did not fight in the car, and the family had many fine outings.

SUMMARY

The method of logical consequences when applied as we have recommended has, in our experience, been invariably successful in ending fighting in the car.

21

BEHAVIOR IN PUBLIC

THE PROBLEM

Mr. Copi invited the Kents for a Sunday cruise and added, "Bring your kids along. I'm sure they'll enjoy it." He was wrong. No one enjoyed the sail—not even the four Kent children. This is what occurred:

Steve and Wendy got into a loud screaming battle.

Susan cried because there was no milk on the boat.

Greg got the boat lines all tangled up.

Mother annoyed the Copis with her yelling "Don't" and "Stop that."

Steve was found rummaging around below decks, opening drawers.

Greg dropped a winch handle overboard after his mother had said, "Don't touch it." Mr. Copi said, "That's nothing," but he well knew it was a forty-dollar loss.

A miserable time was had by everyone. Mr. Copi swore silently that he would never invite those kids again—ever. His wife was driven practically to tears by these bad-tempered children and their shrewish mother. Mr. Kent became almost murderously angry, and when they got home he gave each kid a licking. This disastrous experience was long remembered.

A year later, the family was invited to spend a week with relatives. "How can we accept this invitation?" Mrs. Kent asked her husband. "Our kids are completely undisciplined. Wherever we take them, they act up—getting into things, fighting, demanding, crying. I just don't see how we can accept the invitation."

"Damn it," Mr. Kent muttered. "Some families have outings and visits, and the kids behave beautifully. Why on earth don't we have such kids? What can we do to make them behave? Nothing seems to work, not even hard spanking."

His wife replied, "I just don't know why they act that way. They aren't so bad at home, but when we take them out they're impossible. I wonder if it's because when we're out they know you won't hit them, and they take advantage of this."

"Whatever the reason, we have to do something about it," Father stated. "I am ready to do anything—just anything—to get these kids under control. Why don't you check with some other families or call some doctor or someone to see what can be done."

DISCUSSION

Some children are "good" in the home and "bad" outside. Frequently, school personnel are told, "I can't understand why my Bobby isn't getting along at school. We have no trouble at all with him at home."

Such children are often cowed by their parents, who rule by force and terror. Children constantly controlled by their parents usually have no self-control. They "go wild" and misbehave if the school gives greater freedom.

SOLUTION

1. Discuss with the children the need to be pleasant and concerned for others when you go out so that everyone can have a good time. Explain the behavior you want changed.

2. Discuss the logical consequences should they misbehave. Get their agreement by helping them see that others want to have a good time too.

3. Families should playact eating properly in a restaurant.

4. Parents should first "experiment" with the outside behavior in homes of friends or relatives where failure may not be disastrous.

5. The consequences must be applied immediately, in silence, with no anger shown, and with no second chances.

SOLUTION APPLIED TO THE KENT FAMILY

Mrs. Kent went to an Adlerian family counselor who suggested a plan for dealing with the problem. She discussed it with her husband and they agreed to put it into action.

They called the children in and Mother said, "We want to talk about our going out and having a good time. Do you like it that we can't go sailing again with the Copis because we didn't behave well? And the Robertsons said that we can't go back to their house because there was so much noise and getting into their things." Both children said that they were unhappy with the situation.

Father explained. "We need your agreement that there has to be better behavior so that we can go out with other people." "I guess so," said Wendy.

Mother further explained that, should there be some nonacceptable behavior, they would all go right home so that the children could learn by that consequence that they must behave well. The children agreed, not being too concerned about the whole thing.

Having made sure that everyone understood, Mr. and Mrs. Kent put their training procedure into practice. They suggested having a picnic at a beach. They were going to make a fire, cook frankfurters, and roast marshmallows. Mrs. Kent bought a small air-cushion raft.

Before leaving, she talked with the children about what would be acceptable and nonacceptable behavior. The children agreed not to fight, cry or whine and always to remain in sight. They also agreed that the consequence would be to go right home should anyone's behavior be unacceptable.

And they took off. It was a two-hour ride to the beach, and they got there about eleven. A fire was started, food was taken out, the kids ran into the water. About twelve-thirty, Mother called that the meal was ready; the kids, famished, came to eat. Suddenly there was an explosion: a fight between Wendy and Susan over who was to have the first frankfurter. Other people nearby looked on in surprise at the intensity of the fight. Mr. Kent looked at his wife and nodded. She quickly began to pack. Father deflated the raft and started to carry things back to the car. He threw the frankfurters into a garbage can. Within minutes they were ready to leave. The astonished children, shocked to find the parents' warning coming true, got into the car; the family returned without a stop, getting home in the early afternoon, with everyone hungry, thirsty, tired, and subdued.

The parents felt that the lesson had been learned. They repeated the same expedition the following week, going through the same routine. That day was just perfect.

However, the Kents knew that there was more to be done. One day, Mrs. Reinhardt called. Her family was having a birthday party, to which she invited the Kent children. The conversation went as follows:

"Marge, you know what a nuisance my kids are."

"Oh, Myra, they're normal."

"I hope so. But they are quite a nuisance outside the home. Anyhow, here is what I want to ask you. I am now training them. I want to ask you to promise that if we come to the birthday party and any one of kids misbehaves, you won't interfere if I take them home immediately."

"All right, if that's what you want. Actually, I think it's a good idea. Your kids do sometimes get a little rough."

The next Saturday, as the children were in the car about to go the party, Father turned around to talk to them.

"If any one of you doesn't want to go, let me know and I'll stay home with you, and Mother will drive the others."

The kids all demanded to go, wondering why their father was even asking them.

"If anyone misbehaves at the party, we'll have to take him or her home. Okay?"

Each of the kids indicated understanding.

Mother added. "If Father has to take anyone home, and then someone else misbehaves, I'll take *everyone* home." Again the kids nodded understanding.

They drove off and, sure enough, not long after they arrived, Greg got into a battle with Barry Reinhardt about a toy. Mr. Kent scooped up Greg, and within a minute both were in the car going home, with Greg carrying on in a violent temper tantrum. The rest of the kids had a wonderful time—something that they reported enthusiastically on their return.

When summer arrived, the Kent family spent a weekend with their distant relatives, who complimented the parents on "their wonderful children." The Kents looked at each other and smiled, feeling that their training efforts had really paid off.

FURTHER EXAMPLES

Misbehaving in a Restaurant

The Hams went out for dinner with their eleven-year-old son and twelve-year-old daughter. At the restaurant, both children started jostling each other to sit at Mother's right side. The parents, who had been counseled regarding such behavior, got up and went to another table. The kids looked on in confusion. When the waiter came, Father said, "Is it possible for us to sit at one table and our kids at another?" The waiter, who had seen the situation, said, "Of course." The two pairs, separated, ate in peace.

That was the last time the kids ever pulled that kind of behavior in public.

Annoying Other Guests

The Malterre family went to a summer resort with their two children, five and six. Mrs. Malterre noted that the kids were splashing people in the pool, much to their annoyance. She got up, called to the children, and started to walk away from the pool. The children, afraid to be left alone, followed her, asking why they were leaving. Mother said nothing until she was some distance from the pool.

"I didn't want to talk to you while at the pool," she said. "You are disturbing others, splashing water. Either you stop this, or we'll go back to our cabin."

Both kids promised to stop. They returned to the pool, where no further trouble arose.

That evening at the dinner table, the children started "fooling around"—getting up and down, making noises, and in other ways annoying the other guests. Mother got up, called the kids, and walked back to the cabin with them. She waited for Father, who arrived after having eaten. Mother then returned to the table for her meal. She finished her dinner in peace, and returned to the cabin.

Meanwhile the children were quiet, realizing how they had inconvenienced their parents. They behaved properly at the table for the rest of the vacation.

Role-playing

Whenever the Guralnicks went out to eat, they were embarrassed by the behavior of their two children. The kids simply had unrefined eating habits. The parents had a discussion and evolved a plan.

"We'd like to go out to Sanderson's Steak House," Father said to the family, "but I will not go unless you kids know how to eat properly."

A lot of discussion was held about whether or not the children ate properly. The kids wanted to go there particularly because you could select your steak and cook it yourself.

Finally Father said, "Well, we could go there, but we'll have to practice eating properly. We'll role-play (that's like pretending) that I am the waiter and you are ordering your dinner and eating with good manners. Mother can watch and make notes, and later tell you what she thinks you did right and whether you did anything wrong. We can go to Sanderson's if you both eat properly.

The kids agreed, and at their next meal Father acted the role of waiter. The table was set as at a restaurant. The kids had to get their own salad at a salad bar. When the kids finished their meal, Mother gave her impressions.

"David, when you got to the table, you didn't help your sister, and you sat down first. You didn't put your napkin on your lap. And you were kicking her under the table. Alice, you were playing with your water glass, and you spilled some salad off your plate and spilled some milk on the table. Otherwise you did fine. David, you chewed with your mouth closed and you didn't poke hard with your fork and make noise on your plate. And Alice, you used your knife and fork very nicely, and not once did you use your hands to put salad in your mouth."

Father added, "Well, you did pretty well. Next meal, we'll have another trial, and when you both show you can eat properly, we'll all go to eat at Sanderson's."

SUMMARY

Parents have an obligation to prepare their children for social behavior, and usually the most important factor in such preparation is that the parents themselves act properly.

Children should be shown the way in which to act; they should be informed of the consequences of misbehavior. Consequences should be applied immediately, in silence and in a firm manner, without anger, threats, or scoldings. If others in the family have to be discomfited, this is the price of training. It is a small price to pay for having pleasant family outings and visits.

22

AGGRESSION

THE PROBLEM

When Mr. Niedzielski came home, his three-year-old son ran to him to be picked up and hugged. "Did you bring me something?" little Beau asked.

"No son, nothing today."

"Bad Daddy!" Beau shouted, and hit his father.

"I don't know where he got this," Mother stated, "but he is becoming very aggressive. He hits other children, and now he hits me when I tell him to do something."

"Oh, Doris, it's probably just a stage. Maybe he wants attention. Why don't you give him more love?"

"I don't know about that. He gets a lot of love. If he doesn't get his way, he is so angry that he hits. I think he'd better learn to control his temper or he will have trouble in life."

DISCUSSION

Aggression, as well as other types of misbehavior, is a result of children's discouragement. We find aggressive behavior in children who come from homes in which there are any one or several of the following: a lack of order, much chaos, inconsistency, punishment, and competitiveness between parents. In such situations, children experience anger and frustration, anticipate battling, and believe that punishment and chaos are the only way of life.

Parents must first take stock of the total home situation: Is there a set time for awakening in the morning, for meals, for play, for TV, for homework, for sleep? If not, a necessary procedure is to look for ways to schedule events so that things can operate more smoothly in the home. When parents establish order in their lives their home life will become more peaceful. This sense of peace will then become part of the lives of children. They will know what is coming next and family members will no longer have to fight over every issue. As the children experience life going more smoothly at home, the battles lessen. If the parents cannot create order, we would advise some professional counseling.

You must lessen your own anger and outbursts of temper and hitting the children. Too many parents are weighed down by the details of daily life; work, fixing leaky faucets, paying bills, yelling at the children. They need time to go back to the things that delighted them in their youth: a walk in a beautiful spot, time for exercise or sport, time to work off frustrations, treating themselves to an ice cream cone—or anything else that will enhance their lives, even momentarily.

SOLUTION

1. Establish a schedule. It could include just a few landmarks during the day so that all the family members will know what to expect. For example: Breakfast at 7 A.M., dinner at 6 P.M., bath at 8 P.M., roomtime at 8:30 P.M.

2. Stop your own aggressive behavior. Lighten your own life, have fun, have a "date" with your spouse, leaving the children with a sitter. You also can have family outings, of course.

3. Establish a special time each day with each child and show much love. An individual play time with each child helps the child feel that he or she has you exclusively for ten to fifteen minutes a day and has that time to look forward to *daily*. This special time improves parent-child relationships and prevents behavior problems from the outset.

4. Tell the child that you do not like aggressive behavior and that you will leave the room if the child hits you. Make it clear you will take the child home if the child becomes aggressive while away from home.

5. Give positive, loving attention at other times. Never withhold love while training.

SOLUTION APPLIED TO BEAU

The parents discussed the need for establishing order in their home. They planned together the time for arising, for each meal, etc. They were beginning to realize that their own punishing ways were producing violence in Beau so they decided instead to use consequences for training. Then they talked to their child:

"Beau, from now on when you hit us we will not allow that to continue. We will quickly walk away from you and go into the bathroom or to our bedroom. We will come out when you decide to be nice."

Later that night, when Mother told Beau that it was time for his bath, he ran to hit her. She quickly walked to the bathroom, locked the door, put on the radio and started reading a book. Beau was outraged and started to scream and cry. Twenty minutes later, when he was quiet, Mother came out, looking pleasant, smiled, and gave Beau a hug. She engaged him in a conversation about something she had done that day. Beau tried hitting Mother or Father two more times, then realized that it was more fun to be able to be together with his parents, so he stopped hitting.

FURTHER EXAMPLES

Hitting Other Children

Five-year-old Bobby often hit children wherever he went. It certainly was not pleasant to have him as a guest in one's home. Mother finally got fed up with this behavior and told Bobby just before going to visit Mrs. Kaye and her four-year-old daughter, Sarah, that he must behave and not hit anyone or they would go home. Bobby and Sarah were playing for less than five minutes when he wanted a toy that she had. He hit Sarah, took the toy and she began to cry. In silence, Mother took Bobby by the hand and put him in the car. He screamed that he would not do it again but Mother drove straight home. A few days later Mother took Bobby to the shopping center. He was there for only a few minutes when he hit a strange child who was smaller than he. Mother immediately took him to the car and went home; Bobby screamed and cried all the way home because he wanted to stay at the shopping center. For a while when Bobby and Mother went out he behaved well. A few weeks later he took a poke at a child in a store and Mother immediately took him home. That was the last time he was aggressive.

Spitting at People

Four-year-old Izzy suddenly started spitting at people. His parents were upset and explained that spitting is a nasty habit, but Izzy continued. finally they decided to give Izzy a pitcher of water and a glass and told him to go into the backyard to practice spitting on the ground. At first Izzy thought it was fun but his parents had him continue much longer than he wanted. Izzy finally had his fill and he no longer spit at people.

Biting People

Two-and-one-half-year-old Teddy was biting people. One day, as mother held him, he bit her on the arm. She very quickly put him on the floor and walked away in silence. He was surprised at her reaction and he began to cry. When he stopped crying she came back, sat on the floor and played with him, saying that she would not spend time with him when he bit. Teddy tried biting Mother one more time as she held him and she quickly put him down. Later she again played with him, held him in her lap, and cuddled him. He realized that Mother would not be with him if he bit her and he stopped the behavior.

SUMMARY

The aggressive child is a discouraged child. The first step in training is to stop punishing, since it sets an example for the acceptance of violence. Another necessity is to change a chaotic home into one with order since order produces a sense of peace. Do not stay with a child who hits you: simply leave the room. The child wants to be with you. If the child is aggressive when out of the home, simply take the child home.

23

UNDESIRABLE COMPANIONS

THE PROBLEM

"Come right in, Helene!" Mrs. Jacobs called out.

Obediently, her daughter left her friend and came in.

"Why, Mama?" she asked.

"I don't want you to play with Renee."

"But why, Mama? We have such fun."

"Mother knows best, Helene. You are only ten. I want you to play with nice kids. Why don't you play with the Schwartz children?"

"They're too young."

"Well then, play with the La Brie children."

"I don't like them."

Mother became exasperated. "Well, I don't want to see you with Renee. And if I do see you talking or playing with her again, I'm going to bring you into the house and you'll have to stay in your room the rest of the day."

"But, Ma, it just isn't fair." And Helene began to cry.

DISCUSSION

Children grow up in three arenas—the home, the school, and the street. Parents must train the child in the home and then allow the child to manage school and street problems alone.

The choice of friends tells a great deal about children. If they play only with younger children, we may conclude that they may feel inferior to kids their size and age. They may want to boss younger children. Perhaps they are born "mothers" and want to instruct and protect little children. That they play with older children may indicate that they are looking upward, are ambitious, and want to be big. Or they may be merely playing the kid-brother role.

On the street, children really begin to be on their own. There they can begin to express themselves as individuals with more latitude than they have either at home or at school. No longer are they under the direct control of adults—they can become themselves. With their peers they begin to develop their social being.

On the street, children at first cautiously explore the big wonderful terrifying world of the "outside." They may be hurt by others. They encounter new attitudes. Should they say, "My mother says . . ." they find themselves derided. They are placed in their first loyalty conflict. If they are on the side of home and family, they are laughed at. At times they must become traitors not mentioning mother. . .and later teacher, denying their wisdom and advice and admonitions. They soon become two personalities: they have their street selves and their home selves, each with its own vocabulary.

How surprised parents are when they learn from others the image their child has in the street.

"What!" shrieks the mother when she learns that her son is the neighborhood bully, carries a portfolio of *Playboy* pictures, is the chief tormentor of new kids, is giving free consultations in applied gynecology, instructs in commando techniques, and is the one who deflated Mr. Warfel's car tires last week. Mother is almost in shock as she listens to this "authentic" description, trying to reconcile the boy she knows with this neighborhood monster.

Some children will not go out to play in the street because of their inability to adjust to the world outside. They will obediently sit in front of the house and deal only with "nice" children. Subdued by their parents, they do not learn to deal with life, and they tend to become fearful and discouraged.

Our golden rule regarding the child when the child starts to go out: "Leave the child alone." Let children find their own friends and explore relationships. Young Ronald will be with Franklin this week, with Walter the next, with James the next, and then back to Franklin. These pairings are a kind of mating and, like all voluntary matings, are based on a complex of compatibility factors.

No parent is wise enough to know which of the kids the child goes with are "good" or which are "bad." Isolating a child is not the answer. If the parent has taught the child basic values, the child should be able to meet life without being corrupted, and the parent need not worry.

At least one child in every neighborhood is a "bad" child: sexually precocious, a thief, a liar, a troublemaker. Every parent in the neighborhood would be happy to make a contribution to a moving-away present should this monster leave the area.

SOLUTION

What should be done about such children?

Adopt them! Invite them into your home—feed them, play with them, treat them with love, kindness, and respect—so that they like your own child, get the benefit of your warmth and good sense. Do not be dismayed if they do not know how to behave. Do not be upset if they "attack" you—wild animals will do that before they are tamed. Be ready to see them melt and become normal, sweet, and good. Thus you will be helping your own child and another parent's child as well.

SOLUTION APPLIED TO HELENE

Mrs. Jacobs noticed that Helene was now playing out of sight and becoming more secretive. She realized that her daughter was probably still playing with that naughty Renee. So Mother went to a trusted friend for advice. After initial resistance to the advice, Mother realized that it did make sense, and the following occurred that night:

"Helene, I'd like you to invite some of your friends over for ice cream and cookies."

"Why, Mama?"

"I think it would be a nice thing to do. You can ask some kids from the neighborhood and from school. And please be sure to invite Renee."

"Renee? I thought you didn't . . . I mean, I don't . . . Why do you want her?"

"I changed my mind about her. I'd like to meet her and be friendly with her. Do you think she would come?"

"I don't know."

"Helene, please ask her to come over and talk with me later today, I'd like to invite her myself."

A half hour later, Helene and Renee appeared together, and Mrs. Jacobs graciously invited Renee to the little party. Both kids withdrew, puzzled.

"I thought you said your mother didn't want you to play with me," Renee said to Helene.

"I thought she didn't. I don't understand her."

"Yeah, parents are funny. Let's play house . . ."

As a result of Mrs. Jacob's change of attitude, Renee became a frequent visitor to the Jacobs home. She began to feel at home there, and the two girls played nicely. Other children, some of whom had been told by their parents to avoid Renee, also began to play with her. One day a neighbor came by and talked with Mrs. jacobs.

"I notice that Helene is playing with Renee," said Mrs. Van Natta.

"Oh, yea. I used to forbid her to play with Renee, but I found out that she was not doing as I wished. So I decided to give her permission to do what she was doing anyway. Renee is a human being and it's wrong for us adults to ostracize her. I can see that she is changing. I think we all should feel responsible and should welcome her. Don't you agree?"

"Maybe you're right. We've been making her an outcast. I'll tell my Lori she can play with Renee. Thank you for making me see it differently."

SUMMARY

Parents should allow their children freedom in the arena of the street. In every community there is likely to be at least one "bad" child. It is natural for parents to want to shield their children from the unwholesome influence of such a child, but to try to do so is a mistake. We hope that parents will instead try to help the "bad" child to become "good" by opening their home and encouraging the child to become more cooperative. You may not know it, but another parent may think that *your* children are "bad."

24

DEMANDING ATTENTION

THE PROBLEM

The phone rang, Mrs. Knox, who had been cooking, dried her hands to answer. It was her friend Arlene. As the two ladies were starting a pleasant conversation, four-year-old Pam came running in from the yard and began pulling on Mother's skirt, shouting something about a doll. "Just a minute, Arlene," Mrs. Knox said. She turned to her daughter. "You shouldn't bother me when I'm on the phone." The girl screamed louder about not finding her doll. The exasperated mother went back to the phone. "We have a crisis," she said. "I'll call you later." "That's about the tenth time this week you have interfered with me when I was on the telephone. When will you learn to wait? Now, what is it you want?" And after hearing Pam's complaint, Mrs. Knox went looking for the doll. Later she called her friend back and apologized saying, "I just don't know how to get her to stop interfering with me when I'm on the phone."

DISCUSSION

Some children's main goal in life is getting attention. Parents should train children to know that times do exist to get attention and at other times not to and that they should get attention by useful rather than by useless means. The trick is to learn how to give children the attention they desire but not to succumb to misbehavior such as force or blackmail.

SOLUTION

1. Decide whether or not the child's behavior is an attempt to get undue attention.

2. Think of a proper logical consequence. Ignoring or withdrawing from the behavior will usually work.

3. Inform the child that the behavior bothers you and that you intend not to pay attention when you are bothered. Say that you will listen and play when the child is pleasant. Say these things only once.

4. Put your idea into practice. Be calm and quiet, firm and friendly.

5. Continue your procedure consistently, as long as necessary.

SOLUTION APPLIED TO THE KNOX FAMILY

Mrs. Knox said calmly, "Pam, from now on, when I am on the telephone I don't want you to bother me. I will just not pay attention to you."

Surprised at her mother's calmness, Pam answered, "Yes, Mommy."

Mrs. Knox next called the friend with whom she had most of her conversations. "Listen, Arlene: if I ever mention 'camels' in our phone conversation, you'll know I am dealing with Pam, so you can hang up even though I remain at the phone. I'll pretend that I'm talking to you, while I ignore her."

Several days later, while Mother was on the telephone, Pam ran over and began pulling on her mother's dress. Mrs. Knox hurriedly mentioned "camels" and her friend said, "I'll listen in—don't be concerned about me." A rather unusual scene was then enacted, with Mrs. Knox talking more or less nonsense into the receiver and trying to control herself while Pam shouted and yelled and tugged. Mrs. Knox determinedly talked on. Suddenly Pam changed tactics and began pounding Mother with her fist. Mrs. Knox hung up the receiver and walked to the bathroom and locked herself in. Pam began pounding on the door, shouting. Mrs. Knox turned on the radio. The baffled and indignant Pam began hammering on the door, screaming wildly. Mrs. Knox started a long bath. The pounding ended. Mrs. Knox finished her bath and went back into the living room. Pam was reading a book and looked up. "Hi, sweetheart," Mother said sweetly. She picked up the telephone again, dialed her friend, and reopened their conversation, saying nothing about the incident with Pam.

In the next two weeks, Pam and Mother repeated this performance several times. Then Pam's excessive demands for attention ended.

FURTHER EXAMPLES

Daredevil on the Playground

Mrs. Calia reported that her six-year-old, Vincent, was a daredevil and would do dangerous things when she took him to a playground. He liked to make the swing go high or to climb to the top of the jungle-gym and stand up; he also did other hazardous things.

The counselor asked Mrs. Calia what she did. She replied that she told her son to come down, or to stop it, or to come to her—and that she once even climbed up to get him.

The counselor gave her a simple suggestion: "Turn your back." Vincent soon realized that Mother wasn't looking—and what was the use of acting if she paid no attention? So he gave up the nonsense and stopped his dangerous activities.

Mrs. Calia had not realized that by giving him attention she was provoking her child to do dangerous things.

Refusing to Nap

Often when two-year-old Betty was placed in her bed at naptime, she would get out of bed and make a mess in the room—out of the cabinets would come all the toys, books, and clothes. Mother would scold Betty. And Mother began to think that the child didn't need a nap even though she seemed tired.

Mother enrolled in one of our Family Education Centers. The counselor told her that Betty still needed naps but that she had found a way to get much attention from Mother. Mother was told to put Betty in bed, to do nothing to keep her in bed, and to keep the door to her room closed. If Betty got out of the room, she was to be brought back in silence. A timer or alarm clock set for one hour was to be in the room; when it rang, Betty could come out. If there was a mess, Mother was not to say a word about it; she was not to ask Betty to clean it up, she was not to scold or spank. At a later time, when Betty was occupied, Mother would put things away.

Within two weeks Betty was napping quietly.

Refusing To Dress

The Kefir family was in a rush in the mornings since both parents worked and the children had to be driven to the day care center. Three-year-old Sandy got a lot of attention every morning in that she was constantly being told to hurry. She was slow in dressing and seldom had time to eat breakfast. At the last minute, either Mother or Father ended up dressing her after much nagging, scolding, or spanking.

The parents were advised by the family counselor to tell Sandy only once that it was her job to get ready in the mornings, that they were not going to dress her, and that if necessary, they would put her, undressed, into the car with her clothes, and she could either dress herself or go into her class undressed. On the days when Mother drove, Sandy found that she really was adamant about not dressing her daughter— Sandy learned to dress herself on those days. But Father felt sorry for Sandy and on the days when he drove he would dress her at the last minute; Sandy learned to anticipate this. When Father stopped feeling sorry for his little girl and giving her this service, she quickly began dressing herself.

SUMMARY

Only one answer exists: ignore children when they demand undue attention. Continue with whatever you are doing. Do not talk, scold, or respond in any way to this misbehavior. If you become upset because the child gets your goat, walk away—go into the bathroom, turn the radio on, do not listen to the child, come out when you are calm. In other words, do not be a sucker for the child's provocative, annoying behavior.

Remember, though: children do need and must have considerable attention. Spend time with the child when the child is behaving well. Play, talk, show your affection, take the child on excursions, have a family playtime.

E

SPECIAL
PROBLEMS

PRELIMINARY NOTE

In this part of the book we shall take up a variety of special problems, some quite common, like dawdling, and some relatively uncommon, such as bowel and bladder control. What they all have in common is that they are highly resistant to change. But if parents follow our general theory and practice, these relatively resistant problems will yield.

Many parents feel that children misbehave because they do not feel loved and that if children's emotions are worked on through loving, praising, caring, tender mothering, and the like, the problems will vanish. While we agree that problem behavior can be tackled in this manner and that parents, even if they use logical and natural consequences, should always be loving—and have said so in this book over and over again—we do not think that a lack of love causes these problems or that giving a child more love will erase them.

We believe that the best way for parents to solve these problems is to operate in a strictly logical manner—to refuse to be victimized by children. One action can be worth a thousand words. Tell children a hundred times that you want them to walk beside you—and they may not. But let them get lost once as a result of walking away from you—and they are likely thenceforth to stick with you like a shadow.

25

DAWDLING

THE PROBLEM

The DiSanto family was eating breakfast. Jimmy took only occasional bites, and he sat with his meal in front of him long after the others had finished. Mother urged, "Hurry up, you'll be late for school." Jimmy didn't appear to hear. Mother then suggested that Father do something about the matter, but Father did not know what to do other than to scold and threaten a spanking. And Jimmy continued to dawdle at meals.

DISCUSSION

Procrastination, postponing, and not meeting one's obligations on time are other examples of dawdling. We usually consider it to be a fault of character. We all know people who miss appointments, who forget to do what they are supposed to do. Many have been dawdlers since childhood.

A parent who permits a child to get away with such behavior is also a delinquent. The child should be trained to be considerate of others and to finish whatever is done within a reasonable length of time.

SOLUTION

1. When you and your child are calm, explain (just this once) what you intend to about the dawdling. Thereafter do as you have said you would but do not explain again.

2. If the child is slow in eating, remove all plates, when everyone else has finished. Do not give food between meals. The child will be hungry and eat faster if there is no "payoff" of much attention for dawdling.

3. If the child is slow in dressing, go out alone. If you do not believe that the child can be left alone, put the child and clothes in the car or bus. The child can dress en route or when at the destination.

SOLUTION APPLIED TO THE DISANTO FAMILY

Mother told Jimmy that from now on she would remove his plate when she removed the others from the table. The first morning, Jimmy objected: "I'm hungry; you don't want me to eat." Mother seemed deaf; she did not respond. "You don't care if I starve," cried Jimmy. Mother did not answer but went on washing the dishes. She had to remove Jimmy's plate at only two subsequent meals—thereafter he ate as fast as the others in the family.

FURTHER EXAMPLES

Not Getting Ready On Time

John was a dawdler to an incredible degree, and he drove the rest of the family wild. Finally, the parents consulted a counselor and decided to follow the procedures we recommend. They had the prescribed discussion with the child, and he did begin to hurry up a bit. Not long thereafter, the whole family decided to go to the beach. Everyone agreed to be ready at 10 A.M.

The next day at nine-fifty, everyone was hurrying and scurrying, making sandwiches, packing clothes, food, and games, getting the car filled—except John, who was calmly reading the Sunday paper in his pajamas. At nine fifty-five, he was still engrossed in the comics, apparently oblivious to the tumult about him. At nine fifty-nine everyone was in the car, and at ten o'clock precisely, Father turned the key to start the car.

"We can't go without John," Mother announced flatly. "We can't leave an eight-year-old child home alone all day."

"But we told John that if he dawdled we would go without him," Father said. "No matter that he isn't dressed. We're taking him just as he is!" With this, Father ran back into the house. There was John watching TV. Father got the clothes from John's room and put John and his clothes in the car. John dressed quickly because he didn't want to be seen in his pajamas. After that, he did not dawdle for outings or school.

Slow Eater

Pete was a very slow eater (he did practically everything at a snail's pace). The counselor advised Mother to tell him that she would give him exactly fifteen minutes to eat and that if he hadn't finished in that time he would not be given anything else to eat until the next meal. At the next meal, he had taken only three forkfuls of food at the end of fifteen minutes. By the end of the third day, he was eating as fast as anyone else at the table.

Not Ready to Go to School

Lena was always late for school because she took so much time dressing. Her impatient father invariably had to wait in the car to take her. From home to school was about a twenty-minute walk. Father finally consulted a counselor and took the latter's advice: he simply told Lena that if she wasn't ready by eight-ten, he would leave—and he did. Lena had to walk to school and was even later than usual. Three or four treatments of this sort completely changed her. Subsequently she was right on time.

Late for The Show

Tony wanted to go to the movies and his parents agreed to take him. They mentioned that they would leave at seven-fifteen. When seven-fifteen came around, no Tony. "Perhaps I ought to go look for him," Father said. "No," said Mother. "He will never learn to be responsible for himself if we assume his responsibility. We will go without him." And the parents took off. When Tony showed up at seven-twenty, he looked at the clock and jumped up and down yelling, "Stupid! Stupid!" at himself for not having kept an eye on the time.

SUMMARY

Parents should ask themselves: "What will happen to the child if he or she acts in this irresponsible way as an adult?" They should treat the child in the same way that the world will or as much in that way as is feasible—they should use logical consequences. This is the parents' job; to teach reality.

26

TEMPER
TANTRUMS

THE PROBLEM

The department store had a busy day: all the aisles were clogged with shoppers. Mrs. Tacker was nervous. She was trying to find cloth that matched a swatch she was carrying. She had come to town with her five-year-old, Philip, and he had been darting back and forth from counter to counter, with her in hot pursuit. To calm him down, she had taken him to the sixth floor to see the toys. Now she and Philip were back in the yard goods section, and he was pulling her dress, demanding to go back to the toys. For the fifth time within ten minutes, she begged him to be quiet, telling him that as soon as she bought the cloth she would go there with him. As she talked with him, she anxiously looked for a salesgirl. Philip would have none of this. He got louder and louder—and then it happened! He threw himself down on the floor with a scream and began kicking and thrashing about.

Mrs. Tacker noticed the crowd looking on—some in amusement, some in alarm—and became embarrassed. She tried frantically to make him stop. Finally, she gave in and took him back to the toys.

DISCUSSION

We do not believe that children cannot control themselves— It is not necessary for anyone, young or old to "blow off steam"—to scream, throw things, get drunk, or tell someone off. Under some conditions, such as extreme intoxication or delirium due to illness or drugs, a person may lose all control, but these are highly exceptional circumstances.

People in a normal state are responsible for their behavior. They choose to behave in certain ways so as to get what they want.

Philip had the temper tantrum in order to blackmail Mother into going back to the toy department.

A temper tantrum is always blackmail done in the presence of an audience for the purpose of gaining a goal.

SOLUTION

To cause your child to stop having temper tantrums, you should, when one occurs, remove yourself psychologically and perhaps also physically. Thus you take the wind from the sails of the little tyrant who is trying to blackmail you. The solution is just that simple. The best procedure is to just stand there and look on quietly. If the temper tantrum is in public, we suggest that you go as far as possible from the child while still keeping the child in sight. The purpose of the tantrum is to threaten and harass you. After you make it unmistakably clear that it is not going to have its intended effect, it will soon end.

After it is over, say nothing about it. Above all, don't threaten the child in regards to him or her ever having one. Handle it in the same way. Soon the child will get the message and give up, realizing that you simply will not let yourself be blackmailed.

SOLUTION APPLIED TO PHILIP

Mrs. Tacker consulted an Adlerian family counselor and resolved to follow her advice.

At the next visit to the department store, Philip asked to see the toys and Mother did take him to that floor for a short time. She then led him by the hand to the dress department. He did not wish to stay there long enough for her to do her shopping. Again he threw himself on the floor, screaming and thrashing about. This time Mrs. Tacker walked away, took an escalator to another floor, and asked a sales clerk where she should go to find a missing child. She went to the ladies' room to freshen up, returned to the dress department to make a purchase, and finally went to the lost-and-found office. There she picked up her son. She was pleasant with him and made no reference to his tantrum.

Philip did not have temper tantrums again in public places. At home she handled his tantrums in a similar way (removing herself) and they soon ended once and for all.

FURTHER EXAMPLES

Involving Mother

Jane ran from her room to her mother and began to wail. Immediately Mother ran to the bathroom, locked herself in, and turned on the radio. She didn't even want to know what the wailing was about.

After the wailing stopped, Mother listened a bit longer to the radio and then came out. Jane was waiting for her, her face contorted. Mother realized that these were tears of power.

"Jane, if you begin carrying on again, back I'll go into the bathroom," the mother warned.

Jane and Mother looked at each other, and Jane's pursed lips relaxed. "Harry was in my room and he took my elephant."

Mother listened quietly. "What do you want me to do?"

"Make him give it back to me. He's your son."

"He's your brother. If he took it, ask him to give it back."

"He'll only lie." Once again Jane broke down and opened her mouth to wail—but Mother was already fleeing to the bathroom, where she opened a book. She read for a half hour. When she came out, Jane was playing quietly with her brother.

In this incident perhaps the reader can see a bit more clearly how Adlerians interpret behavior. Jane was "upset" with her brother but she was trying to get Mother to do something. When Mother refused and Jane saw that her tears and cries would avail her nothing, she abandoned her attempt at blackmail.

Father and Mother Treat Child Differently

Two-and-a-half-year-old Don became angry very often. His temper tantrums were frequent and usually involved his kicking the refrigerator door over and over again. Mother went to an Adlerian counseling center and was told to walk away from him whenever he had a tantrum. A few weeks later, at another counseling session, the counselor was surprised when Mother reported that Don was still having tantrums. Mother, it appeared, was faithfully following instructions—she did leave the scene and stay in the bathroom with the radio turned on quite loud; but Father thought her behavior was nonsense, and he would either threaten the boy with a wooden spoon or actually hit him with it if he kicked the refrigerator door. The counselor asked Father to attend a counseling session. When Father too was convinced that the best thing was to walk away, the tantrums ended.

SUMMARY

You, the parent, must not let yourself be overly affected by your child's emotional behavior. Learn to move away when the child exhibits negative emotionalism. Come back when the anger, the violence, the excitement are over. Always keep calm and show no anger yourself.

Be sure to give the child plenty of love and attention at times when behavior is good.

27

NIGHTMARES— EXCESSIVE FEARS

THE PROBLEM

"Aieee!" The blood-chilling scream came out of Alex's room, and both parents sat up in bed. "He's having another nightmare," Mother cried, and she got up and ran to her son's room. Father turned on the light. Three A.M. He too got up. He went into the bathroom, filled a glass with water, and hurried to the side of his son's bed, where his wife was holding and soothing their eight-year-old. "There, there, it was only a dream."

After a few minutes Father went back to bed, but his wife lay down on the bed next to Alex so that he could fall asleep free of fear. A half hour later, she crept into her bed. Her husband had not yet fallen asleep.

"Wonder what it means?" he asked her softly.

"I don't know, but he has been having these nightmares more often.."

"You ought to ask the doctor," her husband suggested.

"I did, and he said that Alex would outgrow them and that we shouldn't pay too much attention to Alex. He told me that if they continued, he would prescribe a mild tranquilizer.

DISCUSSION

A nightmare is a fantasy that a person imagines while asleep in order to scare oneself. What is a child's purpose in having a nightmare and becoming scared?

In Chapter 2, we discuss four goals of children's misbehavior:

1. *attention*—the child wants to keep people busy;

2. *power*—the child wants to show that he or she will not do what others ask;

3. *revenge*—the child feels hurt and wants to hurt back; and

4. *inadequacy*—The child wants to show inability, helplessness.

Alex may be aiming at one (or even more than one) of these goals *without awareness* (nonconsciously). He may have nightmares because he wants, nonconsciously, to keep his parents busy with himself, to keep them under his control, to hurt them, or to show that he is helpless and must be cared for even during the night.

Alex's mother and father were alarmed, gave him water, rocked him, and provided him with company until he fell asleep again. Whatever his goal may have been, this parental activity reinforced Alex's behavior—thereafter he would be likely to continue having nightmares and being fearful.

We believe that Alex's parents should not encourage and strengthen his fears by giving him all this reassurance. On the other hand, we do believe that his parents should convey to Alex that they are concerned for him, want to encourage him, want to help him feel that what has happened is normal and natural and that he has nothing to worry about.

SOLUTION

On hearing a child cry in the night, the parents should wait awhile, move slowly, hoping this cry will be the only one. Only one parent need go to look at the child. Without saying a word, the parent should see if the child has fallen asleep again. If so, the parent should return to bed. If the child is awake and frightened, the parent should give brief reassurance—saying that it was a bad dream, saying good night, and leaving the room. *The attention given should be minimal.*

SOLUTION APPLIED TO ALEX

Alex's parents consulted a family counselor about the nightmares.

The following night, at about 2 A.M., the parents were awakened by a shriek, followed by a loud "Mommeee!" Mother got up slowly, and walked slowly to her son's bedroom. Without turning on the light, she entered the room and said softly, "Now, now, you just had a bad dream; go to sleep." She tucked the blanket around him and left the room. She waited for a few minutes in her room before returning to bed, and then, not hearing anything, went back to sleep.

Prior to the parents' change of procedure, Alex had been screaming out in his sleep about once a week. Six months after the change, Alex's nightmares had ceased completely.

FURTHER EXAMPLES

Fear of Water

Two families, each having a boy about three years old, were on vacation. At the beach, Ron went right into the water but George stayed near his parents.

"Go into the water, George," his father urged.

"Look," Mother said. "Ron, your friend, is in the water."

"Don't be afraid," Father said. "I'll go with you."

The boy stared at the ocean a moment or two, evidently intensely alarmed. Then he ran away from the water, stopping some fifty feet away, apparently terrified.

"I don't know what the kid is afraid of," Father said. "I think I ought to pick him up, take him in the water and prove to him that there's nothing to fear."

"That's what you did last year, and he had nightmares for months afterward," Mother reminded.

"What do you think we ought to do?" Father asked Ron's parents. As it happened, they had some Adlerian education.

"The important thing is to say nothing to him about going into the water. Don't try to encourage him, because that would actually discourage him. It makes no difference whether he really is afraid, or whether he is only trying to prove to himself that he's a baby. The solution is to absolutely ignore him with regard to going into the water. Make no comparisons with our son, Ron. Just enjoy yourself and let him enjoy himself. And let's see what happens. I predict that by the end of our two weeks, if we really leave him alone, he will be in the water."

So George's parents no longer spoke to him about going into the water. And day by day they noted that he was going closer and closer to it. At the end of eight days he was building castles close to the waves as they rolled up on the sand. By the tenth day he was entering the water up to his knees. By the fourteenth and last day he was romping in the water with Ron. At no time did George's parents compliment him or make any other reference to his behavior with regard to the sea.

When they were packing, George asked whether they could come back next year, and the parents said they thought so. George stated proudly, "I went into the water." Father replied, "You sure did." And nothing more was said about the matter.

Mother's Fears Reflected by Daughter

Emma, Two, was brought to a playground and put on a swing. She panicked, screamed, and was taken off. Her parents were disturbed by her behavior, especially since it had already begun to be evident that she was an overly fearful child, afraid of Santa Claus, of animals in the zoo, and the like.

The parents consulted a family counselor. The latter found that Mother herself was a fearful person—afraid of water, or heights, or high speeds in a car. She was highly overprotective of Emma, always worrying about what might happen to her. Father reported that Mother had resisted taking her to a playground because she feared Emma's being hurt.

Mother was told that she was setting a poor example for the child. Her own displays of fear—remarks, excited instructions, and general overconcern—were reinforcing the child's fears. Mother was told to stop her overprotection. However, it developed that she was not able to do so, and the child continued to be fearful.

Then Father was asked to take Emma to the playground, and Mother was asked to stay home. Father watched his daughter but intervened only if real danger threatened—he then acted, but without talking. Soon Emma was playing like any other two-year-old.

Fear of the Neighborhood

After the Baldwin family moved to a new neighborhood, Ross, four, refused to go out; he stayed in and watched television. He would go out only when accompanied by his parents. If they put him out and left him alone, he cried and beat on the door until he was let in.

A family friend suggested that they do nothing, that eventually Ross would go out. However, after three months of his continued fearfulness, the parents felt they had to do something. The talked to a neighbor—a mother with a son Ross's age—and asked her to bring her son over for a visit. The neighbor was sympathetic about the problem and did come in with her son, Joe; but Ross ran into his room upon seeing them. However, since he was on his own grounds, he did emerge after a while, and played a bit with Joe. After several such visits, Ross and Joe were asked to play on the porch, which they did. Soon thereafter, Ross began to visit Joe's house. Within several weeks, Ross was playing on the sidewalk just like any other child.

Fear of Play Area

At a Family Education Center, a five-year-old boy refused to go into the playroom while his parents consulted their counselor, and instead waited at the door of the counseling room. The counselor thought that the child would eventually get tired of waiting in the hallway, but during session after session the child waited outside, refusing to go into the playroom. Finally, the counselor picked up the boy, carried him into the playroom, and put him down, telling him, "You stay here." By the end of the session, the child was happily playing there with other children; and the playroom worker reported that he played well and was no problem. From then on he went willingly to the playroom.

SUMMARY

One person's reactions to a situation can serve to intensify another's feelings about it. This is especially true with regard to parent and child. A parent's fears are likely to be reflected in the child in magnified form.

Fear in its simplest form is reaction to real or apparent physical danger. But fear can arise in other forms that can be just as hard to bear: fear of failure, of strangers, of being unloved, of the unknown.

Parents should realize that all children have some irrational fears. About their child's fears they should take as relaxed an attitude as possible. Most childish fears do not persist if parents act sensibly. If the child does have an irrational, long-lasting fear, the parents should seek professional help.

28

BAD HABITS

(Nose-picking, genital play, stuttering, thumb-sucking, etc.)

THE PROBLEM

"**D**an, hurry up! Your breakfast will get cold," called Mrs. Herzog.

"O.K., Mommy."

Dan, four, wandered into the kitchen, sleepy-eyed.

"For goodness' sakes, take your finger out of your nose!" snapped Mother. Dan immediately complied, putting his hand in his pants pocket.

"How many times do we have to tell you that picking your nose is a disgusting habit? No one will want to play with you or invite you to their home!" Father chided.

Dan hurriedly ate his breakfast and asked for more milk. As Mother went to the refrigerator, up went Dan's finger—right into his nose.

"Dan!" cried Mrs. Herzog. "Will we have to tie your hands behind your back? When will you learn to keep your hands where they belong?"

DISCUSSION

Most parents go through the same procedure in trying to teach children to overcome a bad habit. They usually start with a grimace to show them they are doing a "no-no." Then they tell them to stop. Then they lecture about how terrible it is. Then they try a little humiliation: "Do you want to look stupid?" As a last resort they slap or spank. But the offender just carries on with the ugly habit. Why does this procedure not work?

Our general theory is that practically all behavior is purposeful even though the doer often is unaware of his or her purpose: Unless the behavior is rewarding, i.e., unless it "pays off," the child will not keep it up. But what reward can come from picking one's nose? It upsets everyone. Father and Mother make a fuss about it. If other children are in the house, they are likely to deride the nose-picker. Surely these are not rewards!

Yes, they are! The nose-picker is given what is for children the most important of all rewards: *attention.* A parent actually encourages nose-picking by paying attention to it. Parents often create what they fear, simply by giving attention.

If you are dubious about this point, perhaps we can convince you by having you make—in your imagination—an experiment. Let us suppose that you consider it particularly disgusting for a child to put his or her fingers in his or her ears and that you decide to do what you can to keep your child from ever doing it. So you watch carefully and if the child touches the ears, you say, in a friendly but firm manner, "Don't touch your ears." If you see the hands near the ears, you remind gently, "Don't touch your ears." And if again you see the child actually touch the ears, you push the hand away and give a long lecture on the importance of not touching them. You have your spouse, the grandparents, the baby-sitter, and everyone else also watch out for this behavior. You do this consistently for about one week—and what do you suppose will then be happening? *Your child will be running around with fingers in the ears.*

So, while you think you are training your child

to not speak so rapidly,

to not suck his or her fingers,

to not put his or her fingers in the ears,

to not wet the bed at night, and

to not pick one's nose.

What you are really doing by giving attention to these bad habits is training the child to continue them.

So whether the attention comes in the form of moralistic lectures such as "Peter, don't touch your penis. Doing that isn't nice."

Or whether it comes in the form of *Slap!* "I told you never to pick your nose. Next time I'll hit you twice as hard."

Or whether it comes in the form of "If you don't look like a stupid fool with your thumb in your mouth. . ."

. . . each of these methods is ineffective.

Now, what about anxiety? Many popular columns and books warn parents that children who suck their fingers are anxious or scared. it is possible, of course, that the child *is* anxious and *does* suck on fingers to relieve the anxiety. But where does this leave a parent with regard to treatment of the problem? Should you, as most manuals on child-rearing suggest, give the child more and more love and security? How? If you increase cuddling and playing with the child *for this reason*, you are quite likely to achieve exactly the opposite of what you want: the child probably will associate all this nice cuddling and loving (attention) with the undesired habit and will become more and more inclined to persist in it. Showing your love by cuddling and playing should be done when the child is well behaved; giving loving attention during the display of the undesired habit will encourage the child to continue it.

We take the "tough" attitude of ignoring the child when the child is "demanding" attention by undesired behavior patterns. Giving attention or cuddling when the child is not showing such habits. You should try not to feel angry, and you must certainly not show it—that would also be attention. Therefore, if Jerry is sucking his fingers and looking scared, ignore him. When you later notice that he is playing happily or smiling broadly, at that point give him attention—play with him, pick him up, cuddle him.

SOLUTION

One could make a virtually endless list of bad habits, including chewing nails, playing with genitals, scratching the head, banging the head, humming noisily, scratching the crotch, making "put-put" noises, making funny faces, sticking out the tongue—and so forth and so on. *The solution for all of them is the same: Ignore them.*

Pay them no attention. If you give children attention because of the undesirable habit, you will be rewarding them for it, and they will continue it.

Now, to ignore the habit is often very hard to do. We recommend that, insofar as may be feasible, you walk away from the offender and turn your back to the offensive behavior, doing so as unobtrusively as possible. Say absolutely nothing about the behavior.

Funnily enough, parents often arrive at this solution but without appreciating its full significance: "Well, I finally gave up. I figured there was just nothing I could do, so I stopped even talking about it. And you know what? She stopped!"

SOLUTION APPLIED TO DAN

Mrs. Herzog consulted a counselor and then got her husband's cooperation in carrying out the recommended plan.

"The important thing," she emphasized to Mr. Herzog, "is that we consistently and completely ignore Dan's nose-picking. We must act as if we are not concerned—as if we don't even see it. We should turn away from him, but not in anger, and just talk about something else.

At first Dan's nose-picking increased. On about the tenth day of the treatment, he even tried to attract his parents' attention by very obviously putting his finger in his nose at the dinner table. But the parents conversed about the food and ignored Dan's behavior.

"See?" said Dan, trying all the harder. But Mr. and Mrs. Herzog continued eating and talking to each other.

After that episode, Dan quit nose-picking for two days. Then he tried it once more, with no success. And so he finally gave up the habit.

FURTHER EXAMPLES

Chronic Masturbator

Little Richard, three and a half, was already a chronic masturbator. Mother reported to the counselor that she had done everything she could think of to make him stop, including putting red pepper on his penis. She was informed that all children play with their sex organs but soon lose interest unless parents show interest. It was explained to her that her fear and disgust about this perfectly natural behavior on the part of her son had made him concentrate his interest on his penis and that if she would disregard the child's sex play, he would soon stop it. And this is just what happened. When she lost interest, so did he.

Finger Sucking

When Mrs. Jerome stopped reminding her daughter Janet not to suck her fingers, within several weeks this behavior stopped. Her counselor had pointed out to Mrs. Jerome that because the family dentist had told her the sucking could harm the daughter's mouth, she had become alarmed about it and that her alarm and reminding had intensified Janet's sucking.

Head-banger

Little Laurie was a head-banger. Her favorite pastime was to rock in her crib and bang-bang-bang her head. The mother would rush into the bedroom, shake her daughter, and yell at her. When the counselor spoke with the parents, the father pointed out that if he and his wife were in the home, or if only his wife was there, Laurie banged her head, but that she did not bang it when only he was there. He said that he never worried about the banging and never went to see Laurie about it.

The mother recognized that her intervention "caused" the problem but stated that she just couldn't stand the bang-bang-banging. The counselor suggested that the mother go on a vacation and that a housekeeper come in. The mother indignantly refused this solution and demanded pills of some sort for the child. The counselor informed her that pills would not work.

"Oh, what can I do?" the distraught mother asked. She was told she simply had to stay out of Laurie's room at night, and she finally promised to.

The next day, weeping, she called the counselor and said that her daughter had banged for hours. Couldn't the daughter be given sleeping pills?

"Laurie expects you to come into her room," said the counselor. "Her signal—her command—to you is the banging, and until now you have obeyed. To put her to sleep by giving her pills would not help in the least to train her not to try to summon you."

And so for several days her daughter kept banging, night after night. However, on the fifth night, it stopped once and for all. The little girl finally got the message: no matter how much she banged, no one was going to answer.

Starting to Stutter

With Ken, her pride and joy, Mrs. Chickamoto was visiting a friend, Mrs. Luke.

Mrs. Chickamoto said, "Sylvia, I'm worried about Ken. He seems to be starting to stutter."

"Oh, Rose," her friend replied. "I've been reluctant to say anything, but I see that I have to. You're always correcting him. Please stop it. You're actually reinforcing his speech problem. Just pay no attention. All kids hesitate or try to talk too fast when they're learning to speak."

"I know you're a speech therapist, Sylvia, but do you really think I shouldn't correct Ken when he makes mistakes?"

"I certainly do. I beg you to pay no attention. The most common cause for children's acquiring poor speech habits, especially stuttering, is parents who worry and correct them. The kids want attention and unconsciously begin to stutter to get it."

"Thanks for the tip, Sylvia. I'll try to remember it every time I'm tempted to correct him."

As Ken matured, his language improved, and he did not become a stutterer.

Nightmares

"Doctor, I'm worried about Larry."

"Seems healthy enough to me."

"He's starting to have nightmares," the mother explained.

"What do you do when he has them?"

"I run into his room, wake him up, and tell him he only had a bad dream, and then I get him a glass of water and stay with him until he falls asleep again."

"Well, just go in, check him, and say 'Go to sleep' or 'You had a bad dream.' Don't make a fuss or you will be reinforcing his behavior—he'll begin to have more nightmares and keep you busy with him often at night." (About nightmares, see also Chapter 27.)

Night Light in Bedroom

When Hal demanded that the light in his bedroom be left on, his mother said there was no need for that. He made such a fuss, she finally left it on. Thereafter, every night there was an argument about the light. The parents considered various possibilities, including installation of a night light or leaving the hall light on in such a way that it wouldn't bother him. After considerable discussion, the father suggested (1) that a brighter light be put in the room—one bright enough to keep Hal from sleeping too well with it on, and (2) that a little stool be placed so that Hal could turn the light on or off when he wanted. Mother finally agreed, and Hal was given on-and-off lessons. For several nights he had his light on when he went to bed and it was still on in the morning. And then some mornings the light was off. Mother said nothing. Within two weeks the light was off every morning.

Thumb Sucking

Jean, a college sophomore, went to see a counselor about a school problem. As they talked, Jean confessed that she had sucked her thumb until last year, when she entered college.

"Why did you suck your thumb?" asked the counselor.

"Because I told myself that it comforted me when I was anxious."

"What made you stop?"

"Oh, I would have been embarrassed for my roommate to see it."

SUMMARY

Our essential message regarding bad habits is that, no matter what may have caused them, parental attention sustains them.

Children are insatiably looking for attention. If they discover that behavior such as thumb-sucking, scratching, playing with the genitals, etc., get them attention they are likely to continue that behavior. in effect, the parents are encouraging children to misbehave by rewarding them for poor behavior. And it makes little difference if the attention—the "reward"— comes in the form of punishment: i.e., nagging, slapping, shaming, criticizing, and other unpleasant behavior on the part of parents. Attention is attention. While the children naturally prefer pleasant attention, negative attention is just as likely to sustain the habit.'

In our judgment, there is only one effective way to handle bad habits—*Ignore them.*

Do give your children plenty of attention and love; but do it when they are happy and smiling, *not* when they are demonstrating undesirable behavior.

29

BED-WETTING

THE PROBLEM

After nine-year-old Terry left for school, Mrs. Huff went into his room and looked at the bed. Once Again! There it was—a stain of urine, half dry. Shrugging her shoulders, she picked up the blanket. Yes, it too was wet. She dropped it on the floor, plucked off both sheets, and laid them on the floor with the blanket. She went into the bathroom, came back with a sponge, and cleaned off the rubber sheet. Next she picked up the blanket and sheets and took them to the washing machine. She then went to the linen closet and took out a fresh blanket and sheets. Before starting to remake the bed, she raised her eyes heavenward and groaned, "When *will* he stop?"

DISCUSSION

Bed-wetting is something most children stop completely by the age of five. After that, some children will, now and then, wet the bed, and it is by no means rare for an adult to do so. A few children persist in constant bed-wetting up into adulthood.

Just about every way that conceivable might stop bed-wetting has been tried. Experience has shown that it does not solve the problem to curtail the intake of fluids after dinner, to ridicule the child, to insist on urination before going to bed, to give pills or to awaken the child and insist on urination in the middle of the night.

Some methods do succeed in stopping bed-wetting, but they do so only because they "punish." Some parents, for example, use a buzzer system controlled by a pad that fits under the sheet: the first drop of urine on this pad sets off a device that wakes the child. It is important, however, to note that such methods are not as *psychologically desirable* as the method we advocate.

In our handling of problems, it is fundamental that parents must not reinforce "poor," "unsatisfactory," or "useless " behavior. Often parents do just that about bed-wetting. Probably the very strongest reinforcer for children is attention. If we give children a lot of attention when they wet the bed, they are likely to continue doing it. The answer, in theory, is simple. Whatever attention they have been receiving because of bed-wetting must be stopped or minimized. We must stop talking about it, or asking them to go to the bathroom, or reminding them not to drink, or even waking them up. Also, we must stop giving them "service" for their "useless" behavior. The parent who does such thing for children as making their bed, especially when they are perfectly capable of doing it, is actually encouraging them to continue bed-wetting.

SOLUTION

Our method for stopping bed-wetting by a *child over four is* as follows:

1. In most every case, bed-wetting is a psychological, not physiological problem. (If the cause is a physical condition, this would in all probability have already been discovered by the pediatrician in a previous checkup.) Taking the child to the doctor, especially, for enuresis, may actually harm the child because it may make the

child feel a failure for not succeeding in stopping the bed-wetting. Simply take the child for a general check-up and do not mention your concern in the child's presence. In a phone call before your visit, ask the doctor to check this.

2. In a matter-of-fact way, explain to the child how the problem is going to be handled from now on, and get an agreement to the new routine:

   a. Say that you believe the child is now able to handle the problem. You will not remind the child not to drink, to close the window, or to have clean pajamas ready. You will no longer awaken the child during the night.

   b. If the child should wet the bed, the child is to decide whether or not the child wants to change pajamas and sheets.

      (1) The child may sleep in urine-soaked bedclothes, should the child choose to do so.

      (2) If the child decides to strip the bed, the child is to put the soiled bedclothes is a specified place (we suggest that this be a large plastic garbage can with a tight-fitting lid and that you place it some distance from the bedroom). Say that you will periodically wash whatever is put here: sheets, blankets, pajamas, pillow cases.

      (3) Show where clean bedding is.

      (4) Show how to make the bed and how to clean the rubber or plastic sheet.

3. Never again explain this program, and stick to it without any deviation whatsoever for as long as it necessary—perhaps a year or even longer. Once you have made everything clear, you are going to keep out of the bed-wetting situation completely. *Do not check to see if the bed is wet!* Have faith that someday the child will

stop. Your caring even if you do not verbalize your concern can harm the child because the child will sense your lack of faith in his ability to stop bed-wetting.

APPLICATION TO TERRY'S PROBLEM

Mrs. Huff, acting on advice of the counselor and with the agreement of her husband, called in her son Terry.

"Terry, I want to talk to you about your bed-wetting. And this is it between us on this subject—I don't intend to discuss it anymore in the future. I think you are old enough to take care of everything from now on."

"Gee, Mom, I can't help it. I wet when I'm sleeping. I don't want to."

"I know that, son, and I know that you wanted to go to camp last year and didn't go because of this. Mother hasn't been really helping you, and so now I will do things differently in order to help you to stop."

"How's that?"

"First, I'll never talk with you again about bed-wetting, I won't check your bed anymore, I won't tell you not to drink water before going to bed, I won't change your bed."

"Not change my bed? But it will stink. And I can't sleep in sheets after I wet them. Beside, Eric will sound off about the smell."

"If you should wet, here's what you do. Take all the wet things and put them in the plastic can I'm going to get. I'll wash them from time to time. Then you can make the bed with clean bedding after you wash off your rubber sheet."

"Gee, that ain't fair."

"What isn't fair?"

"That I should change the bed."

"If *you* wet the bed, *you* should change it."

"Suppose I *don't* change it?"

"Then sleep in the wet sheets."

"Don't you care?"

"Of course I do. What I'm doing now is going to help you become a big boy."

"I don't like it."

"Well, if you want, I'll show you how to do everything now, but from then on it will be strictly your problem."

Several weeks later, she noticed that there were no wet bedclothes in the plastic can.

FURTHER EXAMPLES

Child's Bed-Wetting Gained
Admission to Parent's Bed

Gregory, seven, would show up very early in the morning in his parents' bedroom, looking forlorn, the lower half of his pajamas wet with urine. Mother would let him into the bed. Father didn't like the idea of having his wet and smelly son between them, but Mother felt that Gregory might catch cold in a wet bed.

The parents were counseled to let Gregory into their bed only if he was dry. They told Gregory the new rule. He immediately stopped wetting the bed. Because of the rapid change, the counselor strongly suspected that Gregory had been deliberately wetting the bed in order to get into bed with his parents.

After a while, the parents changed the rule: he could come into their bed only on weekends. He immediately went back to bed-wetting, but when the parents showed themselves to be adamant, he gave up bed-wetting the second time—and this time permanently.

Silent Battle

Penny cried when her mother told her the new rules and called her a "bad mother." She refused to change the sheets and kept sleeping in the same pajamas. Soon her room smelled foul. Here was a power contest between mother and daughter.

Mother was distressed by Penny's refusal to accommodate, but her counselor advised her not to allow herself to be blackmailed.

"How long should I wait," Mother wailed, "before I clean up that room?"

The counselor said, "Well, Penny is five years old. I suggest you give up if she hasn't changed her bed by her twelfth birthday."

Mother laughed. "You mean I have to do what is right, no matter what."

The counselor nodded. "That's right: you have to do what's right, no matter what."

The "silent battle" went on for ten days, during which Penny defiantly continued to go to bed without changing pajamas or sheets. The room smelled. The house smelled. But Mother was determined not to give in. On the eleventh day she found sheets, a blanket, and pajamas in the hamper. She felt that the battle was over and that her daughter was on the way to stopping bed-wetting. A month later, there was no more bed-wetting.

Praising Interferes

Joan, five, and her parents came for counseling because although she had been dry at night by the time she was three and a half the child was now wetting her bed. Mother went home and followed all instructions. She showed Joan how to remove the soiled bedclothes and place them in the plastic can, how to wash the rubber sheet, how to get clean sheets and make the bed. But Joan would be dry only about three out of four mornings a week.

Two weeks later, the family came for counseling again. Father stated that he was very proud of Joan for being dry some mornings and that he always told her this on those mornings. The counselor had a hard time convincing him that such praise was interfering with the training program. However, he finally decided to show indifference, to do no inspecting, and to listen to no reports from Joan.

Three weeks later, the family came again for counseling. Joan had been dry every morning for two and a half weeks. She continued to be dry from then on.

SUMMARY

We have recommended a method for stopping bed-wetting that has had a high degree of success. It is essential, however, that parents have faith that the method will work—that the children will eventually stop bed-wetting when they bear the logical consequences of their behavior. Once this procedure has been undertaken, parents must allow sufficient time for change—we suggest at least a year (many children stop within a shorter time). If the child gets a rash or similar physical condition as a result of the procedure, do not give it up. A parent should never give in to the child's demands for attention and service.

If the child is brain-damaged or has a physical peculiarity affecting the ability to retain urine, of course, a physician's suggestions should be followed. Although it is sometimes difficult to know whether the cause of the bed-wetting is physical or psychological, ordinarily—and in this respect our advice differs from that of most family counselors—parents should not consult a physician specifically about the bed-wetting problem. The child should, of course, have regular medical checkups.

Why does this method work? Awake or asleep, children are still themselves, and their behavior—awake or asleep—tells us a lot about the child. Alfred Adler noted that a person's sleep posture told a great deal about personality. A child who wets the bed is giving us a message. Perhaps the child is saying, "I am only a baby and can't control myself. You have to do things for me." No matter what the message is, the wise parent can return a message or two, including: "You are old enough to take care of yourself" and "I shall not be victimized by you." In cases observed by us, at least 90 percent of chronic bed-wetters stop within a month when the method is followed consistently and intelligently.

Let us review the high points of this procedure:

—The parent must decide that enough is enough.

—The parent must explain the procedure carefully emphasizing that the child is old enough to take care of self.

—The parent must answer only briefly and nonchalantly.

—The parent must expect success and refuse to be surprised by it.

—The parent must avoid any attempt by the child to reinvolve the parent in the problem—it must be strictly the child's own problem.

If this method, properly followed, does not work within a year, other methods may be considered. The use of an electric gadget may then be advisable. However, it should be used *only if the child wants it, and will monitor it.* Incidentally, the prices for these buzzers range from about twenty to several hundred dollars—yet, regardless of price, they all do the same job.

30

CONTROL OF BOWELS AND BLADDER

THE PROBLEM

Mrs. Shea looked out the window and saw four-year-old Wilson's wet pants; they were almost too much for her to take. Only yesterday her neighbor had asked, "Is there something wrong with your Wilson? I mean about his . . . control? Have you seen a doctor about it?"

Mrs. Shea had seen a doctor about this problem several times; he had confidently told her, "Some kids are slower than others in controlling their body wastes. Just be patient. He'll get over his incontinence. There is nothing physically wrong with him." And she had said, "But, Doctor, he wasn't doing this last year—he was using the toilet."

Through the window she yelled with determined fury: "Wilson!" Her son stopped, turned around, and slowly started toward the house. "Hurry!" she shouted. How she wanted to punch him! Oh, she just knew he *could* control himself. He just wanted to play and was too lazy to come in. When would he learn? Wilson still moved slowly and Mrs. Shea screamed, *"Hurry! Right now! And I mean right now!"* Now Wilson was at the door, looking guilty and fearful. She gave him a tremendous slap, then grabbed him by the wrist and dragged him along the floor. She noticed feces coming down his pant leg, and this further enraged her. She dragged him into the bathroom.

A half-hour later, a white-faced Wilson was in his room, having been told: "Never again am I going to let you out; you're just a baby; you're too lazy to care; you have no consideration for me; you can control yourself, you just don't want to; you want to drive me crazy."

DISCUSSION

When we learn from parents that a child has had bowel or bladder control in the past but is now soiling clothing, we suspect that one or both parents are trying to overcontrol the child. No parent can control a child's bowels. A child who is in a power struggle with a parent or who feels resented because of much punishment learns that soiling clothing really hits the parent hard. The child is not aware that he or she does the soiling to show the parents that they can't make the child stop or otherwise to bother them, but those goals usually underlie soiling behavior. Parents become angry, scold, and punish; this reinforces the behavior, and so it continues.

SOLUTION

To solve the problem of incontinence, parents must first stop trying to control the child's behavior—not only in soiling, but in general. They must admit their defeat to themselves and even to the child and start using logical consequences.

A logical consequence for soiling is to have to clean oneself and to put on clean clothes. This is a messy job which the child will not like any more than does the parent. At a calm time, the parent should tell the child that if he or she again soils clothes, the child will have to handle the situation—will have to go into the bathroom, clean up, put on clean clothes, and put dirty clothes in a covered container. This procedure should be explained only once. Thereafter, when soiling occurs, the parent must not look annoyed, hurt, or angry, and should ignore the presence of the child while soiled. Thus the parents become noninvolved; the child has the responsibility. The child will soon cease soiling because it no longer works: it does not bring parental attention—the child no longer gets the service of being cleaned by a parent but instead must do the distasteful task. Regardless of whether the child's unconscious objective in misbehavior has been power or revenge, it now brings no payoff-anger or hurt from the parents.

Parents should not withhold love while training. When the child is behaving well, they should give positive, loving attention. They should establish a time for playing. If others are involved in the training—neighbors or other family members—parents should get their cooperation so that they too will act as do the parents in solving this problem.

SOLUTION APPLIED TO WILSON

After discussing the problem with a family counselor, Mrs. Shea spoke to Wilson in a quiet, loving way: "Wilson, I feel that you are now a big boy and that I should no longer treat you like a baby. You can do so many things for yourself now, and you do them so well. I believe that I was wrong to yell and spank you when you did not use the toilet. From now on, when you make in your pants, you can be a big boy and clean yourself. There are towels, washcloth, and soap in the bathroom for you. You know where your clothes are in your dresser drawers. After you clean yourself, put the dirty clothes in this container I just bought, and then get out clean clothes and put them on."

"But, Mommy, I won't get myself as clean as you do."

"That's all right, Wilson. Do as well as you can. I'm sure that you are big enough to do a good job."

Since the neighbor was quite annoyed with having Wilson around when his pants were dirty, Mrs. Shea went over to tell her of the new training procedure. She asked the neighbor to tell Wilson to go home if he had a mess in his pants. The neighbor gladly agreed to cooperate.

That afternoon, Wilson soiled his pants while he was outside. Mrs. Shea, looking out the window, noticed what had happened, but she did nothing about it. Later Wilson came into the house and stood right by her. She continued to read her magazine. He finally went into the bathroom and cleaned himself. He put the dirty clothes into the covered container, but he left the bathroom quite messy. He put on clean clothes and went to watch TV.

Sometime later, while Wilson was not observing her, Mrs. Shea tidied up the bathroom and threw the dirty clothes into the washer. Wilson continued soiling his pants two more days; Mother continued the same procedure. When he was not soiled, she gave Wilson loving attention and played with him. Father also played with him for a short while after dinner. On the third day, Wilson did not soil himself but used the toilet. During the next week or two, he did have several more "accidents," but each time he cleaned himself. And from then on he used the toilet.

FURTHER EXAMPLES

One of Children Wetting Self, Others Are Not

Robert, Gary, and Don came with their mother to one of our Family Education Centers. Mother said that her most pressing problem was Gary's wetting himself when he was at home, especially when the children were going to bed; they all shared a room, and the other boys complained about the odor. She was told to inform Gary that from now on he must clean himself, etc. She was also told that she must stay out of the arguments among the children. The next time the family was counseled, Mother reported that the problem had stopped—like a miracle.

When she no longer gave Gary the service of cleaning him and stopped protecting the other children from him, the children settled the matter themselves and the problem ceased.

Soiling on School Bus

Roger, six, was soiling his pants at home and in school. The teacher got a change of clothes for him from Mother and told Roger that whenever he had that problem he should go to the boys' toilet, clean himself, and put on the clean things. After doing this only once, he stopped soiling in school. But then he soiled on the bus going home from school. Mother was upset. She cleaned Roger scolded and spanked, but the soiling continued.

She discussed the matter with the teacher and decided to try the teacher's method. It worked. Roger stopped soiling on the bus and at home.

SUMMARY

Learning by sad experience is very effective. The method we call natural and logical consequences can sometimes be difficult for the parent, but it works.

31

MORALITY

(Lying, stealing, etc.)

THE PROBLEM

"**W**here did you get that toy?" Mother asked.

"I found it."

"Where?"

"In the street."

"It looks like Steve's."

"I don't know."

"Isn't it Steve's?"

"I don't know.."

"You do know it belongs to Steve. You go right next door and give it back to him."

Bill hung his head and started for Steve's. Mother watched him go and said to herself: "I just hate liars. And Bill is becoming a liar—possibly a thief."

DISCUSSION

A tragic irony of family life is that parents' behavior may create exactly the kind of child they do not like. In some cases this can be readily seen: the father who wants a brave son pushes him and scares him, and the child becomes a coward, with the father speeding this development along by criticism and sarcasm. Sometimes the process is not so obvious, as in the case of the overfearful mother who ends up with an overfearful child.

Handling character problems is a touchy matter. On the one hand, we certainly don't want a child to think that morally unacceptable conduct is all right; on the other hand, we don't want to frighten to such a degree that the child is afraid to admit and discuss it.

Overreacting to a child's misbehavior may actually reinforce it through giving it so much attention that the child becomes inclined to repeat it, attention being, a most desirable reward. So remember: when you scold a child for something, you may actually be encouraging the child to do it again.

SOLUTION

With regard to problems involving stealing, lying, or other conduct offensive to morality, the wisest parents are those who prevent their ever arising. The best prevention is a good parent-child relationship—one based on mutual respect, which fosters frankness, openness, honesty, trustworthiness. The child most likely to lie or steal is one who has been punished often.

When children have stolen or lied, it is best, if possible to avoid putting them on the spot. They naturally want to protect themselves from unpleasant consequences and will be tempted to lie—indeed, a head-on confrontation is usually almost certain to elicit a denial. Not saying or doing anything at the moment is usually best. Later, when you and the children are calm and in harmony, you and they can discuss the matter. Do not try to trap them or corner them, but do encourage truthfulness (tactfully make it as painless as possible). Practically always you will be able to get agreement to the moral principles involved, as well as to whatever restitution may be called for.

Angry lecturing and condemning are likely to do more harm than good. A parent should refrain from talking to the child like this: "You're a thief and a liar! Not only did you steal it but then, when I asked, you lied. People go to hell for lying and stealing." Such statements will probably make the child fearful and will certainly damage self-respect.

SOLUTION APPLIED TO BILL

Mother called Bill and asked him to sit down. She smiled at him.

"Bill, I want to talk to you a bit. I found a toy in the living room and I knew it wasn't yours. I thought I recognized it, and so I called Steve's mother, and she told me Steve was crying because he couldn't find his toy. I don't know whether he lent it to you and you forgot to return it, or whether you found it somewhere and then took it home—but you ought to keep in mind that you should never take home anyone else's things. Do you understand?"

"Yes, Mother."

"Fine. O.K., dear. I just wanted to make sure you understood. Please take the toy to Steve."

A little later, Mother played a game with Bill. Each felt good about the other.

FURTHER EXAMPLES

Countering with Similar Behavior

Marlene began telling a series of outrageous lies about what she had done and what had happened; both Father and Mother looked at one another and smiled. They listened carefully, and then they too began to lie, telling big colorful tales. Marlene caught on, and she began to laugh. "I was only fibbing," she said, and her parents also laughed and confessed that they too were fibbing. In this manner they did not shame her, but let her know they knew she was fabricating a wild story.

Child Bears Tales about Another Child

"Mommy!" Sandra screamed. "Patty has my doll and won't give it to me."

Mrs. Hapenny listened carefully, smiling at her daughter, and said, "My feet hurt—the shoes I got a couple of days ago are so tight."

"Huh?" the puzzled daughter said, "Mommy, didn't you hear what I said?"

"Yes, I did, dear. Thank you for giving me the information, but my shoes are tight, and my feet hurt."

"Aren't you going to do anything to Patty?" Sandra was amazed.

Ordinarily Mother would give her sister Patty a strong scolding. Disappointed, Sandra cried, "I don't care about your stupid shoes."

"I am sorry to hear this," Mother stated, then turned and walked away.

If a child bears tales about another child, one way for you, the parent, to handle the situation is to listen politely and then give the talebearer a complaint of your own—about the price of eggs, the weather, or whatnot. The message is clear: *I don't pay attention to talebearing.*

Taking Things of Others

His parents were quite worried about seven-year-old Herbert.

"It isn't that he's really a thief," the mother explained to the counselor, "but he takes things that don't belong to him. He comes into our bedroom and takes anything. We check his room. One time he had our wedding license; another time, my husband's medals. He takes anything he can lay his hands on."

The father added, "He takes things from his brother and sister, and now he's starting to go into neighbors' homes. We just don't know how to handle him."

The counselor then had a conversation with the boy in the presence of his parents. To their surprise, the counselor did not ask about stealing; instead, he asked Herbert what made him happy and what made him unhappy. Herbert said the main thing that made him unhappy was that his mother wouldn't let him ride his bike where he wanted to go with his friends. Herbert particularly wanted to go up a hill so he could come down rapidly.

"Why didn't you ask him about stealing?" the father asked after Herbert had left the room.

"After all, you covered the topic with him. But what is this about the bicycle?" asked the counselor.

"He's too young to ride a bike and come down a hill. He would have to cross a street, and he could get run over."

"But Herbert thinks he is old enough to do it."

"Well, I don't."

"Maybe you ought to let him do it. Most children are very conservative—they don't want to try anything they think is overly dangerous."

"What has this got to do with his stealing?"

"They may be connected. Why not think it over and see what happens if you let him use his bike on the hill?"

Several weeks later, the parents were interviewed again. They reported that the stealing had stopped, and they were pleased.

"And how about the bicycle?" the counselor asked.

"Fine—he manages quite well. He does a lot of riding with his friends. We're letting him go where he wants."

"Do you see any connection between the stealing and the bike?"

"No—I still don't see any connection," the father replied.

"Herbert knew that you didn't like his taking your things. he was doing this to get even with you for not letting him ride with his friends. Now that he can do what his friends do, he is no longer angry with you and does not feel that he wants to punish you. You have improved your relationship with him by showing you have confidence in him."

Stealing To Have as Much as Others

Wallace was stealing because he didn't have as much allowance as others in his social circle. The solution was to give Wallace an opportunity to earn money. The parents found a number of jobs around the house (in addition to his chores) for which they agreed to pay him at a rate equal to the legal minimum wage. Wallace could now shine shoes, put stamps in trading books, wash the car, rake the lawn, clean out the pantry, and do other things to make enough money to buy the various items he wanted. The stealing stopped.

Smoking Pot

When a neighbor identified that rather peculiar smell emanating from Howard's room as marijuana, both parents panicked. They searched the room and found a bag filled with a tobacco-like substance. Their son was a drug addict! They visualized him shoving a needle into his arm, the next step after smoking pot! They called their family doctor, who told them that in his opinion marijuana was no more dangerous than tobacco, although neither substance should be recommended for use.

A psychiatrist counseled them to say nothing to the son but to watch him carefully to see if he showed personality changes or if he should appear to be "stoned" (intoxicated). The psychiatrist particularly cautioned them against talking to their son about marijuana.

The parents were relieved after the interview. They watched their son for any symptoms, but noted none. After a couple of months, they no longer noticed the odor and assumed that he had stopped smoking marijuana.

Unbeknownst to them, Howard had informed his school counselor that he had smoked pot but hadn't liked it much—that it did nothing for him and, besides, was too expensive.

Because his parents said nothing to him, Howard handled the situation on his own—and he gave up smoking pot. A friend of his had parents who, under similar circumstances, panicked, and called the police. The boy was interrogated, he denied everything, the police could find no evidence of marijuana, and nothing was done. But the relationship between the child and his parents was severely damaged. And the boy continued to sneak pot whenever he could.

Saying Four-letter Words

When little Karen, four, said *that* four-letter word, her mother looked horrified. "Where did you learn it?" Mother asked.

"What does it mean?" Karen asked.

"Oh, it's a terrible word," Mother said. "Nice girls never use it."

Mother consulted a book on child psychology. It explained that sometimes a child will say naughty words just to get attention and that the best thing to do is to completely ignore them. Next time Karen said the word, Mother showed no reaction at all. And the next time or two also. Karen stopped using the word.

SUMMARY

Problems of a moral character are difficult to deal with. In general, we suggest that when a problem of this nature first arises, a hands-off policy be followed (if that is feasible), in the hope that the first "offense" will be the last. If the problem persists and the common-sense measures we have recommended do not work, we advise the parents to see a professional counselor.

F

BUILDING
A COOPERATIVE
FAMILY

32

COMMUNICATING

Parents frequently complain that they are not able to communicate with their children. What these parents mean is that they do not send or receive positive thoughts. And only too often the reason is that they have no positive feelings!

Sally comes home from school. Mother issues a barrage: "Why are you so late? You know I worry. You should be home doing your homework. You shouldn't be going with those wild kids." Sally gives her mother an ugly look and disappears into her room.

Talking should be reserved for positive purposes; giving information, telling stories, problem-solving, recounting and sharing thoughts and feelings. Parents who show good will generally have children who show good will.

Avoid words at a time of conflict. Being silent is effective communication, and it allows you to cool off. Our suggestions for logical consequences (Chapter 5) should help you discipline your children in a respectful manner. It will help maintain a good relationship with your children.

IMPLEMENTING POSITIVE MESSAGES

1. **Accept the child.** Children must believe they are fundamentally O.K. and that you love them no matter what they say or do. You may not like what they do, but you like them as persons. Just a simple word or two will usually suffice: "O.K.," or "I feel that way too at times." A smile, wink, nose wrinkle, or hug needs no words at all, but tells children you accept them.

2. **Display affection.** Some parents show affection only when the child is very young. We need physical contact and warmth throughout life. Accept and encourage your child's affection too.

3. **Minimize competition between children.** The person who loses in a competition does not feel good. A better procedure is to encourage cooperation.

4. **Modulate your tone of voice.** A pleasant voice is more winning than one that is loud and harsh.

5. **Watch nonverbal messages.** Angry facial expressions convey negative attitudes. Calm down; smile.

6. **Admit your own imperfections.** Admitting your errors allows the child to see you as human and indicates that you are not always right and know so.

7. **Show appreciation.** Let children know how much you appreciate them, not only what they do.

8. **Show your enthusiasm and spontaneity.** Pleasant times together build good relationships.

9. **Give "I will" not "You should" messages.** Don't say "You shouldn't fight with your brother." Say "I will leave the room when you and your brother fight."

EFFECTIVE LISTENING

1. **Do not be judgmental.** Acknowledge that children have a right to have their own ideas even if they do not agree with yours.

2. **Be an active listener.** If the child seems to want to say something, pay attention. Jerry: "Mom, I felt bad in school today; I flunked a test." Mother (stopping bed-making and sitting down with Jerry): "Do you want to tell me about it?"

3. **Try to understand a child's words.** Time is needed for language skill to develop, and a young child may say something inappropriate. Mark (age four): "Grandma, Daddy is going to take me to a funeral." Grandmother (perplexed, but trying to understand): "What will you do there?" Mark: "Oh, you know, there are rides, and things to throw and to win." Grandmother: "Oh, yes; you and Dad are going to a carnival?" Mark: "Yeh."

4. **Reflect a child's feelings.** At times children's words do not tell the whole story, and they may not know their feelings. If parents can show they understand the feelings, they have a better rapport. Paul: "Dad, look at my truck. Hugh broke it. He's a jerk! I'm going to get one of his toys and break it!" Father: "You feel angry and want to get even." Paul: "That's right."

BUILD POSITIVE RELATIONSHIPS

Our book tries to teach parents how to build positive relationships with their children. Good communications are vital in this process. For more on communications with children, read more on this topic.

So essential is communication that we believe our most important advice to all parents is to establish a family council, a structured device for effective communications, to be discussed in the next chapter.

33

THE FAMILY
COUNCIL

Were we to be limited to only one recommendation to help create a happy, cooperative family, we would say: *"Start a family council."*

People who live together inevitably have conflicts of interest at times. The family council gives invaluable training in human relationships. Each member receives practice in understanding others' opinions, feelings, and behavior. Parents as well as children learn how to get along within the family. This knowledge can be useful too in dealing with the outside world, the community.

We are going to give a detailed description of a family council, for experience shows that many parents who start one do not succeed because they do not understand important elements.

GUIDELINES

Membership

Everyone in the family, whether it be a two-person family (such as mother and son) or a multiperson family (such as grandfather, parents, six children, and a boarder), is a potential member. Even children too young to talk are included: membership encourages them to feel that they really belong to the family and are an important part of it.

Structure

The family council is *not* a discussion around the dinner table, or a discussion while driving. It is a formal meeting of everyone in the family. It has a chairman and a secretary. Everyone serves a turn as chairman. Those able to read and write may take turns being secretary, to keep and read minutes. Fixed rules of procedure are followed.

Scheduling Meetings

The council meets periodically, on a schedule drawn up in advance, such as every Tuesday night after a certain television program, or every Saturday morning right after breakfast.

One of the reasons for failure of a council is happenings like this: someone asks, "Should we have our family council tonight?" Someone else says, "Is there anything that anyone wants to bring up tonight?" And if no one answers, someone says, "Well, let's not have one tonight." Missing meetings destroys continuity and weakens the institution.

Attendance

People are invited, not required, to attend the family council, and a member may leave a meeting at any time.

Order

Order in the meeting is determined by *feet:* If anyone misbehaves to such a degree that the session is unpleasant, any person who is sufficiently annoyed can leave—and in this way votes with the feet! The purpose of the council is sensible discussion, controlled communication—clear discussion, attentive listening. If a member disturbs the meeting, only the chairman can ask that person to behave; if that person still does not behave, then anyone annoyed can leave. *But a member cannot be expelled from a meeting because of unpleasant behavior.*

Procedures

Discussions are open and unrestricted. Anyone can say whatever he or she wishes, and no one can shut up the person who has the floor (not even the chairman). The council is an open forum with complete freedom of expression. If someone wishes to talk and talk, others can get up and leave if they don't want to listen.

(To have a time and place where anyone can get anything off his or her chest, with others listening politely, is a kind of therapy, often needed by people.)

Issues

The family council is an open forum for grievances, issues, problems, matters of common concern. It is not so much a means for John and Jane to settle their quarrels, or for Mother to pick on Bill, but rather for the discussion of an issue or problem that affects the family.

The general rule is that any member except the chairman can bring up any subject. Other members may object if it is a subject that doesn't affect the whole family. The chairman rules on admissibility of an item.

Consensus

We recommend consensus. Some parents think a majority vote is enough to settle issues, but majority votes do not work well because someone loses. Issues should be discussed to reach a consensus in the same manner as labor and management negotiate on and on until they come to a decision. If unanimity is not possible, the issue should be tabled until the next meeting.

Purposes

The council meeting is a means to discuss anything of common importance. To give illustrations of the kinds of matters that may come up in a family meeting:

Jon wanted some friends to stay overnight. The council *discussed how many guests could be accommodated and under what conditions.* An understanding was reached about overnight visitors.

Bert asked if he could earn some money doing jobs in the family because he needed money for a corsage for the eighth-grade dance. Father and Mother prepared a list of jobs he could have and also set prices: shoes shined—fifty cents, etc.

Father announced that he wanted to buy a new car. He told the children the make of car he intended to purchase. He wanted the children's opinions about colors. The majority opinion was red, and Father agreed.

Mother complained that the children weren't doing their chores on time, and there was a discussion of what to do. The children agreed on times.

Eleanor complained that Frank played his record player too loudly and kept her awake. Frank agreed to use headphones after 10 P.M.

Father informed the children that a cousin, after an operation, was coming to stay with them for two months.

Plans were made for a family picnic the following week.

Parents asked the children if they wanted complete charge of their own rooms and, with the children agreeing, rules were established for parents' and children's behavior relative to the rooms.

Equality

The essence of the family council, and its major value, is equality. Father is just another member. So is Mother. The youngest and the oldest are equal. Each, if old enough, can and should have a turn at being chairman.

STARTING A FAMILY COUNCIL

1. Parents should make sure they agree on the concepts of the family council.

2. Parents must realize that they themselves are the greatest hazard to the family council because they may attempt to use it for their own purposes, as another way to manipulate children.

3. Parents inform the children of their intention to start a family council and invite them to join. Parents will meet whether or not children attend. Almost all children will be interested, and they will ask questions about how the council works. The parents explain, adding that many details will have to be worked consensually.

4. A date and a time are established for the first meeting.

5. At the time indicated, the family council meets. Anyone not showing up should not be reminded!

6. The first meeting should include the working out of organizational details: *Should we have a secretary? How do we select chairmen? How often shall we meet? How long should meetings last? What kinds of things should we take up?* The parents can give opinions about procedures, but the final decision should be based on consensus. This meeting also should include some family fun—e.g., a treat, such as ice cream, served after the meeting.

Other Points to Consider

1. Decisions can be made that affect absent members.

2. Decisions hold only until the next meeting. If anyone wants changes, they should be discussed at the next meeting.

3. Parents should always be examples for the children. They should attend every meeting on time. They should have the meeting even if children do not attend.

4. If a decision is made, parents must keep to it.

5. Parents should refuse to make decisions for the family that should be settled at the family council. "Take it up at the family council" should be a constant refrain in the family.

6. Meetings are not to be canceled except by unanimous agreement. Parents should not agree to cancel except for extraordinary reasons. That there seems to be nothing to bring up is not a valid reason for canceling a meeting.

7. No emergency meeting should be held unless every member agrees to have it.

8. Meetings should be time-limited—short at first (fifteen minutes), then later perhaps a half hour or forty-five minutes, as required.

9. Among rules that may be considered are the following:

   a. Chairship to be rotated in some automatic way, such as by age or alphabetically.

   b. Chairperson is to accept no new topic until all have had an opportunity to discuss the present one.

   c. Chairperson is not to discuss an issue brought up by others until all have had their say; then the chairperson may come in.

HAZARDS TO THE FAMILY COUNCIL

Some of these have already been mentioned, but they deserve repetition:

1. Father or mother dominates.

2. Parents complain too much during sessions and use the family council to manipulate children.

3. Meetings do not take place on time.

4. One of the parents avoids attending.

5. Parents make decisions that should be made by the family council.

6. Decisions are not upheld.

7. Sessions are canceled for reason of "nothing to bring up."

8. People become discouraged when consensus is not reached immediately.

A FAMILY COUNCIL IN ACTION

The following is an excerpt from a typical family council. Present are the mother, the father, their daughter, Denise (thirteen), and their son, Sam (eleven).

Sam (chairman): O.K., it's my turn this time. Who wants the floor?

Denise: Me. Can I have my own bike?

(No one says anything.)

Sam: Who are you asking?

Denise: Well—Dad.

(Father does not answer.)

Sam: Well, apparently they don't want to answer you.

Mother: Denise knows why we don't answer. She lost her bike because she didn't put a lock on it when she went to the store. She was careless. Father and I have told her we do not feel obligated to replace it.

Denise: Well, how can I get a bike? I need one.

Father: One way is to wait and see if the police recover your bike. Meantime, you are lucky that your brother lets you use his. Another way is to start working. Mother and I can give you some paying jobs. Another way is to use whatever money you have and buy a secondhand one.

Denise: Oh, well, if that is how you feel. . .

Father: We explained that if you left your bike unattended, it might get stolen.

(Silence for a while.)

Sam: O.K., anything else?

Mother: Yes. Father and I want to see an opera next week, and we're willing to buy tickets for you if either or both of you want to go along with us.

Sam: Do we *have* to go?

Mother: No, just if you want to. Tickets are expensive.

Denise: I want to go. Will there be ballet in it?

Father: I don't think so.

Denise: What's the name of the opera?

Mother: *Carmen.*

Denise: O.K., I'll go.

Sam: I don't want to go.

Father: Then we'll get just three tickets.

Mother: I have something else to bring up. (Gets nod from Sam, the chairman.) It has to do with the towels in your bathrooms. If they're wet, I wish you would hang them on your towel racks and not just drop them on the floor.

Denise: I wish you would get all my towels one color and Sam's another color.

Mother: I think that's a good idea. Pink for you and blue for Sam.

Sam: I want brown, not blue.

Mother: Fine. I'll get brown ones for you.

Father: May I have the floor? (Sam nods.) Somebody has been smoking cigarettes in the house. I found some butts in the garbage can one day. You know how Mother and I feel about it.

Denise: It wasn't me.

Sam: Well, it wasn't me.

Father: Whoever it was, you know Mother and I don't want any cigarette smoking in the house. If you want to ruin your health, don't do it in this house. (Kids nod in agreement.)

Sam: Anyone want to take up anything else? (Waits to see.) O.K. Then I have a beef I want to take up. How come all the kids in the neighborhood get twenty dollars a month allowance and we only get two dollars a week?

Father: Why do you say "All the kids get twenty dollars"?

Sam: I asked, and that's what they all tell me.

Father: How many have you asked?

Sam: Lots. Everybody I asked.

Mother: We don't have to do what everyone else does.

Denise: He's right. We don't get enough. Prices have gone up, you know. . .

We hope we have given enough of a sample to clarify the procedure of a family council.

SUMMARY

The most important advice we can give parents is to establish a family council. However, do not start one unless you really understand the procedures and also the hazards. To succeed, you must operate in a democratic spirit.

An effective family council will help a family cure itself of almost anything that ails it. Families, like individuals, are organisms; and organisms, given an opportunity, are self-correcting. So whatever your problems, it is highly likely that they can cure themselves if a family council is established and maintained.

One last bit of advice: even if you do understand how to run a family council, and do keep to all the rules, you may lose your faith in its potential if your children try to sabotage it. Stick to it through thick and thin, doggedly continuing for at least a year—and somewhere along the line the children will suddenly catch on to the idea that this is their way of participating in real decisions in the family.

34

FUN IN THE FAMILY

Many parents do not know how to play with their children and often are too rigid to join them in play. Yet playing in the family is fun for all—parents and children. Play can teach equality, mutual respect, responsibility, and new skills. It can teach order and, most of all, can cement a fundamental feeling of love and togetherness. It's true: The family that plays together stays together.

In families where a strained relationship exists, if the parents offer to play, the children may refuse. Suggestions we are now going to make for starting family play will prevent any such rebuff.

STARTING FAMILY PLAY

1. Father and mother should decide to play some simple game themselves. (Suggestions are as follows.)

2. We suggest about fifteen to twenty minutes of play in an evening.

3. Decide upon a particular time (perhaps after the dishes are done).

4. Play the same game at the same time every possible day of the week.

5. If the children look on, ask if they would like to join you. If all say "yes," continue to play, finishing the round, and then let them join in. If all should say "No," continue playing for the regular fifteen to twenty minutes. If some want to join and others do not, bring into the game those who wish to play. Do not try to induce the others to play.

6. Here is a vital point: If a child, whether player or nonplayer, does anything that is unfair, or makes a commotion, or gets into a quarrel, or tries to get his or her way unfairly, or violates a rule, you should *say absolutely nothing—but stop playing! Do not answer questions or explain why you stopped.* As far as you are concerned, the game is over.

7. The next day, at the same time, start to play as usual. If any child wants to join in, fine. Nothing is said about behavior. If no child joins in, fine. You continue playing. If the day before three kids were playing but today only two want to play, fine. If the one who does not join is the troublemaker of yesterday, fine. If that child too wants to join, fine. *But again: if any disruption of player or nonplayer occurs, you stop playing, refuse to answer questions, and do something else.* But play again the next day.

8. After a week of play, you should change the game. Play the new game for a week.

9. We suggest about two weeks of playing according to this system. At the end of the second week, have a discussion with the children to see if there is some game that they

all would like to play. *Consensus*—i.e., unanimous agreement—is called for. If this is not achieved, you say, "If you kids can't agree on what you want to play, we will decide what *we* want to play, and if you then want to join us, you may." If there is a consensus, the game chosen should be played during a whole week. Too rapid changing requires too many explanations and causes confusion. Keeping to a game for a week sharpens skill, and records can be kept.

10. If ever the children annoy you with demands for more play after the fifteen or twenty minutes, you should just move away. If they persist, use the bathroom technique (see pages 32 and 33).

PRINCIPLES TO FOLLOW

Here are principles to follow in playing games with your children:

Do not play so as to let them win.

Some children will be less capable than others: permit them to handicap themselves. If Johnny, playing toss cards, wants to sit almost over the hat, that is up to him. But if Jenny makes fun of Johnny for doing so, and if her doing so bothers you, just get up and leave the game. This will teach Jenny not to do that. Don't worry about unfair advantages. If a child does take an unfair advantage in the form of a handicap where the child cannot lose, soon the child will learn it is no fun to win all the time and will accordingly adjust his handicap.

SUITABLE GAMES

The games should have some or all of these features: (1) be old favorites, (2) call for inexpensive equipment, (3) be simple to explain, (4) be fair for a wide range of ages, (5) have a good deal of action. Here are some examples of suitable ones, or you can make up your own family games.

Toss

Lines are drawn a certain distance from the wall, with each person having a designated line. Father and Mother may each be ten feet from the wall, behind their line. Jimmy, age nine, may be eight feet from the wall, and Janet, age five, may set herself two feet from it. Then in turn, perhaps by age, each tries to toss an object closer to the wall than anyone else. The objects tossed can be slippers, buttons, coins, etc. We suggest colored counters, such as buttons or poker chips.

Boccie

This can be an outdoor or an indoor game. It requires a golf ball and tinted tennis balls. One player (later, the last winner) tosses out the *pallina* (the smaller ball) and then, in turn, each of the other players tosses two tennis balls, trying to put them as near the *pallina* as possible. If one of your tennis balls stops closest to the *pallina*, you get one point; if both, you get two points. Children can handicap themselves. Each person should throw from where the pallina was tossed, except that if a child wants to get closer to it, that is okay.

Guess

Each person has a certain number of counters, say ten. Then a small object, say a ring or a coin, is given to a player. The player puts his or her hands out of sight and then brings the fists out. In one of the fists is the object. The player says, "Guess." Anyone who thinks he or she knows in which hand the object is guesses. If he or she guesses right, that person gets a counter from the one who had the coin; if he does not guess correctly, he or she gives one up to the player.

Incidentally, this simple game is played in a different version, with the hands under a small fur skin, by American Indians, who will play it by the hour. Its fascination comes from the subtle clues that are given to try to misdirect the guesser. This game can bore children if they play it for only a few minutes, but it will fascinate them if they play it long enough.

Bombs Away

Here is a simple game, fair to all, regardless of age. The player kneels on a chair (or couch), facing the back, holding in one hand a "bomb." This may be a short pencil, a clothespin, a coin, etc. The player drops it on a target, which usually is a milk bottle, a milk carton, etc. The size of the bomb and the opening of the target should be such that the best player will get about fifty percent success.

Balloon Volley Ball

A nickel balloon can really take a lot of abuse and be the center of a lot of fun. The "net" may be a towel strung in a doorway, or a set of chair tops, or even a table. The opposing sides knock the balloon back and forth over the "net." If the balloon hits the "net," the side that knocked it yields one point to the other side.

SPECTATOR FUN

In this category we put reading or looking and, of course, television.

We recommend that parents read aloud to children, selecting books or magazines at the child's level. It is advisable to have a regular time for reading and to have it last a predetermined number of minutes. Books such as the Pooh stories, *The Wind in the Willows, Otto of the Silver Hand,* and the Uncle Remus stories are a good way to introduce children to good literature. Older children can take a turn at doing the reading aloud.

With reference to television, we have a number of comments and suggestions.

No conclusive evidence is available to support that television-watching is harmful, even if violence or sex is shown; and we do not believe in censorship. However, we do believe that parents ought to join in watching children's programs, laughing along with them. Remember, at heart we are all kids—or should be—and able to have fun.

We have found that if parents give children permission to watch television as much as they wish, they will at first, especially if television has heretofore been rationed, watch practically continuously, but soon will begin to show signs of discrimination, and later will take television in their stride. We must trust children to show good sense. If you make all decisions for children, how will they learn responsibility?

If, with only one set, several would-be viewers want to watch different programs at the same time, consensus should be sought. The situation is one from which children can learn much about arbitrating differences.

OUTDOOR ACTIVITIES

We strongly recommend beach-going, picnics, bicycle trips, hikes, camping, and other forms of outdoor togetherness. But too much car driving, motorcycling, or motorboating—excessive "motor means"—should be avoided. Give the children an opportunity to interact with nature, and to experience nature's rules. Back-packing, canoe trips, and the like can be creative, character-building experiences.

Part of the fun is the planning—deciding what to do for a week-end or for a summer. Planning places to go, equipment to get, things to do—these weld the family together, whether the project be snorkeling in the Caribbean, a canoe trip to Wisconsin, back-packing in Colorado, or fishing in the local pond.

The basic notion is that a family can be fun. However, parents should learn to use natural and logical consequences rather than their voice as a means of control. Allow children to make mistakes so that they can learn. If you can take an adventuresome, friendly, and accepting attitude, you will have children who will always remember the fun you had together. You'll find this statement from your grown-up kids very gratifying: "Gee, we used to have so much fun with Mom and Dad . . ."

G

HELPING
OTHER
FAMILIES

35

FORM A PARENTS' STUDY GROUP

Our last suggestion for a happy, efficient, orderly home: start a Parents' Study Group. First we shall tell you why, and then, how.

The most basic philosophic principle of Adlerian psychology is *social interest*. The word that Adler used was *Gemeinschaftsgefühl*, which means "feeling for humanity" or "being part of mankind." All major human problems are due to deficits in social interest. The thief, the murderer, the drug addict, the alcoholic, the ne'er-do-well, the lazy one, the cynic, the pessimist, the neurotic, the psychotic—all are deficient in social interest. The normal, happy, successful person likes people and is liked by them. They care for others.

This does not necessarily mean that they are do-gooders, or that they go around with Thanksgiving baskets, or that they contribute to charity—although people who do these things are likely to have a good deal of social interest—but it means that they care for the welfare of others. They *participate*. They give of themselves.

We suggest that you consider starting a Parents' Study Group for these reasons:

1. By so doing, you become an example to your own children that your concern is more than just yourself and your immediate family.

2. You will be able to help other parents understand their children, deal with their problems, and build a better family and a better neighborhood.

3. You will get good ideas from others.

4. You will make additional friends.

5. You will get satisfaction from seeing others get help for their problems.

Thousands of Parents' Study Groups have been started by housewives using Adlerian-based texts. Most parents who started such groups were not professionals, had no experience at first, but all of them had fun and profited from them.

A Parents' Study Group essentially consists of a group of parents, frequently all mothers, or mothers and fathers, who meet for about one and one-half to two hours, one day a week, for about a dozen weeks, each studying the same book. One member of the group becomes the group leader, and participates by assigning chapters to read in this book and uses as a discussion source, *An Action Guide for Effective Discipline in the Home and School* by Margaret Cater. At the meeting, he or she begins to ask questions, guides the discussion, refers the group back to the book—but never gives his or her opinions. The book, not the study group leader, is the teacher.

Such groups ordinarily meet at members' houses or in a church, school building, or community hall. Often, the group hires a babysitter to take care of young children while the meeting goes on. Usually, one person purchases the books, from a bookseller, from an Adlerian organization, such as the American Society of Adlerian Psychology in Chicago, or directly from the publisher. The total "dues" should cover the cost of the book, the baby-sitter, and coffee for the twelve or so weeks.

Let us now consider how such groups are started and run. A variety of ways, naturally, can be utilized but here are some possible beginnings.

1. You can inform the school principal in your neighborhood that you would like to start a Parents' Study Group, and leave your phone number so that anyone interested can call you; you can begin to make arrangements. Or you can leave this information with a minister, a community worker, scout master, doctor—anyone who gets in contact with a number of people.

2. You make up a simple announcement, such as the following, which you can post on any bulletin board, say in a shopping center or a laundromat.

ANNOUNCING A PARENTS' STUDY GROUP

If you are interested in joining a group to study children's behavior and to solve problems in the family, please call this number.

(Name)
Telephone)

---

3. You can mention your intention to some friends, asking them to ask other friends, perhaps setting a date and place for a preliminary discussion.

In the meantime, you should select a text. Naturally, we believe that our book is suitable. Parents should examine several books before selecting the one that appears best for the particular group.

In running a group of this kind, one person ought to serve as leader. Frequently, the organizer of the group is, but need not be. The leader should read the whole book rapidly at least once, and then should go through it carefully, breaking it down into, say, ten parts, each part to take one session.

If you choose to use this book as the text book, an *Action Guide* by Margaret Cater is available. The study questions are outlined and many suggestions are provided to facilitate the learning from the Parent Study Group. The *Action Guide* may be obtained from Accelerated Development Inc., Publishers, 3400 Kilgore Ave, Muncie, Indiana 47304 or telephone (317) 284-7511 or order toll free 1-800-222-1166.

The leader must remember that the book, not the leader is the teacher. He or she gives no advice! It would be completely out of the spirit of a Parents' Study Group to give advice. The leader should look in the index if necessary, and then say, "On this point, I think if we look at page _____ we will find something. Let me read what it says. . . ." In other words, the leader does not serve as an expert.

After a group is finished, usually one or more of the parents will decide to start another group. In this manner, the organizer of the first group may be responsible for thousands of parents being reached within several years.

The next possibility—and we have many instances of this— is that parents may start a Family Education Center based on Adlerian principles. To do this, they would get in touch with the American Society of Adlerian Psychology for information. Your local library can get the address of this society for you, or of the *Journal of Individual Psychology*, the organization's magazine. Speakers, organizational experts, or other knowledgeable individuals located in your area may be arranged for, or if no one is available close by, information can be mailed to you.

Several dozen Adlerian Family Education Centers exist in the United States and Canada, so the possibility is strong that some expertise will be in your immediate vicinity. These centers can do a number of things:

1. Arrange for informational meetings to parents.

2. Speak at PTAs, women's groups, service groups.

3. Coordinate Parents' Study Groups.

4. Actually do public family counseling (using a certified counselor).

5. Arrange for TV showing of Adlerian family counseling, video tapes and films.

Most of these centers operate at very low cost, generally meeting in church, school, or social organization buildings. They usually charge annual dues, sell books, have fund drives to maintain themselves. Usually no one pays for services and no one gets paid for services. If the organization gets very large, a paid administrator can be hired. We have seen a number of such Family Education Centers start out of the humble beginning of a Parents' Study Group.

For all the reasons we have explained, we strongly suggest that the readers of this book consider calling a group of parents together to study this book or one of the books suggested. Not only would you be helping others in difficulty, but you would be helping yourselves due to the power of the group, which clarifies, intensifies, and facilitates the messages within these Adlerian books.

36

CHANGE YOURSELF: HOW TO BECOME A MORE POSITIVE, LOVING, AND LESS ANGRY PERSON*

In working with parents over the course of many years, we have often found that they need help before they can be effective in creating a harmonious home. Usually they want to make suggested changes but their negative attitudes prevent them from operating successfully and producing desired results. Here are some ideas and drills which can be helpful to change negative attitudes.

*The ideas in this chapter came from Robert and Loy Young.

UNCONDITIONAL LOVE

Unconditional love is total acceptance given no matter how negative the other person may be toward you. It is an uninterrupted expression of love. However, this does not mean that we must love the behavior or actions of the other person. We love the doer but not necessarily the deed. If we were always to love the deed, we would be doing a disservice to the other person since they might become a tyrant toward us and show us little respect.

We can discipline and love a child at the same time. This is not an easy challenge, but with perseverance it can be done. When a child misbehaves, it is natural not to be pleased. However, it is entirely possible not to become upset and angry. Simply decide that you want to give unconditional love to your child, that you want to accept the child in a loving way with all the assets and flaws. Then look for the child's good purpose (see p. 264) which will help you not to get angry. The next step is to use consistently the methods for retraining as described in this book. Learning to give unconditional love to others is a huge task which takes time and patience, but it is worthwhile and rewarding. Children who grow up with unconditional love have high self-esteem and are more likely to be successful, contributing, happy members of society.

POSITIVITY

To improve our relationships with the family as well as elsewhere, we must be positive in all our interactions. A universal law is *like attracts like*. If we are negative in our thoughts or actions, we produce negativity in the people who surround us. They reflect our negativity. On the other hand, if we are positive in our interaction, others reflect our positive actions and thoughts.

Do you notice that on days when you do not feel up to par, your children seem to sense this and that is when they misbehave most? One way we can train ourselves to become more positive in our lives and thus improve the atmosphere of our homes or other places is by doing the following drill:

Positivity Drill

1. Remember a time when you felt negative about someone. Say aloud how you were feeling.

2. Say the words: "I cancel it."

3. Replace the thought with a positive one about the person or situation.

Example 1

1. My friend, Ima, is too fat.

2. I cancel it.

3. Ima is very helpful to people.

Example 2

1. I am clumsy (or stupid, or make too many mistakes).

2. I cancel it.

3. I am sensitive and generous.

LOOK FOR THE GOOD PURPOSE

In our relationships with others we may run into conflict and conclude that they are out to "get" us. We feel angry, put down, hurt. It is very helpful to look for the *good purpose* (good intention) of the other person even if we have difficulty finding it. Although that person may have a good purpose, the actions may seem inappropriate to you. For example: Mother screams at her children but they continue to disobey her. Her good purpose in screaming is to get their cooperation and is a function of her frustration.

Mother is upset that Ted, eight, hits his brother, Tim, three, because he wants Tim to help him put away the toys that he was playing with. His good purpose is: He wants to teach Tim to do the right thing. His behavior is neither appropriate nor effective; however, he does not know this. If Mother can see the good purpose she can then handle the situation without anger. (Of course she should let the children handle their battles by themselves. See Chapter 19.)

In raising our children as well as in our relationships with others, often the helpful procedure is to look for the other person's good purpose. We then do not remain angry or hurt for long and can thus improve our relationships.

CRITICISM

We are often most critical of a trait in another person which we see and dislike in ourselves. For example, Mary says, "Joe talks too much." We could ask Mary if she sometimes talks too much and most likely she will say, "Yes." Or she might say, "Sometimes I talk too much, but certainly not as much as Joe does." If Mary can change that trait in herself, she might then be able to help Joe also. If he finds her less critical, more encouraging, and less talkative, he probably will modify his talkativeness. And Mary will become a more positive person by changing her attitude of criticism to one of acceptance and good will.

Criticism Drill

1. What are you critical of in another person?

2. Do you have that trait or do you enact that quality in your own life at times?

3. What can you do to overcome that trait or action?

Example 1

1. Moe says, "Frieda is selfish."

2. Moe looks into himself to see if he is ever selfish and he realizes that at times he takes the bigger piece of cake or the steak that looks best.

3. Moe now realizes that at times he, too, is selfish. He decides to change and to offer his wife the best item of food at times. She probably will become less selfish as a result of his givingness.

Example 2

1. Mother says, "I can't stand that my sixteen-year-old, Martin, is late for school so often."

2. Mother asks herself if she is ever late for appointments and she says that she is not.

3. Mother looks deeper into herself, asking if she is ever late with anything and she suddenly realizes that she procrastinates in tasks that she does not like to do.

4. Mother asks herself how she can change that trait and she decides to adhere to her schedule for things that must be done.

5. This not only improves Mother's life, but she sets a good example for her son, becomes far less critical of him, and she becomes a more accepting person.

HANDLING NEGATIVE EMOTIONS

Believe it or not, we have control over our emotions. We actually select them to suit our purposes. For example, when someone does something of which you do not approve, you can be indifferent, angry, upset or understanding, to name a few reactions. We have a choice. No one "makes us angry;" we decide whether or not to get angry.

Although it is not good to destroy others with your negative emotions by certain negative behavior such as yelling, blaming others and having temper fits, it also is not good to suppress your emotions. Suppressed emotions can lead to physical illness. For this reason we need to learn to transmute negative feelings to positive feelings by looking for the good in every situation. For example: (1) If you lose something you are upset, but the good side is that thereby you are learning to pay close attention to details so that you do not continue to lose things: (2) If you are in a hurry and make everyone rush to suit your tempo, they will not do that for very long without some resistance. The good part is that you will learn to be more patient, a much desired quality.

Being aware of the frequency of the times when you are expecting to get your own way in your relationships with others and seeking for the good will help tremendously in your becoming less agitated and negatively emotional.

Whether or not you have difficulty applying our suggestions to help your family become more harmonious, we suggest that you try the suggestions and drills of this chapter. They have helped many people become more positive in their interactions and improve in their general well-being.

Part II

EFFECTIVE DISCIPLINE IN THE SCHOOL

H

THE TEACHER'S DILEMMA

PRELIMINARY NOTE

Mr. Ray finally arrived at home after the third day of the semester on what seemed to be the longest day of his life. He had a terrible headache and felt sick to his stomach. His energy was depleted. His fifth grade class was giving him a hard time. Mr. Ray had thought that this class, his second year of teaching, would be much easier than last year, his first. However, these children were even worse than last year's. He was completely puzzled and wondered why he is always getting the very worst class in the school. Could it be that his principal was deliberately giving him the worst behavior problems?

37

EXAMPLE

Mrs. Ray just got home and was alarmed to see her husband looking so pale lying on the couch in almost a stupor. *"What's wrong?"* she asked.

Mr. Ray: *Oh, you won't believe the day I had.*

Mrs. R: *What happened?*

Mr. R: *Well, about a half hour after the starting bell rang I was called out of the room for just a moment by Mrs. Morse, the teacher next door to me. She felt that she should tell me that the principal was upset with me about how noisy my class was yesterday. It was really nice of her to tell me but I don't know what good it did. Anyway, when I went back into the room, it was empty. Not one of my 25 pupils was in the room. I ran down the corridor and couldn't find them so I ran back into the room. As I entered, I saw one child peeking out of the cloak room. So, I went to see what he was doing there and that's where they all were, playing this kind of trick on me. I was really scared, to not see them at first. They thought* it very funny to have "disappeared." I really lost my temper and yelled at them to get back in their seats or else!

Mrs. R: Did they behave after that?

Mr. R: For a little while. Then all of a sudden everyone in the class dropped a pencil—just like an orchestration, all at once. Of course, I told them in no uncertain terms that they shouldn't do that and they had better behave. About a half hour later most of them went to sharpen their pencils; they were just grinding them down! I was so upset because I told them that they must ask me for permission to leave their seats, but they didn't listen to me.

Mrs. R: That's awful—those kids must be emotionally disturbed or delinquent or something.

Mr. R: Yeah, they're a pretty bad lot. But that's not all. I finally got them into their reading groups but while I was working with one group, the other two groups were very noisy even though I had given them an assignment to keep them busy and quiet. I made some of the worst ones stay in for recess and they sure were mad at me. It served them right, though.

Mrs. R: I'm really sorry that you had such a bad day.

Mr. R: That's not all. In the lunch room several of them started to throw some of their lunch at each other. I was so embarrassed; another teacher had to come and yell at them to stop it. And, the afternoon was not much better. In fact, I had to run to the rest room to vomit my lunch after we got back into the room. It was really an awful day!

38

MOVING TOWARD DEMOCRATIC DISCIPLINE

What is happening in our schools to allow for such a predicament? Although one may believe that Mr. Ray's class is unusually outrageous, in general we are witnessing a young people's rebellion to the point of revolution against adults and their traditional ways of child-rearing in both the home and the school. Children will no longer accept the traditional idea of adults acting in superiority over them. The above example demonstrates how teachers can no longer force children to behave as they did in their own childhood classrooms. In the older, traditional approach one word or look from the teacher and children behaved or else! Statements such as, "Children should be seen and not heard," "Spare the rod and spoil the child," "Do it because I say so," were used in every home and school—but these statements do not work today!

Our society's shift from autocracy to democracy and our moving toward social equality is presenting challenges which most of us are not well prepared to meet. In the distant past people were given titles to reflect their control over others—kings, emperors, noblemen, and a string of other ranks down to the lowly and humble serf. But in the home of the serf, the man was king. His wife had to obey him and she had no rights. She couldn't even inherit his property; it went to the oldest son. In those days everyone knew his/her place. They explicitly knew to whom they were either inferior or superior. Of course, children were subservient to all others.

The "inferiors" grew tired of this. Minorities protested and demanded equal rights. Unions were organized. Women challenged the principle of male supremacy. People are now insisting on equal treatment in all sectors. And this includes the children!

Children born into a family in where a struggle exists for equal rights easily conclude that they have rights too. As our children fight for their rights, they are no longer willing to submit to the arbitrary rule of adults. Punishment or threats of punishment will no longer keep the youngsters in line, at least not for very long. Both teachers and parents must learn new methods for childrearing—democratic methods which will win children over to a willingness to cooperate.

In a democracy, not only do you have rights, but you have responsibility. Our children frequently do not see this. They have been brought up by overly protective adults to believe that they have all the rights and the parents and teachers have all the responsibilities. Though well-meaning, adults often act as children's servants. What shall we do? We must raise our young to become responsible for themselves and concerned for the well-being of others. They must learn mutual/equal rights and responsibilities. This is quite a challenge.

Many teachers are aware of autocratic methods not working but they are confused and think that they simply have to stop being autocratic. Simply avoiding autocratic methods leads to permissiveness or anarchy—a lack of order in which chaos develops. We need to study democratic methods in detail in order to implement them in the classroom and the home. The intention of the authors is to assist adults in learning the theory and technology of raising our young in effective, democratic discipline.

I

AUTOCRATIC & DEMOCRATIC CLASSROOM ATMOSPHERES

39

AUTOCRATIC METHODS

T eachers strive very hard to complete the semester's huge number of academic requirements. In addition many reports are to be filed, records need to be kept, meetings are to be attended, etc, etc. The job of the teacher is very demanding. Because of feeling pressured, teachers inadvertently resort to autocratic ways of dealing with the children which are not very effective. They usually experienced some of these methods which are quite discouraging in their own childhood classrooms. Let's look at some of them:

1. *Fault finding and nagging:* "How many times do I have to tell you that you should have your materials ready to work with?" "John, pay attention!" "Betty, look at the blackboard."

2. *Threats:* In all probability no educational method is used more often than this: Teacher shrieking, "Jack, you're so slow; I'll give you five more minutes and if you're not finished by then I'm going to take 50% off your grade!"

3. **Punishment:**   Some teachers cannot imagine how a class can run smoothly without punishments. "I told you to stop talking to your neighbor but you will not! Go to the principal's office right now." "You have to stay in for recess because you broke a rule."

4. **Rewards:**   The problems of using rewards are (a) they are seen by children as their just due and they are not willing to do further work unless another reward is given, (b) children expect bigger and better rewards as time goes on, (c) there is no inner motivation in rewards, and (d) children do not experience the simple joys of accomplishment and of learning for the sake of learning something which is interesting when they work toward a pay off.

5. **Moralizing, preaching:** "When I was your age . . ." "You know you should plan ahead so you get your homework done!"

6. **Stereotyping, labeling:**   "You're the lazy one in our class." "You're a procrastinator." "You're the baby."

7. **Being sarcastic:**   "Look at the big shot." "Someone's gotten up on the wrong side of the bed this morning."

8. **Taking full responsibility:**   The teachers see the classroom as their own. In autocratic classrooms teachers run it all. There is no shared responsibility.

Teachers without realizing they are doing so frequently use the preceding discouraging methods in their classrooms although they are not conducive to the growth of the children. Teachers become discouraged because of their own frustration and wanting to get something done quickly or not knowing more encouraging techniques. The preceding methods have been used for centuries in our autocratic child training and doing so is a "habit" which is not easy to discard. Discouragement is the greatest obstacle to learning. Children who are discouraged are deprived of experiencing their own strength and ability to solve difficult situations. Discouraged children usually are not motivated to learn or to participate in a useful way.

40

DEMOCRATIC
METHODS

T he democratic process is a respectful form of governing pupils with their cooperation. It is a stronger form of discipline because the class helps formulate and then fully agrees with the disciplinary measures. When a child misbehaves and is uncooperative, the problem is not the teacher's alone—it is also the problem of the class and must be handled by the group. This aids the teacher in not being the only responsible person for the classroom's actions.

Democratic methods are encouraging. Instead of threatening, punishing, preaching to get the children to perform, teachers use ways of winning the children toward cooperation so that the classroom is unified. This unification is what simplifies teachers' work because of the cooperation and shared responsibility.

One way of winning cooperation at the first day of school is for teachers not to have already decided and decorated the room according to their own tastes. The dialogue could be as follows:

Teacher: *If you notice I did not hang pictures or fix our classroom in any way. I do not believe it is my own classroom; I believe it is OUR classroom. What would you like to have in our room to make it look nice?*

Fred: *In my last classroom I brought a fish bowl and a fish.*

Teacher: *That sounds very good; you could do that again if you wish.*

Susan: *I think we should draw some pictures ourselves and hang them around the room.*

Teacher: *That is a good idea. We could do that after our first drawing lesson.*

Carole: *I have a rabbit I could bring to school.*

Teacher: *OK, you could bring your rabbit and we'll plan how it will be cared for and what to do with it on weekends.*

These plans continue until all ideas have been heard.

Teacher: *What do you think we could do for fun, just to enjoy ourselves?*

Blanche: *We could go on field trips.*

Todd: *We could take a picnic lunch with us on field trips.*

Jane: *We could play a game together at recess.*

Fanny: *We could have parties.*

Teacher: *All of these are wonderful ideas. I'll find them to be fun for me too. How would you like to have a party right now?*

Jane: *Oh, but we don't have any refreshments, no cake like at a birthday party.*

Teacher: *Well, do we have to have refreshments to enjoy each other's company? What could we do instead of eating?*

Sam: *We could tell what we did during the summer.*

Earl: *We could sit on the floor in a circle and talk together about the summer.*

Teacher: *Let me see the hands of those who would like to have that kind of a party right now for 20 minutes.*

All the children raise their hands. It is obvious that they are very happy and enthusiastic about this first encounter with their teacher.

Some teachers will fear that the class will get out of hand if such a first day were to happen and that little work would be accomplished for the rest of the year. In actuality, just the opposite will happen. If the children enjoy being in the classroom they will be much more ready to work.

Notice that the teacher said that the party would last 20 minutes. He has an academic task ready to go to immediately following the party.

This first day encounter not only set the pace for decorating the room and for enjoying the classroom, it became the first classroom discussion of the year. The children were being trained in a most important aspect of the democratic group, the class discussion. More information on class discussion will be presented in another section of this book.

41

AUTOCRATIC
AND DEMOCRATIC
LEADERSHIP STYLES

For a democratic society to exist and thrive, it is necessary that its citizens be self-disciplined, self-reliant, and self-determined. In a democracy, power and responsibility are vested in the people, but when the people have not learned how to exercise their powers and fulfill their responsibilities the democracy soon finds itself in serious trouble.

Each family and classroom literally is a cradle of democracy. In the family, children should learn the attitudes, patterns of behavior and the acceptance of responsibility that will enable them to participate in a democratic form of life. If children fail to learn to live democratically in the family, then the school has the job of teaching democratic living. If neither the home nor school teaches democratic living, how can we expect children to accept the requirements of democratic living later when they grow into adulthood? If they fail to learn the ways of democratic living in the family and school WHERE THEN WILL THEY LEARN?

AUTOCRATIC & DEMOCRATIC LEADERSHIP STYLES

AUTOCRATIC BOSS	DEMOCRATIC LEADER
Adult is the boss	Adult leads
Speaks in a sharp voice	Speaks in a friendly voice
Gives commands	Invites, asks, requests
Applies power and force	Exercises influence, persuades
Demands cooperation	Wins cooperation
"You must do this"	"This is what I will do"
Imposes ideas	Sells ideas
Relies on domination	Guides
Depends on criticism to control	Encourages the other person to
Finds fault	do better
Punishes those who differ	Acknowledges achievement
Tells the other person	Helps the other person to im-
"I decide; you obey"	prove
Monopolizes responsibility	Is willing to discuss quietly
	"I suggest and help you decide"
	Shares responsibility

Figure 41.1. Differences between autocratic and democratic leadership styles.

Parents and teachers who follow autocratic approaches stunt their children's growth and deprive them of the opportunity to learn to live cooperatively in equality. Parents and teachers who teach democratic approaches train their children to think for themselves and to learn the great benefits of harmonious, cooperative, democratic living.

Some of the preceding were adapted from various writings of Rudolf Dreikurs, M.D., by Practical Parenting Publications, Columbia, Missouri.

J

BUILDING A DEMOCRATIC GROUP

PRELIMINARY NOTE

Politicians have observed that democracy is the best form of government, but the challenge is to make it work. No less can be said of democracy in the classroom. It is the most effective atmosphere for establishing order and maximum learning and it is a challenge for teachers to make it work. The use of classroom discussion is one solution for this challenge since it enables teachers to increase cooperative behavior and mutual respect, to encourage all children to participate usefully, to promote academic interest, and to deal effectively with behavior problems.

Teachers generally assume that they must single-handedly teach, correct, and control each individual child in the class. The size of the class then becomes an awesome factor since teachers feel unable to give what they consider the necessary personal attention to each child. However, if teachers know how to be group leaders, then they teach only one class, which consists of twenty, thirty, or fifty children. The difference between these viewpoints of teachers' roles is huge. When teachers are only concerned with each individual child they constantly neglect the others when occupied with one. On the other hand, teachers who are skilled group leaders regard each child as an integral part of the whole class, and use the entire group to assist the disturbing child.

Dreikurs taught that teachers must learn to develop wide-range vision so that they have the ability to see everything that occurs in the group at any given moment. At no time should concern with one child preoccupy teachers so that they neglect the total class situation. No misbehavior should go unnoticed. Each disturbance even in the far corner of the room will effect the whole class as it becomes contagious, spreading restlessness and lack of interest throughout the room.

If teachers use the cooperation of the group instead of their own authority for the correction of behavior, the misbehaving child begins to feel that he/she belongs to the group. This lessens the child's discouragement and helps change the behavior. The group feels less frustrated about the situation and enjoys the opportunity to contribute to the group's improvement. All benefit.

Many teachers feel that they cannot afford to take time away from academics for discussions. However, the time spent on guidance is generally a good investment. The class atmosphere improves and eventually more time becomes available for academics as behavior problems lessen. Some schools report fewer incidents of vandalism and that even students with delinquent behavior become cooperative when they are integrated into the group through regular classroom discussions.

As teachers use discussions they discover that the children are eager to participate. They enjoy expressing their opinions since that gives them a greater sense of significance and belonging. Children usually learn to wait for help with social problems until the discussion time rather than running immediately to their teacher for help. They either wait patiently until time for the discussion period or solve the problem for themselves. And, waiting is beneficial since the original tempers subside and a less emotional discussion can occur if needed.

Some teachers resist classroom discussions because value issues arise and they believe these should be handled by the home and church. However, schools must educate for total living rather than only for the three R's. Besides, to remain free of values in schools is impossible and the children are aware of teachers' values whether they are consciously verbalized or not. During discussions students generally formulate their own beliefs, attitudes, and value systems.

Just what does a classroom discussion consist of? It is the democratic interchange of ideas involving a group of pupils and their teacher talking and thinking together about situations relevant to the group. It is not just conversation since it has direction, looks at problem areas, and deals with unpleasant issues which are generally ignored in conversation.

Children have a deep need to discuss with adults issues which really matter to them. They have very few opportunities to do so. They need to feel accepted, and not ridiculed or hushed when having the freedom to talk about situations which are controversial. They need this type of self-expression and the opportunity to make simple but real decisions.

42

WHAT CHILDREN LEARN IN CLASSROOM DISCUSSIONS

Classroom discussions are aimed at teaching many skills:

1. Learning to listen to others
2. Understanding self, other pupils and teacher
3. Understanding the goals of behavior
4. Developing empathy and concern for each other
5. Developing compassion and acceptance for others
6. Learning mutual respect
7. Replacing competition with mutual empathy and help
8. Developing a cohesive group
9. Learning that others have similar inferiority feelings helps develop self confidence
10. Learning problem solving
11. Improving personal relationships
12. Profiting from other's experiences as well as one's own

43

GUIDELINES FOR CLASSROOM DISCUSSIONS

1. Hold classroom discussion any time during the week, however, having a regular time established gives it as much importance as academic subjects and the group can look forward to a specified time in which to bring up problems. Once or twice a week or daily discussions can be scheduled. If the teacher finds that something occurs which needs immediate attention, a discussion can be held at the moment.

2. Have the class and teacher sit in a circle or semi-circle which enables everyone to see each other.

3. End discussions before children become restless or bored. Depending on the age of the pupils ten minutes to a half hour is useful.

4. Hold discussions on any academic subject to get the children to see the relevance to their lives and to encourage their involvement.

5. Have a discussion regarding a child's behavior at the time of disturbance. It alleviates the emotional stress of the moment.

6. Use stories as a basis for discussion. This can be done initially to establish trust and to help the class understand behavior.

7. Invite all children to voice their opinions. A shy child could be encouraged by asking his/her thoughts. No one must talk if he/she does not want to. Some learn by listening. Children could be asked to comment on each other's opinions.

8. Respect each child's statements no matter how ridiculous they may seem.

9. Accept no one as "the expert." Ask the class, "Who has something to say about that?"

10. Use brainstorming to help find a variety of solutions to a problem. Evaluate each idea after all suggestions are given.

11. Use open ended questions because they are more effective than closed questions. Ask: "Who has an idea about that?" "What would you choose?" "Why?" Closed questions are answered by yes or no and stifle discussion.

12. Focus on solutions and not fault-finding (what people are doing wrong). The purpose of the discussion is to help find better ways of living.

13. Retain a sense of humor. It is very helpful to teacher and students.

14. Recognize that time is short; encourage sticking to the subject.

15. Share responsibility. Ask, "What can we do about it?"

16. Assure the children and make certain that classroom discussions are not used to evaluate or to grade pupils.

44

GROUND RULES FOR CLASSROOM DISCUSSIONS

T eacher and pupils need to establish ground rules for the classroom discussion. They should be few and simple:

1. Everyone has equal opportunity to speak. Raise hands to take turns talking while others listen attentively.

2. Everyone has a right to speak without being interrupted and without fear of negative consequences.

3. Everyone must use mutual respect and not give comments which hurt others.

4. Stick to the subject.

45

TOPICS FOR CLASSROOM DISCUSSIONS

Stories, thought provoking topics, concerns of the group are subjects for discussion. Within the first week of school possible discussions could center around regarding decorating the room with pupil participation, assigning responsibilities, the organization of committees, planning work schedules, order in the corridors, going to the restroom, to have or not have homework, and so forth.

Problems between class members, fighting, stealing, cheating, friendships, shyness, aggression, vocations are excellent choices for discussion.

Asking open-ended questions can lead to stimulating discussions:

"Suppose you are now grown up. If you had enough money so that you did not have to work, what would you do with your life?"

"Are children equal to adults?"

"What do we mean by equality—equal in what ways?"

"Do you want to go to college? Why?"

"Is your school work related to your lives outside of school?"

"Why do we study history?"

46

GENERAL STRUCTURE OF A CLASSROOM DISCUSSION

In their book, *Discipline Without Tears*, Rudolf Dreikurs and Pearl Cassel suggested that the following headings be written on the blackboard at the beginning of the discussion period:

1. Good things of the past week

2. Ways in which we can improve next week

3. Personal problems

4. Responsibilities

5. Future plans.

Each topic is to be discussed for approximately six minutes in a 30 minute session. The chairperson has the responsibility to keep the discussion on track if it should wander. The teacher serves as chairperson at the beginning of the semester until he/she trains the children to take over the leadership.

Dreikurs and Cassel reminded us that teachers must realize that leading effective group discussion is a skill which improves with practice and teachers should not abandon the discussions due to initial frustrating experiences. The class needs to develop group discussion techniques and most children are not used to adults asking their opinions, or encouraging them to identify and solve their own problems. Time is needed to become proficient in classroom discussions.

Preceding material was printed with permission from Pearl Cassel.

47

STORIES FOR CLASSROOM USE

When starting group discussions, the use of stories helps to encourage talking about behavior if the class is not yet ready to discuss their own behavior problems. Reading stories or making up stories of your own which are pertinent to present behavior situations are a good introduction and training ground for the class. Stories about children or animals free children to express themselves without taking situations personally. The following are some examples of the use of stories.

STORY A: THE FOX AND THE GRAPES
(Aesop fable)

Once there was a hungry fox taking his morning walk. He saw some beautiful tempting grapes hanging from a vine a few feet above his head. He thought, "I bet those grapes are wonderful. They look so good." He leaped and snapped at the grapes but couldn't quite reach them. He then thought, "I just have to keep trying to get them, they would make a marvelous breakfast." So he leaped and snapped and leaped again, but he could never quite reach the grapes. He tried so many times that he got completely exhausted. It was some time before he got enough strength to drag himself limping away. As he went along he grumbled to himself, "What sour things those grapes are! No one would want to eat them."

Class Discussion

Teacher: *What do you think of the fox?*

Paul: *I think it is funny that he tried hard to get the grapes and then said they weren't good.*

Teacher: What do you think, Jeremy?

Jeremy: *I don't think it is funny. He wanted the grapes and couldn't get them.*

Teacher: *Do you think he tried hard enough?*

Fred: *Sure, he was tired from trying so hard.*

Teacher: *Who else has a thought?*

Elsa: *He really didn't know if the grapes were sour or not. He didn't get to taste them.*

Teacher: *That is true, why do you think he said that?*

Fred: *I think he just made it up.*

Teacher: *Why did he make up that idea?*

Jenny: *I think he felt bad so he said that about the grapes.*

Laura: *He probably was angry.*

Teacher: *At whom do you think he was angry?*

Lisa: *Maybe he was angry at the grapes for being too high up.*

Teacher: *Who else do you think he might have been angry at?*

Paula: *There was no one else there to be angry at.*

Teacher: *Think about it.*

Lisa: *Oh, I know, he might have been angry at himself because he tried so hard and didn't even get one grape.*

Teacher: *So why did he say that the grapes were sour?*

Lisa: *Because he didn't want to look like he was stupid for trying so hard. So he said that they weren't good anyway.*

Teacher: *Do you think anyone else ever does that?*

John: *Yeah, sometimes when we play a game and my brother loses he says it wasn't a good game anyway.*

Teacher: *Anyone else see some people act that way?*

Paula: *I think lots of people do that sometimes.*

Teacher: *How many of you have ever done that?*

Most of the children and the teacher raise their hand.

The above type of discussion with the teacher asking questions and not giving the answers may be used with other stories to teach about human behavior.

STORY B: CONSEQUENCES VS. PUNISHMENT

Third graders, Jim and Seth, were good friends. They often played together after school and sometimes they got into mischief together. Each of the boys had a different way to deal with their mothers. Jim had to ask his mother for permission to do anything at all after school and then he would do it if she said it was okay or not do it if she said no.

Seth and his mother had made an agreement a few months ago. He and his mother made a list of things that were okay for him to do after school, like go to the playground, build things in the open field near their home, play at the small creek, and so forth. He would not have to ask for permission to do these things but he had to be home on time for their early dinner. If he wanted to do things that were not on their list, he would have to ask her permission.

One day Jim and Seth decided that they wanted to go to the large shopping center. Jim knew that his mother would say that he couldn't go and Seth knew that the shopping center was not on his list of places he could go without special permission. They had to cross Grand Avenue, a large street with no stop light to tell them when to cross. They knew it was dangerous but they thought nothing could happen to them anyway. So, off they went to the shopping center.

When they got there they were walking around looking at many things as they were trying to find their favorite store to which they had gone with their parents sometimes—the toy store. They found the toy store and spent time there looking at the many toys. They really had a good time doing that. As they were leaving the store Mrs. Jones, their neighbor, saw them coming out of the store.

Mrs. Jones said: "Hello boys, did you shop for toys?"

"No," said Jim, "we were just looking around."

"Are your mothers here? I would like to say hello to them."

"No," said Seth, "we came by ourselves."

"Oh," said Mrs. Jones.

The boys walked around some more and then went home.

When Jim got to his house his mother was standing in the doorway and she looked very angry.

"Where have you been?" she said.

"Oh, nowhere, just playing," answered Jim.

"Well, Mrs. Jones said she saw you and Seth at the shopping center. Do you realize how dangerous it is to walk there and cross Grand Avenue? You know that you should not do that without an adult being with you." She was very angry and talked in a loud voice. "As punishment, you will get a good spanking when your father gets home and I will not let you watch TV for the rest of the week."

"But Mom," Jim started to say, but his mother was no longer in the room. Jim was very upset.

When Seth got home, his mother was in the kitchen making dinner. He went to the kitchen and saw that she looked upset or something. After he said hello to her she said, "Mrs. Jones phoned me a little while ago and said that she saw you at the shopping center. You know that you are not supposed to go there without me or some other adult." She was upset but not yelling.

"Yes, Mom, but we were careful going there and it isn't very far away; it just takes a short while to walk there." Seth felt bad for upsetting his mother.

"That was not on our agreement list and you know it is dangerous to cross Grand Avenue, and we had an agreement that you were not to go there without an adult to supervise your crossing that street or to walk around there."

"Yeah, but we were careful."

"What do you think should be your logical consequence for not keeping your agreement?" said Mother.

"I don't know, I have to think about it. Well, I guess I could ask you for permission for doing anything I would like to do when I leave the house, like I used to do when I was younger, before we made the agreement that I could go to nearby places and cross only certain streets and not have to ask your permission for those."

"Well, that sounds like a good consequence. I think it shows that you understand that agreements must be kept and that we have to be careful to not do dangerous things." How long do you think this consequence should last?"

Seth thought about it and then asked: "Do you think we could try that for two weeks and if I always ask for your permission you will let me try again to go only where I'm supposed to go that's on the list without asking you?"

Mother thought about it and decided that would be okay.

Questions For Discussion In Classroom

1. What is a consequence?

2. How do you think Jim felt when he got home and his mother was yelling at him and decided his punishment?

3. How do you think Seth felt when he and his mother talked over the situation?

4. What do you think of Jim's punishment?

5. What do you think of Seth's logical consequence?

6. What is the difference between punishment and logical consequences?

7. Which home would you rather live in, the one with the punishment or the one with consequences? Why?

8. When you are a parent some day, which do you think you would like to do to teach your children the best way to do things?

Ask additional questions as ideas are brought up in the discussion. Allow the children to give their own thoughts. They may not agree with you. You could ask further questions to have them think of your objections to their thoughts. Do not make those children wrong who do not agree with your ideas. You cannot force them to think in your way; that would start a huge power struggle.

STORY C: THE BULLY

Bill, nine-years-old, is big for his age. When playing in the school playground or on the street near his home, he often will pick on children who are smaller—bump into them or hit them.

One day Bill hit six-year-old Don who fought back. They fought each other for a while. Don didn't have a chance since Bill was bigger and stronger. Pretty soon Don had a bloody nose and went home crying.

Don's mother felt sorry for her son and angry at Bill: "That big bully," she said, "something must be done about him. I guess we'll talk it over with Dad tonight and see what he thinks should be done."

This story is left open ended so that your class could discuss what should be done. Perhaps your class could write several endings.

Questions For Discussion In Classroom

1. Why do you think Bill picks on smaller children?

2. Is Bill a happy boy?

3. What should his teachers do?

4. What should Don do?

5. What do you think about Don?

6. What should Don's parents do?

7. What should Bill's parents do?

8. What do you think would be a good ending to the story?

9. What do smaller kids do to annoy bigger ones or bullies?

STORY D: FORGETFUL JESSY

Jessy is a very forgetful boy. He often forgets his school supplies or to return his books on time in the class which I teach.

Our class was joining a school excursion on a Monday. The permission slips were sent home one week in advance of the trip. I told the children that it was very important that the permission slips be returned as soon as possible and those who do not bring these slips by the Thursday before the excursion would not be able to go. The school had to know how many children were going in order to reserve the right number of buses. Everyone agreed and all of the children handed in their signed permission slips by Thursday except Jessy and two other children.

On Friday I called the three children aside and told them nicely that the deadline for permissions slips had passed and they could not go on the field trip.

Early Monday morning Jessy and his mother brought in the permission slip. I explained to them that I could not accept the Permission slip because the count had been made and Jessy was already told on Friday that he couldn't go.

Of course, Jessy was disappointed but he is beginning to remember more things now.

Questions For Discussion In Classroom

1. Why did the teacher not allow Jessy to go on the excursion?

2. Was that fair?

3. Why was it important for the permission slips to be returned on time?

4. Who would like to make up another question to ask about the story?

STORY E: THE NEW CLASSMEMBER

Ronald's father is a military man and his work takes him to live in different places every year or two. This means that his entire family moves to a new city and Ronald changes to a new school more often than most children. He was in kindergarten and first grade in Utah, then he went to second and third grade in Minnesota, and now at age ten he is starting fifth grade in Indiana. The school semester started two months ago.

Now, as his mother is driving him to the new school, Ronald is remembering his first few months at the school he just left in Minnesota. He didn't know anyone when he went into the classroom the first day and being alone was a little scarey. Mrs. Kelly, his teacher, showed him to his seat when he walked into the room and she went back to her desk. He felt strange and shy among all the children who knew each other. He also felt uncomfortable, so he kind of looked out of the corners of his eyes at the things hanging on the walls and at the other children. No one said a word to him.

The first recess seemed awful to him because he stood around all by himself in the playground. He didn't talk to anyone and no one talked to him. At lunch, he sat at a table with other children but again no one talked to him. It took several months until he became friends with Paul, a boy in his classroom.

Both Ronald and Paul were shy and would usually stand around all alone. One day Ronald decided to smile at Paul and talk about the spelling test they just finished. Paul asked him if he would like to come to his house after school so that they could study their next spelling words together. Ronald was happy to get that invitation and he excitedly ran home after school to ask his mother's permission. They studied together that day and many other days too. They had some games that they both enjoyed so they had fun together and became good friends.

Since he finally had a friend, Ronald began to feel better about being in the Minnesota school; later he made a few more friends at school and in his neighborhood. Now that they moved to Indiana, he was sorry to have left that school and a little scared because of going into a new classroom today. He was also a little excited about seeing all the things that would be new to him. He wondered what the kids and teacher would be like, what the classroom would look like, and how long it would take for him to make friends in this new place.

They arrived at the school, finished enrolling in the office and Ronald entered his new classroom. A teacher with a warm smile got up from her desk and walked to the door to greet him. She said: "Hello, I'm Mrs. Goodwell; you must be Ronald. It is good to have you in our class. I hope you will be happy here and that you'll learn many new things." She then turned to the other children and said, "Children, this is Ronald, a new pupil who came all the way from Minnesota. Maybe he will tell us about that place a little later."

As Mrs. Goodwell was talking in such a friendly way, Ronald felt a warm glow of relief going through him. He knew that this new classroom would be different than his last one. Didn't she already say that they would like to listen to him tell about Minnesota. He could tell them a lot about it.

Just before recess, Mrs. Goodwell said, "Boys and girls, since this is Ronald's first day here, he doesn't know any of you. Who would like to play with him at recess and introduce him to some of your classmates?" Robert, one of the boys, raised his hand and so did some others. Mrs. Goodwell appointed Robert. Then she said, "And now, at lunch time who would like to take Ronald to the cafeteria and show him the lunch procedure, sit with him while eating, and introduce him to the other children at your table?" Mary and Jane both raised their hands at the same time, so Mrs. Goodwell appointed both of them. Again Ronald felt the warm glow—he was beginning to feel like he was part of the group.

Ronald had a good first day in his new school. When Mother picked him up at the end of the day, he couldn't wait to tell her all about his day—the teacher, the classroom, what he had for lunch, and especially the new children he met.

The next day Mrs. Goodwell asked Ronald to tell the children about Minnesota. He felt good to tell them something he knew very well, and the boys and girls listened to what he had to say. When he finished Mrs. Goodwell asked if they had any questions to ask Ronald. Some of them asked him questions which he answered with much self-confidence. He felt proud to be able to give his classmates that information. Mrs. Goodwell suggested that the children could ask Ronald more questions during recess or lunch.

On Monday there was an especially nice way to begin the week in school. The children and Mrs. Goodwell planned at the beginning of the semester that each Monday morning they would have one-half hour to walk around the classroom, talk to each other, and share how they spent their weekend. It was such fun to get to know the boys and girls that way. They felt so good about being in school that when the time was up they got down to their studies and worked very hard.

As time went by Ronald found all the fun things like sharing with classmates, field trips, making friends, and surprise things helped him enjoy school so much. He and his classmates were always willing to help Mrs. Goodwell in any way that she suggested would be good for the whole class. And, strangely, there were no bad kids in that class!

Questions For Discussion In Classroom

1. What was the difference between the teacher in the Minnesota school and the one in Indiana?

2. If you had your choice, which classroom would you choose to be in?

3. Do you think children could enjoy fun activities in school and learn their school work?

4. Would the fun things take away too much time from the school work?

5. How could the teacher set it up so that their work could be completed?

STORY F: GETTING UP—I and II

The following two stories were taken from this book's Parenting Section, Problems of Routine Living—GETTING UP. They are about the same family; first, before studying this book and second, after studying the book. They are appropriate for classroom discussion and will give the children a comparison between an autocratic and a democratic home. Most narratives of family life in the book can be used in class discussions. Teachers can make up questions for lively discussions about children's behavior.

Getting Up—I

See the example given in this book in Topic 8 "Getting Up" with the example given at the beginning of that Topic.

Questions For Discussion In Classroom

1. What do you think is the reason that Harry and Ellen didn't get up on time?

2. Why was father upset?

3. What is it that some kids get up by themselves, watch the time, dress quickly, eat breakfast and are ready to leave on time?

4. What would be the consequence if the children did not eat their breakfast before leaving for school?

5. How do you feel when your parents talk about how hard things were when they were kids and that they did better than you?

Getting Up—II

Harry and Ellen's parents had a discussion with them.

See the "Application to Harry and Ellen's Problem" in this book in Topic 8 "Getting up—II"

Questions For Classroom Discussion

1. How would you feel if you were tardy when you got to school?

2. Was the teacher fair or unfair to have Harry stay 45 minutes after school?

3. In which story, the first or second, were Harry and Ellen learning to behave in a responsible way?

4. What do you think of children having their own alarm clocks?

5. Which way would you like your parents to act: as in Story I or Story II?

6. What does it mean to "Learn things the hard way?"

Most children's stories are suitable for discussions regarding social relationships. The children might enjoy bringing a story to class for discussion. Teachers can select from many children's books at the library. Sources are given at the end of this chapter.

48

CLASS COUNCIL

Following a period of time in which the class has had training in group discussions, the teacher might suggest that they have their own "government" in the form of a class council which would meet once or twice a week. They could discuss anything they wish. Children usually agree with enthusiasm. It takes time and patience to work at it because it is a challenge. Children are generally not used to making their own decisions and to solving problems peacefully. It usually works out successfully if they stick with it for several weeks. A most important aspect is for the teacher not to give up. He/she must encourage the children to see the advantages, to practice the council discussions and to continue working at it. The opinion of the council carries more weight than that of the teacher. Problems are usually solved more easily with the council than with the authority of the teacher alone. Children are allowed to bring up any concerns that they may have, e.g., fights with other children in school and elsewhere, concerns about situations with siblings, concerns regarding the teacher such as unfairness, busy work, and other problems that they wish to discuss. The better the relationship of teacher and pupils, the freer the children will feel to bring up any issues.

Two or three class members are selected by the class to form the council for perhaps two weeks at which time the group would elect a new council. All class members have a turn to serve on the council. At first the teacher must take more leadership until the children become trained in leadership. Later he/she can be an observer stating an opinion only when needed. The teacher should sit with the children and actively listen to the procedure, never using that time to do paper work or other tasks. If the teacher does not seem interested, the council will fail because children will become disinterested and restless. The council must be held regularly and be considered an important part of the school program.

For more details on classroom discussion and class council please see: *Maintaining Sanity in the Classroom* by Rudolf Dreikurs, Bernice Bronia Grunwald and Floy C. Pepper.

49

SOURCES FOR CLASSROOM DISCUSSION STORIES

1. Dreikurs, R., Grunwald, B., & Pepper, F. (1971). *Maintaining Sanity in the Classroom*, pp. 120-136. New York: Harper & Row.

2. LaPointe, V., & Overtoom, C.G. (1979). *Socio-teleo analysis: Stories for classroom discussion.* Glendale, AZ: Available from Socio-Teleoanalysis, P.O. Box 460, Glendale, AZ. 85311.

3. Dreyer, S.S. (1977, Vol 1; 1980, Vol.2). *The bookfinder: A guide to children's literature about the needs and problems of youth aged 2-15.* Circle Pines, MN: American Guidance Service.

4. Dinkmeyer, D., McKay, G., Dinkmeyer, D., Jr. (1980). *Systematic training for effective teaching. Teacher's resource book.* Circle Pines, MN: American Guidance Service.

5. Dreikurs, R., & Cassel, P. (1972). *Discipline without tears.* Ontario, Canada: The Alfred Adler Institute of Ontario, P.O. Box 5043, Station A, Toronto 1 Ontario.

ENCOURAGEMENT

"A child needs encouragement like a plant needs sun and water. Unfortunately those who need encouragement most, get it the least because they behave in such a way that our reaction to them pushes them further into discouragement and rebellion."

Dreikurs and Cassel

PRELIMINARY NOTE

Looking up the word, "encouragement," in *Webster's Collegiate Dictionary* throws helpful light on the meaning:

Encouragement: To inspire with courage, spirit, or hope. (En means to put into or promote. Courage has to do with one's moral or mental strength to venture, persevere and withstand fear, danger or difficulty.)

When we use the word "encouragement" we are referring to the act or process of inspiring and stimulating children to develop courage and confidence, to generate in them the inner strength to try, to keep at it, and to endure fear, danger, and difficulties. When adults encourage children they contribute to their healthy growth toward maturity. We should try helping them grow into adulthood as creative, self-disciplined, self-determined, self-reliant, self-confident persons.

**Quotes From Rudolf Dreikurs'
Various Writings on Encouragement**

"The lack of encouragement can be considered the basic cause for misbehavior. A misbehaving child is a discouraged child. Children so dearly want to be a real part of the classroom. Yet, in their attempts to do their part, to gain recognition, to find different ways, we confront them with our doubts of their ability. We do this either directly with discouraging words or by tone of voice or actions that show adult superiority. All too often, we get across to the children that we consider them inept, unskilled, and generally inferior—if not impossible. We reject them as being weak and inferior—an attitude which in itself produces an atmosphere of discouragement. Encouragement, then, is a continuous process aimed at giving children a sense of self-respect and feelings of accomplishment. From earliest infancy the child needs help in finding his place through achievement. We also discourage children through overprotection. Children need to learn to take bumps and rebuffs in stride. A bruised knee will mend. Bruised courage may last a lifetime."

In order to help children reach their potential, we must help them strengthen their courage. Too many people waste their potential and lose their courage by trying to be perfect, to never make a mistake, and by wondering how good they are or worrying about how inadequate they might be. Encouragement is directed toward increasing children's self-esteem, their belief in themselves just as they are with some flaws.

50

BECOMING AN ENCOURAGING TEACHER

The first task in becoming an encouraging teacher is to start encouraging oneself. We must learn to feel positive about ourselves, accepting our limitations and mistakes, not allowing these to keep us from feeling likeable, lovable, and capable. Our self-esteem is at the root of having a happy effective life.

The negative beliefs which lower our self-esteem and keep us from relating effectively with our class members and others can be changed. We generally are not aware of these beliefs and when they are called to our attention we could give consideration to changing them. One or more mof the following negative beliefs are often held by teachers.

NEGATIVE BELIEFS

1. I must control the classroom.

   To control the classroom is impossible; no one allows control over themselves and certainly not pupils these days. With the help of class members in making rules and consequences for improper behavior, teachers' jobs are easier because their responsibility is shared with the young people. In using classroom discussion weekly, sharing and cooperation are possible.

2. I know better.

This is a very common belief but we must ask ourselves, "Do I really know better than others? I think I do but others think the same." Keeping this in mind one can look for other persons' differing viewpoints and acknowledge that although we do not agree, we can be friendly.

3. I do not like my imperfections and do not want to show them.

We must develop "the courage to be imperfect." That is, accept our flaws and realize that people will accept us even more than when we want to show that we are perfect. This helps class members, especially, to accept their teachers and it helps us with our self-esteem to be able to accept our own imperfections.

4. I must never show my vulnerability.

We fear showing that we are vulnerable to criticism, open to attack or being challenged. If we fear showing our hurt or being wounded, we seem tense. Young people and others will enjoy being with us when we are less tense and seem natural—not worrying about being wounded by others.

5. My personal relationships are not good; I can't keep friends. Therefore, I really am inadequate.

Again, we must accept imperfections in relationships as well as in other areas. We could work on improving them as everyone we know must do.

6. The children should like me.

Some children do not like any adults or other children, or even themselves. They are struggling to cope with life. Expecting them to like us is unrealistic. However, in time children who do not seem to like us may become fond of us providing they become encouraged by us.

7. The children should trust me.

   As in number 6, this is unrealistic since many children do not trust anyone, especially adults; however, in time they may become more trusting.

8. The children should treat me fairly.

   Some children have never been treated fairly, themselves and they may truly believe that we are unfair to them—that is a matter of interpreting fairness. Just because an adult is fair to a child does not mean that the child interprets those acts as being fair. Children are at times completely unaware of fair treatment. They can take it for granted.

We need to encourage ourselves and the first step is to observe our many beliefs (some are included in the previous list) which may be discouraging to ourselves. Give consideration to those which you may hold and look for alternative ideas which may be more encouraging. For example: Mrs. Brown was always careful to be pleasant, never show her true feelings, so that she would not show her vulnerability. Her class of sixth graders would be mischievous at times and she did not know what to do. One day she became so upset that she broke into tears. The children were so astounded that they became very quiet. The next day they asked her if they could be more helpful. She used that as an opportunity for a class discussion which turned the classroom atmosphere into a sharing one. Her class was easier to teach for the remainder of the semester. We are not advocating the use of tears but teachers do need to acknowledge their humanness as one way of encouraging themselves.

51

HOW WE INADVERTENTLY DISCOURAGE STUDENTS

All of us want to help our young people and we often think we are encouraging when in actuality we are not.

1. Giving Undue Attention

If children believe that they cannot find their place in the classroom by proper behavior, they are likely to try to find their place by behaving improperly to gain attention. They would at least be noticed which they feel is better than being ignored. If the teacher gives a lot of attention to the child's negative behavior by scolding, reminding, etc., doing so is not encouraging since it keeps him/her from becoming a cooperative member of the class.

2. Correcting Errors

We generally want to be helpful and we correct children all the time. This will lead to their believing that more is wrong with them than right and that nothing is good enough for us.

3. Overly High Expectations

Our expecting higher performance, saying, "you can do better," are discouraging words although we mean for them to be encouraging. The pupil may already be trying very hard to do better.

4. Scolding, Reprimanding, or Shaming

These are usually done to be helpful to children but actually are the result of teachers feeling frustrated and not knowing how to be encouraging. These show a lack of respect for children.

5. Not Believing in the Children's Abilities

If we do not believe in children's abilities, they will not believe in them either. We must show faith in children's being able to perform the classroom tasks even if it takes additional time for them to learn.

6. Paying Attention to Tattling

The tattler tries to make himself/herself look good and the offender look bad. The teacher is caught in the middle of this negative game. To not get involved is better than listening to tattling even though we want to help the "victim." Victims learn to help themselves if we do not rescue them. We can say, "I think you can handle it," or, "I think he/she can handle it."

WORDS THAT DISCOURAGE

We generally do not mean to use discouraging words, but we do so without realization. The following are discouraging words that many of us use in our classrooms:

"You should try harder."

"Your sister was in my class two years ago and she was such a good pupil."

"No, it looks like you are going to spill that water for the plants. Let Phillip help you."

"You are just too slow. Let me help you with it."

"Give me your hand so you won't get hurt. We have to be careful."

"You might fall our of the swing and get hit. Be careful."

"Will, I see that you turned in a paper that is a mess again. When will you ever learn!"

"You're just like Bobby. Why can't you do better?"

"What's wrong with you. I tell you over and over again.."

"Shame on you. Sit in this chair until you learn to behave."

"I guess we'll have to give you 'time out' again. When will you ever learn?"

52

HOW TO
ENCOURAGE

We have been writing about inadvertently discouraging our young people. Now we'll focus on being truly encouraging.

1. Encouraging young people is most effective if it starts at the very beginning of the school year. If the teacher is friendly toward each child by standing in the doorway, smiling and shaking hands as they enter the classroom, they will feel encouraged by feeling welcomed into the class and being part of the group.

2. The power of the group can be encouraging from the beginning. Allowing the children to introduce themselves, giving a little information about themselves and what they did during vacation can help them start group cohesiveness and friendships.

3. Allowing a half-hour unstructured conversation time each Monday (another day will do as well) morning

when the children can mill around speaking with a few classmates to cement relationships in the group. This is encouraging and they will enjoy this activity. Most teachers fear that the class will get out of hand or that they will miss too much valuable academic time. However, not much academics can be accomplished if the class is not cohesive and encouraged.

4. The child's worth does not depend on his/her accomplishments. We often act as if the child has value only when he/she does well. Children need to know that you like them just as they are, flaws and all. Being friendly in the classroom and especially on the school grounds is effective. Just say a friendly "Hello," or ask a question, "How was your game yesterday?"

5. Children who have a short attention span or who are slow workers will be encouraged if the teacher divides assignments into many short tasks. This will increase the attention span and with each complete task the children will be encouraged; tasks become more enjoyable since within the period children can accomplish many assignments.

6. Listen closely to what children have to say. Frequently children feel discounted because adults do not listen to them or really try to understand what they are saying. If you repeat their essential message, it will help them feel heard.

7. Use humor. Teachers are frequently trying so hard to teach that they seem far too serious and not much fun to be around. Everyone's load is lightened when we can laugh at situations. Of course we do not want to laugh at anyone and put him/her down.

8. Children tend to view adults as people who never make mistakes, easily handling difficult tasks. They do not see how many attempts it took for the adult to get something right. Allow children to see you make some mistakes, or tell them about one that you made at home.

9. Encourage the children when they are not expecting it. They will be pleased with your response.

10. If class members are poor in a subject. Allow them to teach some task in that subject after they learn it. Let them use the book if needed.

11. You may motivate slow children by sitting down to work next to them at the beginning of a project. This may inspire them to continue on their own.

12. Acknowledge a job well done and give recognition for effort if it isn't done well.

13. Emphasize that children are learning and that grades are not as important as the lessons they are learning. Help them to see the many things they have learned and to see their improvements.

14. Help children see that they can learn even more from their mistakes than from correct responses. Ask, "If you have five incorrect words which you corrected and ten right, which words would you learn from the most?" They will see that they learn from mistakes.

15. Ask the children to help you. Give special tasks to help with classroom needs. They will feel proud and encouraged.

16. Never do for children what they can do for themselves. If they can put on their own shoes but not tie them neatly, let them do it. At another time give them lessons in tying laces.

17. The teacher should not give up when a child is having a difficult time. If the teacher gives up, so will the child.

18. When parents visit the classroom say something encouraging about their child as he/she listens to the conversation.

19. Send a "Happygram" (happy note) to the child's parents when their child does something well. Teachers mostly send negative reports to parents.

20. In class discussions ask for children's opinions. "Which subject should we study first, social studies or mathematics?" "Who saw our principal on the news last night? What do you think of what he said?"

ENCOURAGING WORDS

Encouraging words and actions build self-esteem. Be generous with your encouraging words.

Words That Stimulate Cooperation

Good	Really	I like that
I agree	Excellent	You don't say
I see	Thank you	How considerate
Exactly	Good idea	Fine
Please	I'm glad	O.K.
That's right	Great	Fine job
I'll buy that	I'm happy	Would you help me?

Conversation Door Openers

Tell me about it	Shoot, I'm listening
I'd like to hear about it	Sounds like you've got troubles
Tell me more, please	
Want to talk about it?	Seems pretty important to you
Let's discuss it	
Let's hear your side	Tell me the whole story

Facial Expressions That Tell
the Other Person He/She is O.K.

Smiling	Wrinkling nose
Winking	Giggling
Nodding head	Looking interested
Laughing	Grinning in friendly fashion

Nearness That Tells The Other Person He/She is O.K.

Walking together
Sitting down beside
Talking/listening

Eating together
Playing games together
Solving a problem together

Physical Contacts That Tell The Other He/She's O.K.

Patting back
Stroking arm

Patting shoulder
Shaking hand

Encouraging Responses

You look happy about it
I really appreciate _____
I like the way you work
Let's try it together

You do a good job of _____
That shows a lot of effort
You have improved in _____
You seem pleased with it

53

ENCOURAGEMENT VERSUS PRAISE

Most of us tend to think of encouragement being the same as praise. However, important differences do exist.

At the beginning of this chapter we have Webster's definition for "encouragement": To inspire with courage, spirit, or hope. (En means to put into or promote. Courage has to do with one's moral or mental strength to venture, persevere and withstand fear, danger or difficulty.)

Now we'll give Webster's definition of "Praise": To express favorable judgement; to admire; to glorify by ascription of perfection.

Judging other people is risky, whether the judgement is favorable or unfavorable. When we tell other people (even children) how good they are and how well they did, they may actually have been thinking that they did poorly. By our praise, we may not only embarrass them but also weaken their trust in our intelligence and ability to observe. They may conclude: "If they find me so great, they must not be very smart." Moreover, when we stress perfection of performance and glorify the performer it can easily lead to self-centeredness and conceit that may handicap children throughout their entire lives.

Unlike encouragement which leads to independent thought and behavior, praise tends to contribute to children's dependency on the approval of others as their reason for action and their test of success. We want to encourage inner motivation for the satisfaction of learning and cooperative behavior.

ENCOURAGEMENT AND PRAISE CONTRASTED

1. Encouragement: "I think the table you built will be useful in your family and that they will enjoy it."

   Child's possible reaction: "I am capable and helpful."

   Praise: "You are such a wonderful carpenter—you did a fantastic job on that table."

   Child's possible reaction: "I really was disappointed with it. I should have done better. He doesn't know much about carpentry or tables."

2. Encouragement: "I'm glad that you're happy in school and that you enjoy learning your math."

   Child's possible reaction: "I'm doing OK and my teacher shares my enjoyment."

   Praise: "You are a wonderful pupil and I'm so proud of this assignment—it's perfect."

   Child's possible reaction: "I'm really only appreciated when I get good grades. If I didn't get top grades, teacher wouldn't like me and I'd feel worthless."

3. Of course, we do not praise people who did a poor job or when they fail; however, that is the time they need encouragement the very most.

4. Praise is given to people who succeed and when the task is complete. If we praise children, "Darlene, you are the best reader. You read it perfectly, not a single mistake," she may think she has failed if that kind of statement is not forthcoming at the next occasion.

5. When children expect to be PRAISED they may work toward obtaining the praise only to measure up to the demands of others. Such children will feel worthless unless they meet other's demands by pleasing them. They will not work for the goal of helping in a task for the good of the whole.

6. If children are lavishly PRAISED, "Fred, you did such a good job in your spelling; it is wonderful that you got all the words right." Fred may not feel good at all since it may feel discouraging to him if he is worried that he could not do as well on the next test.

NOTE: The authors wish to acknowledge Ken Marlin for his many years of successfully teaching families the Adler/Dreikurs techniques in Practical Parenting, Columbia, Missouri. Much of the preceding was adapted for schools from his publications.

54

ENCOURAGEMENT COUNCIL

In the 1970s when working in Illinois as a school social worker, Bruce Painter, Genevieve Painter's son, devised "The Encouragement Council" for discouraged families. This process proved to be very effective. The authors are grateful for his permission to use this material. The following is an adaptation for teachers and children:

A teacher and a child, both of whom are discouraged, may come to an impasse where nothing seems to mend their relationship. Doing an Encouragement Council together can be a fresh start in building a more positive relationship, leading both persons to feeling mutual equality and respect. Through this process they can learn to give each other encouragement, appreciation, and closeness and begin to solve their conflicts.

The format is a series of questions read by the teacher which both the teacher and child answer as truthfully as possible. The first two questions are warm-ups to help them begin to relate and build rapport. We are giving two sets of questions initially: (a) for the child who feels inadequate and helpless and (b) for the child who is acting out. After two or three meetings similar questions can be used for both types of discouraged children. The teacher is not to correct the child's responses. Simply ask the questions, allow the child to answer and do not respond to the answers.

QUESTIONS FOR THE TEACHER AND CHILD WHO FEELS INADEQUATE AND HELPLESS

1. What do you like to do for fun?

   [Teacher reads the question.
   Child answers the question.
   Teacher does not comment.
   Teacher answers the question.
   Teacher reads the next question.
   They alternate answering first on each of the following questions.]

2. What are you looking forward to doing sometime this week?

   [This time teacher answers first.]

3. What do you do well?

4. What do you like about yourself?

5. With a bit of work what do you think you could do well?

Possibly the very discouraged pupil will not be able to answer questions 3, 4, and 5 because he/she does not feel that anything is OK. The teacher should answer all of the questions regarding him/herself and if no answer is forthcoming from the child the teacher then asks the child each question again. If no answer is given this time, then help by encouraging the child. The teacher could say what he/she thinks the child does well and they could discuss it, doing the same for questions 4 and 5.

Leave this session with a friendly handshake; the teacher could tell the child his/her appreciation for working together on the process. Make an appointment to do an Encouragement Council again a week later. Continue to meet weekly until the relationship has improved and the child is feeling encouraged.

QUESTIONS FOR THE TEACHER AND ACTING OUT CHILD

The teacher reads each question; teacher and child alternate answering first on each subsequent question.

1. What do you like to do for fun?

2. What is your favorite TV program?

3. What are you proud of in yourself?

4. In your relationships with classmates what is there about you that shows that you have natural leadership ability?

5. If you were to use your leadership ability to help others more, what would you like to do?

6. What do I appreciate about you and what do you appreciate about me?

The acting out child will most likely be willing and able to answer these questions. At the end of the session shake hands and make an appointment to do an Encouragement Council again a week later. Continue to meet weekly until the relationship with each other and the classroom behavior improve.

WARM-UP QUESTIONS FOR FUTURE SESSIONS

Each session should start with two or three warm-up questions. For warm-up questions at session two use the first two questions from the first session. For future sessions use two or three from those which follow for either the withdrawn or acting out child.

1. What did you do for fun with parents or brothers and sisters this last week?

2. What do you like to do for fun with a friend?

3. What did you do for fun when you were in school this last week?

4. What is your favorite TV program?

5. What did you enjoy seeing on TV this last week?

6. What is the most enjoyable thing you did this last week?

7. What do you like about yourself? (This can be used for warm-up with the discouraged child after he/she has done it with teacher's help in previous sessions. It also can be used for warm-up with the acting out child.)

8. What do you like about your family?

QUESTIONS FOR FURTHER SESSIONS

These questions can be used for either the withdrawn or acting out child. Both the teacher and class member answer the questions.

1. What do you like about our classroom?

2. What would you like to see the classroom do to make all of us more friendly?

3. What could you and I do together for fun for ten minutes after school?

4. What have you improved upon recently?

5. What has the class improved upon recently?

6. What did someone at home or school do for you this week that made you feel good?

7. What did you do for someone in the family or school that made you feel good?

8. What would you like to do for someone this week?

9. What would you like to improve upon in your life?

10. What makes you feel close to another person?

11. What would you need from me that would make you feel better about me or closer to me?

12. What do you need from another person?

13. What might you like help with in your life?

The teacher could choose four to six questions to ask at each weekly Encouragement Council, starting with two warm-up questions. Repeating questions at future meetings is effective. Give encouragement to children with whom you are meeting at other times. During classroom discussions help integrate these children into the group and encourage a classmate to become a buddy. When they feel belonging to the group they will no longer be discouraged, withdraw or act out— they will be encouraged, feel unity with others and improve their behavior.

The Encouragement Council can be used with different persons, i.e., principal-child, counselor-child, social worker-child, principal-teacher, family members. It may be used by more than two people at a session; however, with discouraged children a one-to-one ratio is suggested to overcome the severe discouragement and build the adult-child or adult-adolescent relationship.

55

PRINCIPAL-CHILD ENCOURAGEMENT PROCESS

Although Dr. John Platt is no longer at Elk Grove, California School District, he and his staff had done many years of very effective, innovative Adler/Dreikurs work. The following process was sent to principals of their school system and later to members of the North American Society of Adlerian Psychology. The authors wish to thank Dr. Platt and Mr. Glen Brunswick, principal of Florin School, for permission to share the Figures 55.1 and 55.2 with our readers.

From Elk Grove School District
Elk Grove, California

To: Principals

From: Dr. John Platt

RE: Encouragement Process

At Florin, Glenn Brunswick, has begun a program in which he is working with
the teachers on being more encouraging to their students.

Basically, it goes something like this:

1. Teachers are requested to send students to the principal's office during one
of two periods a week (one-half hour on Monday for primary students, one-half
hour on Friday for intermediate students) with <u>Referral for Student Improvement</u>.
(See enclosed.) This <u>can</u> and <u>should</u> include some of the students who aren't
doing too will, behaviorally or academically.

An example of one referral ---

"Jimmy has been really trying harder when in his reading group - We are proud
of his desire to work hard at learning to read." (This boy has been doing
poorly in his academic work and has been a behavioral problem in class, but
for two days he had been "quieter" in his reading group.)

2. The principal reads the note to the child and makes a comment.

3. He then takes a few minutes to type or write a short note to the parents on
the "Florin-o-gram". He sends it in the mail. Glenn believes that discouraged
children probably have discouraged parents who need to know once in a while
that their child does something positive. This takes two or three minutes a
note.

4. The children get a "smily face" with a short comment written on it about
their improvement.

5. With this procedure being implemented at Florin, the principal has an
opportunity to see students for other than disciplinary reasons. Glenn says he
enjoys his opportunity. (I have watched when the kids come to Glenn's office
with these notes and the looks on their faces is something else - especially
the looks on some of the children that have been in the office for negative
kinds of behavior.)

6. Another added sidelight is the importance that it has for school - home
relations. Many parents have mentioned these complimentary notes when they
meet with the teacher for conferences.

Figure 55.1. Encouragement process in Elk Grove, California,
School. Used with permission.

REFERRAL FOR STUDENT IMPROVEMENT

To: Principal, From:_____ Date _____

Student: _____ Time: Check DAILY ANNOUNCEMENTS

STATEMENT OR DESCRIPTION OF ACCOMPLISHMENT/SERVICE: _____

_____

_____

_____

Directions: Teacher is asked to check below recommended action by Principal.

____ Note of commendation to student
____ Letter to parent
____ Acknowledgement in DAILY ANNOUNCEMENTS
____ Article in school monthly newsletter
____ Article in Elk Grove Citizen & So. Sacto News
     (Green Sheet)
____ Nomination for Student of the Month Picture Display

(cut on dotted line)

— —

A SALUTE FROM THE PRINCIPAL !

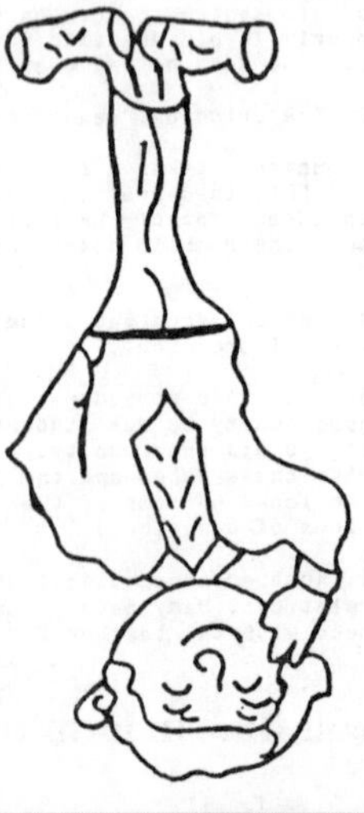

Date:_____

F L O R I N - O - G R A M

FLORIN ELEMENTARY SCHOOL
7300 Kara Drive
383-0530

Figure 55.2. Referral for student improvement with illustrated note from principal. Used with permission.

56

ENCOURAGEMENT EXAMPLES WRITTEN BY TEACHERS

The following examples of encouragement were submitted by Dr. Painter's students enrolled in Adlerian classes for teacher training at Hawaii Pacific College. These examples are of children of various ages.

Situation 1

One of my pupils had many reversals in writing and a very difficult time in forming his letters.

I used to take him aside and show him how to form the letters and compare his to the ones properly written so he could see what he was doing wrong. The results were that his poor writing became worse.

I later stopped the comparisons. I starred or circled all the letters that had been properly formed. He got so he would discuss the one he felt was best and why. He was only comparing his work against himself, not against what I had shown as being "the proper way." I think having taken the focus away from what he was doing wrong and zeroing in on what he was doing right encouraged him. It showed what he could do and lessened discouragement. It also gave him the opportunity to work towards his own goals of improvement and not mine. He made great progress in writing but even more important, he began to talk more positively about himself.

Situation 2

We had a 16 year old boy, Chuck, who was very discouraged, had never had a friend his own age. We also had another boy who said he wanted to help someone. Cedrick was very popular, a basketball player and streetwise. So I suggested that he become Chuck's friend and suggested the same to Chuck. Chuck was on cloud-nine to think that Cedrick was taking an interest in him and he came to school and reported: "Me and Cedrick played basketball last night."

Soon Chuck was "rapping" and even walking taller, emulating Cedrick and even got himself on our school's basketball team (he didn't know how to play before). Other children began being interested in Chuck with his new social skills and prestigious friend.

When Chuck graduated he made a fine speech. He never would have been able to have talked in front of a group before his friendship with Cedrick and the other boys.

Situation 3

I had an opportunity to help out in a 2nd grade classroom. The children learned that I played on a hockey team, which is a big deal to them in this community. One boy named John was particularly interested because hockey was his favorite sport and was involved in the program in town. I gave a lecture about hockey to his class and *encouraged him to share his knowledge with his peers.* John was great and helped his classmates try to figure out the sport, i.e., rules, equipment, etc. Upon leaving I invited John to come to the locker room after my next game to say "Hi." He did come, met all the guys whom he idolized and got plenty of encouragement from them, too. John was thrilled and so was I knowing what a great thrill that would have been when I was his age.

Situation 4

I teach psychology in high school. I acquired Mark, a tenth grade boy, who was constantly disruptive in class. I found it necessary to change his seat and talk to him many times about his constant talking. I noticed that other children were either annoyed or entertained by his clowning.

During our reading periods he was reading aloud while others were reading silently. He seemed to read very well and with feeling, so I decided to ask him to read aloud for all of us. He loved it! After that, he always asked to read. It was enjoyably to hear him, and the other children listened quietly. Of course I told him he read very well.

Previously, his disruptive behavior and work resulted in an F grade. Therefore, his grade went up to a B his effort was sincere.

At the end of the school year, I gave an award for perfect attendance and punctuality. Mark was one of the recipients. I'll never forget the look in his eyes when he learned of his grade and award. He said he didn't realize he could earn a B in psychology. He had failed many other classes.

Situation 5

Jenny was becoming discouraged about her ability in class.

To give her some encouragement I brought the group together and we discussed how each of us had problems learning something, and how that didn't make us any less special. I then passed out slips of paper to each person including myself, and had them write one thing that they especially liked about each person. The papers were collected and given to the appropriate persons. At the end they were reminded that having difficulty in something did not make them any less special, and that any time they felt bad about the way they did something that they should look at the papers.

After this Jenny seemed to have better feelings about herself and the class in general improved and became less competitive.

Situation 6

I have a younger sister, Christina, who is now in the 2nd grade (7 years old) and tends to use both power and attention goals while at school. She will refuse to hand in homework or work in a group. She is a very creative child, but it seems the teachers say she can never think of anything to write about during their "writing periods." So I decided to have a talk with her. I encouraged her by recalling the times in the past when she had been so creative at home. Yet she still said she couldn't write about anything. I also encouraged her to think of absolutely anything when she was having difficulty, and write about it. The next day she came home and said that she had only thought of birds when asked to write. So instead of refusing to write because she didn't think her ideas were good, she wrote on birds. And as days went past, we thought of ways to think of subjects (i.e., things seen on the school bus, subjects on television). After realizing that her ideas were not idiotic, and that no one would laugh at her, she began to have many ideas. She now has no problem in school with this and I like to think that I had a part, if only a small one, in encouraging her to feel that she was okay and imaginative just like any other child.

Situation 7

My daughter Kristin is 9 years old and in the 3rd grade. She was not doing very well in spelling and complained that she was "stupid." When we started to practice the words she became frustrated with me because I wasn't giving them in the order she wanted. I realized she was creating a battlefield and I had to retreat.

I told her I knew she could do it but needed to feel better about herself. "I think you are very smart," I said, "Sometimes we have to help ourselves feel better. Come with me . . . " We went upstairs to the mirror in my bedroom. "Let's look in the mirror and tell each other "We're terrific and do it." She was hesitant and wouldn't make eye contact with herself. I put her on my lap, gave her a big hug and looking into the mirror told her she was smart and could learn her spelling words. She broke a tiny smile. I said it again with more enthusiasm and then asked her to say it.

She began to say "You're terrific" as she looked into the mirror and began to smile. Her whole body lightened up and she was feeling encouraged. So was I.

We talked about how she could pass her spelling test. She said she wanted to study her words with Heather, her friend.

When she came home the next day she said "I knew it, Mom—I not only got 100 on my test but 6 extra points for spelling East Longmeadow, MA (our town)."

Situation 8

I have a cousin about 9 years old who is the youngest of nine children. Once when I was staying with them, he was trying to learn his multiplication tables. It was hard for him to learn and he mixed up many numbers. His brothers and sisters were not helpful. The next youngest would call out the answer when I was quizzing him or laugh at him. Some of the older ones would just say, things like "I cannot believe you don't know them yet. They are easy."

This is what I did. I told him that I would quiz him for 10 minutes every day before dinner for the four days before his test. I did not let anyone else listen. While quizzing him, if he missed, I did not tell him it was easy, he was stupid, or say, "Oh come on, you know that!." I simply would tell him the answer and then ask another one. I acknowledged him for knowing as many as he did. I gave him some time to practice with me to help him learn what he missed. I used encouragement for what he had learned and for what he did not yet know. He quickly learned his multiplication tables.

Situation 9

In working with a childhood diabetic in a residential treatment unit, I sensed that his anger over what he saw as his "curse" in life, the diabetic condition, had left him very discouraged. The discouragement had given rise to a whole "repertoire" of misbehaviors, the most important of which included manipulative tactics to keep his mother—whom he blamed for the disorder—under control. The "encouragement" was an entire treatment effort, directed by myself, but participated in by other staff. It included several areas of intervention:

1. **Teaching**—the boy learned to have competence in personally controlling his disorder by being encouraged to move toward total self-control of daily insulin intake, observance of beneficial dietary intake, and monitoring of physical feelings during activity. He was acknowledged for mastery at each level of self-involvement and with each accomplishment, he moved to a higher level of self-control until he soon performed such tasks as giving his own shots with only casual observation by staff.

2. **De-isolation**—one of my tactics in my relationship with him was to introduce him to other juvenile diabetics who had succeeded in surviving—even functioning productively—despite the disorder. They shared with him their bad feelings and how they resolved problems.

3. **Recognition**—I emphasized what I felt his main areas of competence were (such as his posttest reading level of 7th grade—for a 5th grade boy, after a 10-month period in our program) and explained to him that he was the choicemaker in establishing whether or not the diabetes would hold him back from his intellectual gifts and talents.

This treatment assisted him in feeling competent and responsible for himself. It minimized his tendency toward self pity and showed him that there were better elements of the world to "control" than his mother—such as his own physiology and his own possibilities for intellectual achievement. He was greatly encouraged.

Situation 10

I worked for a while with a 19 year old male who was a resident at a state institution in New York. He was labeled a maniac depressive and was not very responsive to others.

At the beginning of our relationship I thought that he under estimated himself by saying that he couldn't do things. This ranged from athletic games to going out of the institution to get a job. I started encouraging him by doing many activities and pointing out how good he was. I even asked him to help me with my form in bowling because he looked better than I. After a while his confidence increased and his skills in many things improved. He became more relaxed with people and when he was offered a job in the institution store he accepted it and knew that he could handle it. I let him know that I thought he was great because he was so easily able to handle new situations and that I thought he set an example of courage for me to follow. He performed better and he tried to rid himself of other barriers.

Situation 11

I worked in a day care center several years ago. Four-year old Scotty had moved to a new house recently and had just started at his new school. He was a very dominant child; he would often disrupt the class by distracting the other children with jokes or strange noises.

After we developed a friendship I began encouraging him by mentioning how much I liked it when he was quiet when I spoke because then we were able to have a nice conversation, and have a good time with each other. Gradually he generalized the one-on-one conversation to large group situations and learned to participate well in class discussions by taking a turn instead of disrupting.

Situation 12

Five year old Greta went to day care each day with the school patrol when she left kindergarten. She continually ran across the streets and would not obey the patrols.

Our discussion focused on the dangers of this. I conferenced first with Greta, then the single mother, then the class.

A positive approach was taken. Greta could be helpful with the younger children going to day care; we at school could be proud of her. We met daily and her good behavior was encouraged. A daily "Happy Face" was given to her and an end of the week "Happy-gram" was sent to her mother.

Greta was delighted to be a more grown up responsible person who could receive attention by being helpful.

Situation 13

One of the most significant ways in which I have been encouraging to children has been in my teaching blind children.

This has been primarily through my attitude of coveying that they are delightful, wonderful people to be finding ways in which they can meet life situations in a sighted world, in a successful, enjoyable creative manner.

In essence it is sharing the notion that it is good, and fun to be alive and that there are ways of using our own resources to meet the requirements of any situation.

Situation 14

Dawn is a very intelligent and demanding four year old. She came to preschool in November and really caused incredible chaos. Her attention span was very short, her interaction with others disastrous and yet she was very appealing. Within a few months of encouraging her with play during free time and show 'n tell time—whether she brought something or not to talk about, such as showing us what she was wearing, she was glowing and her behavior improved.

Situation 15

Over a period of four years, I had an opportunity to work with a child beginning his high school education. The boy was extremely discouraged, confused, and disoriented.

His parents were separated and later divorced. His father was unemployed and an alcoholic. After his parent's divorce, he lived with his father. His self-esteem and sense of worth were very low.

In order to encourage him and raise his self-esteem, we worked first on identifying his academic goals. He had great reading ability and a desire to read. I encouraged him to read, especially about his family concerns. I suggested that he read Eric Fromm's *Art of Loving,* especially for the purpose of self-love.

The most important aspect of encouragement, however, was that of achieving a sense of responsibility to make him aware that he is in charge of his behavior, that he is responsible for it, and must assume the consequences. Reinforcing the correct decisions and carefully evaluating the incorrect was further encouragement.

His self-esteem has risen and he has been accepted at an excellent college.

Situation 16

This is how I encouraged my 7th grade pupil who read at the 3rd grade level. He also misbehaved a great deal.

I did the following:

1. I arranged for him to be one of two boys to have the special task of going to the grade 3-4 classroom to hear the younger children read and to have him read the simple books to them. He went once a week for several months. He enjoyed this very much.

2. I suggested that his reading would improve if he read to one of his parents or another family member 4 to 5 times per week for a 15 to 20 minutes period. The parents agreed and so did the boy. After several weeks the parents called. They were very excited about the great improvement, and were anxious to continue. He completed a supplementary reading book of 150 pages, and made a fine report on it. Parent-child relationships improved, too.

3. I called upon him to read regularly during the oral reading period. After class I found one aspect of the reading on which to commend him. He smiled and a warm feeling came between us. If difficult words came up, I gently suggested how to pronounce them.

4. When he wrote a short story about automobiles, I had him go to the principal to read it to him.

5. I presented him with an achievement award on his improved reading ability. In addition, I gave him another award commending him on the concern he displayed for the younger children. The year ended with the parents reporting that he was reading more and taking a greater interest in education generally.

Situation 17

I was employed at a day camp to teach swimming. All of the children wanted to be able to swim because their friends could swim. Few of them wanted to admit that they were afraid of not being able to float, put head under water, and so forth.

The main "goal" was to fit into the peer group, for no one wanted to be left out. There was one girl in particular that I became fond of and she was not capable of putting her face or head in the water. I could relate to her fear and I knew that deep down she wanted to overcome this problem.

I paid particular attention to the girl and let her know that I would not force her. When she trusted me and saw that I kept my word, we began to make progress. She always tried 100%. She knew deep down that I really wanted to help her and every day I said a positive thing to her. I even made it a point to talk to her mother often to tell of her daughter's progress.

By the end of the summer this girl was truly happy and felt good about herself. She had made tremendous progress— overcoming fear and starting to float and swim—because I never gave up on her for I knew with time that she would be capable. I think, however, that I was more overwhelmed to watch her smile from ear to ear than she was to have conquered her problem. How nice to encourage another human being!!!

Situation 18

I teach 7th and 8th grade Home Economics. In the 8th grade Family Relations unit I work on self-esteem, self-respect (the pupils call it personality—they would like to know how others see them) so I have them send Valentines to each other.

They are each given a sheet of paper and asked to write the names of each child in the class in alphabetical order from the board. After each name they are to write one nice personality trait for each person on the list. Sheets are collected with the assurance that information will be held in confidence. Using a dittoed Valentine card for each child. I collate the traits given, putting at the top traits mentioned most. They are thrilled with their cards—some share with others, some don't.

Situation 19

I am a school counselor. A twelve year old boy was called a trouble maker, both at home and school. He was constantly punished or blamed. The parents brought him to my office for me to handle his severe misbehavior. They also warned me that he might be very impolite or nasty.

The first session I had with him I spent building support, trying to make friends with him. We talked about his interests, what he likes, dislikes, and what he is good at. During this conversation I gave him positive feedback whenever I thought he did something good. I also told him my opinion when he asked for it.

By accepting the boy we made a good relationship which was very helpful for further counseling.

1

GOALS OF
CHILDREN'S
BEHAVIORS

PRELIMINARY NOTE

Alfred Adler wrote about a man who was seen jumping in front of a fireplace. That behavior seemed psychotic or what we might call, "weird," when he was being observed. However, when it was discovered that the man simply wanted to jump on the mantle so that he could better see what was up there, the behavior was understood and no longer seemed weird. His goal or purpose was realized.

Adlerian psychology is concerned with the goal or purpose of behavior rather than the cause since we can never be certain of the cause. For example, mother pampers and over-protects Gary and his brother in their early years. Gary has much difficulty in preschool by expecting constant attention and having temper tantrums when he does not have his way. Gary's brother, two years older, is cooperative in school and presents no behavior problems. Yet, she raised Gary and his brother similarly.

Early in life, by trial and error, children unconsciously organize the perception of their experiences as they attempt to understand life, the world, other people, and themselves. This forms each one's "biased apperception," their belief systems. In addition, children are social beings trying to find a place of belonging with others.

We could say that Gary developed a belief that he should have much attention and have his own way. He is never concerned about the well-being of others. His behavior is the result of his misunderstanding regarding social belonging. He has not learned to find his place in a group through socially useful ways. He wants to belong to the group but uses behavior which promotes his self-interest. He is unconcerned for others.

On the other hand, Gary's brother developed the belief that he should cooperate with others. He chooses to belong through being cooperative for the well-being of all in the group. All people are decision makers. Each of the boys made their own decisions, according to their purposes, regarding their courses of behavior.

Gary is fortunate that his preschool teacher is skilled in working with children like him. She handles his power plays, ignores his constant bids for attention, and acknowledges him when he behaves well. As a result Gary's self-esteem is enhanced as he begins to feel encouraged. He now seldom misbehaves. Without being aware of it Gary has made a non-conscious decision to change his non-cooperative goals of attention getting and power, to cooperation and participation in school. However, his home behavior remains the same since mother made no changes in responding to his attention getting and power. Not knowing better, she reinforces the negative behavior and Gary continues it at home.

All children want to belong. They use cooperative behavior when they feel encouraged and non-cooperative behavior when they feel discouraged. The children decide.

Adlerian Psychology tries to understand the creative power of life which expresses itself in the desire to develop, to strive, to achieve, to belong. This power is *teleological* or purposeful; it expresses itself in the striving after a goal. An important aspect is to understand the individual context, the goals of an individual's life, which mark the line of direction for all of one's thoughts and movements.

Children want desperately to belong to the group—the family, the classroom, their peers. If all goes well, they do what is required and they feel a sense of belonging through useful participation. However, when children become discouraged for any reason, their sense of belonging is restricted and turns from cooperative participation to trying desperately for acceptance through disturbing behavior. What occurs is as though they say silently, "If I do this, they will see that I am really somebody and deserve attention," or, "If I stand up against the demands of this teacher, she will see that I, too, have power; I'll win my place with my power." As stated previously, this is not done with awareness. Children generally select their goals of behavior at an unconscious level.

While parents and teachers do not cause a child's deficiencies and misbehavior, they make them possible through their responses to the child. They understand the child's goals and learn effective responses to promote cooperation in the home and school.

57

GOALS OF MISBEHAVIOR— THEORY

We have established that each child operates from a biased apperception, those unconscious assumptions which direct relationships with others. A child's behavior has a definite purpose, is oriented toward a goal. Adults who recognize the child's mistaken goals have an opportunity to change them. If they do not know or understand the goals, they inadvertently reinforce the misbehavior and it continues.

When children feel affirmed, loved, and encouraged, they feel that they belong to the group, are worthwhile and accepted. Their goal then is cooperation. However, when they do not feel accepted and their self-esteem is low, they feel discouraged. At such times they do not feel belonging through constructive means, so they start to misbehave in order to find their place. Unconsciously they feel that they will be recognized through their disturbing behavior. They begin to operate in one of four behavior which Adler mentioned in his writings and ined and organized for teaching purposes.

....serving hundreds of misbehaving children, Dreikurs identified the following goals of children's misbehavior:

1. Attention getting

2. Power

3. Revenge

4. Displaying inadequacy

Dreikurs and colleagues made many attempts to discover more than these four goals but these are the only ones that they found which operate as motives in the lives of children under eleven or twelve years of age.

Adolescents also operate within these goals but their relationships to their peers become more important and they pursue a wider variety of behavior patterns in order to find their place in the group. Their disturbing behavior always represents a mistaken effort to find their place but can no longer be entirely explained in terms of the four goals. In addition, the goals of peer acceptance, excitement seeking, sexual relationships, or material possessions, are in operation. They also like to show their independence by doing whatever adults object to—choice of music, dress, language, drugs, driving too fast, and so forth. Teachers and counselors need to become familiar with children's private logic, their individual apperception, in order to help them. Through group and individual discussions, changes can occur. However, most school personnel need special training in these areas.

These four goals of misbehavior denote a progression in the children's level of discouragement and alienation. Children functioning in the revenge mode are more discouraged than those striving for undue attention and power; those who display inadequacy are the most discouraged of all.

GOAL 1: UNDUE ATTENTION

Most young children seek an undue amount of attention through negative behavior as a result of the way in which they are brought up in our culture. They have few opportunities to gain recognition through contributing to the family in useful ways. Adults or older siblings do everything important that has to be done. In former days a child could make a vital contribution if growing up on a farm; many necessary chores could be given to even a very young child. Today's children consider emptying the waste baskets and throwing out the garbage quite lowly compared to the chores of adults and older siblings. In our urban lives most children make no real contribution to the well-being of others.

When children are deprived of opportunities to gain status through useful means, they seek proof of status in the classroom and the home through trying to get non-ceasing attention. Through their faulty apperception they believe that if only people would pay attention to them they would have a place of recognition. Soon they develop an insatiable appetite for attention, expecting an adoring audience at all times.

Usually children first try to find a place through pleasant and acceptable actions—being cute, being funny, clowning, and so forth. However, these are considered misbehaviors not only because they become annoying, but the goal is not to cooperate. The goal is simply the desire to elevate oneself to gain special attention. Adults finally get tired of such antics and when children do not receive praise or recognition for their stunts, the good performances end; they go into negative behavior to find their place.

Some children strive for attention in more passive ways—by being helpless, being a goody-goody, being teacher's pet. Again, these are not done to contribute or to cooperate but only to elevate oneself, to receive undue attention.

When such children do not receive constant attention from passive behavior they become more discouraged and desperate, going into action by being a total nuisance—the walking question mark who asks questions not for the information but to keep the teacher busy, the mischief maker, the clown, the show-off.

Others become "lazy" because it gets them extra service and attention. The teacher coaxes, reminds, reassures, and keeps busy giving extra service.

Children who demand attention cannot tolerate being ignored. They would accept punishment, humiliation, and even physical pain just to get the attention which they crave. They even prefer being beaten to being ignored. By coaxing, reminding, nagging, giving extra service or paddling, the teacher reinforces attention-getting behavior and it, of course, continues.

GOAL 2: POWER

The struggle for power, the second goal of misbehavior, usually occurs after adults have tried forcibly to stop children's demands for attention. The struggle for power is more fierce than attention seeking-behavior; the action is more hostile, and the emotions are more violent. Children become determined to defeat adults, gaining tremendous satisfaction by proving that they can do whatever they wish and by refusing to do what they ought to do. Power-seeking children want to be the bosses. They operate on the faulty logic, "I am important only when you do what I want you to do."

Children who seek power may do so actively or passively. They may have temper tantrums, argue, contradict, or continue forbidden acts. They may passively rebel by being stubborn, by quietly refusing to do their work, by forgetting, by being silent, or by using tears (water power).

The power struggle is a mutual battle. Adults and children are equally involved in trying to defeat each other. Both try to prove that the other cannot boss them. Each say, "You will," and the other responds, "I won't," either verbally or non-verbally.

Power-seeking children may defiantly give in to adults for a while. However, when they feel controlled, they become even more aggressive and develop a greater surge of power. Adults may win the battle temporarily, but they lose the relationship.

Adults are unable to win the power struggle. No final victory of parents or teachers is possible. Children always win in the end because they are not restricted in their fighting methods by any sense of responsibility, moral obligation, or the demand for conformity. Children can throw a temper tantrum in the middle of the grocery store but mothers must stifle their rage because of what others will think. Furthermore, adults teach the children what they most likely do not want to teach—the one who has the most power wins in life by defeating others.

All further attempts to correct children by using power—punishment, nagging, preaching, angry outburst—are defeated since power is being reinforced; the unacceptable behavior continues. If adults do not learn better methods of training, children become even more rebellious and then seek revenge.

GOAL 3: REVENGE

Revenge is the third goal of misbehavior. Revenge-seeking children are so deeply discouraged that they try to find their place by hurting others as they feel others hurt them. Their efforts to gain power seem hopeless; they feel ostracized and unlovable since they do not endear themselves to most people. Their actions are vicious, violent, and destructive. They understand the specific vulnerability of each person and how they can hurt them the most. They are openly defiant and are either delinquent or potentially delinquent. All delinquent children use revenge behavior. They believe that others are unfair and hurt them so they retaliate by hurting back.

Adults respond to the defiant behavior with anger, frustration, and increasingly severe punishment, all to no avail since children in turn respond to adults similarly, but even more so. This vicious circle of punitive behavior develops a pattern of interaction where neither are willing to terminate their viciousness and neither are in control.

Revenge-seeking behavior is far more serious than attention and power- seeking. The family relationship must be improved and to do so professional help may be needed.

GOAL 4: DISPLAYING INADEQUACY

Displaying inadequacy, Goal 4, is used by children who are so discouraged that they no longer hope to find significance in any way. They expect only defeat and failure, and they hide behind a display of real or imagined inferiority. They see further defeat as the greatest danger and try to avoid it by proving their inadequacy to themselves and all others. They use their feelings of inability as a protection so that nothing will be expected of them. They protect themselves from further humiliation and embarrassment by simply not participating and looking lost and sad.

Adults expect little performance from such children and they can be even more upset with children's massive passivity than with their assault of power and revenge. Children who operate with assumed inadequacy unconsciously believe that their weakness is their greatest strength and it actually is since both parents and teachers are very upset with their declarations of bankruptcy.

All these various goals can lead to demonstrated inadequacy. Either passive or overtly antagonistic children can become so discouraged that they cannot hope for finding success in any way; therefore they turn to displaying inadequacy. Children who are consumed with insatiable attention-getting and are unable to find what they consider enough attention or those who are finally beaten down from pursuing power and revengeful behavior also may become so discouraged that they display inadequacy as a protection from further humiliation. And adults become equally discouraged.

58

IDENTIFYING GOALS

To help children change from negative to positive behavior their goal must be identified. You can determine the goal first by observing children's actions and interactions with others and second, by observing your own feelings.

UNDUE ATTENTION

Children seeking undue attention keep adults busy with them. They will talk out of turn, run around, not do their work and in general do what the adult thinks is not appropriate. When the adult offers attention, "Paul, I said you should stop it!" they stop momentarily and start the misbehavior again or something similar.

The adult usually feels irritated.

POWER

Children who are in a power struggle with adults will not stop the misbehavior and they will even increase it. They say either verbally or non-verbally, "I won't and you can't make me do it."

The adult usually feels angry, threatened or defeated.

REVENGE

Children who are in revenge continue strong negative behavior, when adults tell them to stop they may change to even more violent action.

The adult usually feels hurt.

DISPLAYING INADEQUACY

Children who display inadequacy look and seem helpless. They are generally quiet and withdrawn. No matter what the adult does, they continue with this misbehavior. Although this is not always considered misbehavior since they are not disturbing others, we think of it as misbehavior because they are not cooperating or participating in classroom activities.

The adult feels helpless.

Understanding their goals helps adults not only change children's immediate behavior but their motivation for inappropriate behavior.

59

REVEALING THE GOAL TO THE CHILD

When teachers suspect the child's goal of misbehavior they can confirm under which goal the child is operating as well as reveal the goal to the child. We do not advocate that parents reveal goals to their children; this process should only be done by those who are professionally trained—teachers, counselors, and others in the helping professions.

To ask a child, "Why did you do that?" is futile. The child's answer, "I don't know," infuriates the adult but in most cases that is really true. The child usually acts impulsively without being aware of the motives. Instead of asking the child, "Why?" the adult should inform the child of his/her goals, the purpose of the behavior. Information about the purpose of the behavior can help the child understand him/herself in order to change the negative attitudes and understanding self is the first step toward improvement.

These discussions should never occur immediately after a misbehavior when both parties are upset. Some time must lapse before the discussion. It should be done in a calm manner and simply involve the information regarding the goals without criticizing or reproaching. This can be done privately; however, once the atmosphere is such that classroom discussions occur regularly and a sense of trust is present, it can be done in the group, with the children participating. The mutual understanding can be very helpful for the entire class.

Dr. Dreikurs taught his pupils a simple technique to reveal the goals to the child which, when correct, results in the child showing a "recognition reflex," a roguish smile, a twinkle in the eyes, a slight facial tenseness, or looking downward. The recognition reflex is a confirmation as to which goal is operating.

Dreikurs' wording is in the form of guessing, with simple statements which even very young children can understand. Only one goal is dealt with at a time starting with goal one and continuing with each successive goal.

Attention: "Could it be that you want to keep me busy with you?"

Power: "Could it be that you show me, 'I do what I want.'" or "Could it be that you want to be the boss?"

Revenge: "Could it be that you feel hurt and you want to hurt back?"

Assumed Inadequacy: "Could it be that you want to be left alone?" or, "Could it be that you feel stupid and don't want anyone to find out?" or, "Could it be that you just can't help it?"

60

HOW TO CORRECT MISTAKEN GOALS

Once children show the recognition reflex adults can change their approach in order to correct the misbehavior. To not act on one's first impulse is best because to do so will tend to intensify the misbehavior rather than correct it. One needs to check oneself from responding to children in habitual ways, e.g., lecturing, scolding, punishing, and rewarding (bribing). These fortify the mistaken goals. A more effective way is to not say or do what is usually done, but rather to plan new actions which are unexpected. This throws children off guard and changes occur more readily. An important procedure is to be both firm and kind at the same time, to practice mutual respect and to be encouraging.

CORRECTING ATTENTION SEEKING BEHAVIOR

For children who are making a bid for undue attention the best action is to ignore them and to avoid showing any annoyance. Children will continue the misbehavior if nagged, lectured, or reminded. Dreikurs taught a technique which is effective: After disclosing the goal to the child, negotiate the amount of attention she/he is to receive:

> Teacher: Harold, would you like me to give you attention on a regular basis?

> Harold: Yes.

> Teacher: How would it be if I gave you attention five times in the next hour?

> Harold: OK.

> Within the next hour the teacher will give Harold a minimum amount of attention, five times. He/she will say during the class activities: "Harold one." And a little later, "Harold two." "Harold three," and so forth until five. Of course, this is not the kind of attention the child would like; it becomes quite tiring and unexciting which allows the child to see how ridiculous his attention getting is.

Children need to be given attention when they are not looking for it and are being cooperative. Finding tasks which can be helpful for the teacher or another pupil are encouraging procedures.

Both natural and logical consequences can be used to correct attention getting behavior.

CORRECTING POWER BEHAVIOR

If teachers fight with power-seeking children, those children will win. One must avoid showing one's anger. Adults must realize that they are as much in the power struggle as the child is and the best procedure is to extricate oneself from the conflict. One may as well admit to the child and to the class that this child is powerful: "You are a very powerful person. I cannot make you do it and I know that I can't."

Power driven children are quite ambitious. Teachers can redirect such children's ambition toward the useful side of life. They can be given tasks to help a classmate or a child in a lower grade. They also can be given tasks to help the teacher which will seem to give them prestige. The teacher can appeal to this child to help him/her. Any methods of encouragement are, of course, effective.

Natural consequences are effective with power driven children but logical consequences result in being punitive, therefore they are ineffective in the midst of a power struggle.

CORRECTING REVENGEFUL BEHAVIOR

Adults must avoid showing their hurt feelings and must avoid retaliating even though they are provoked to feel like it. Children who show revengeful behavior are difficult to deal with and may need professional help in addition to that provided by the school's regular staff members. These children could be taught how to be more cooperative and to feel equal by being shown love and respect. They can be given a model of self-respect by being treated with equality no matter how vicious they may become.

Adults generally feel like punishing such a child; however, punishment makes matters worse since the child will further punish the adult. As in power, the adult cannot win in this game. Not punishing but rather by doing something unexpected is far more useful. For example, doing something very kind and showing your love at a time when the child's revenge is strong will take him/her by surprise and may start turning the situation around because the child may think of the possibility that he/she is likeable. The adult must be persistent and not show further hurt if the child rejects the attempts at kindness.

At the time of classroom discussions, games of encouragement are very useful for all the children, and especially for the revengeful child. Have the children sit in a circle. One child says something he/she likes about another child. That child then selects another child to whom he/she offers a positive comment. This continues until all have a turn. The adult may have to assist the person who must say something to the revengeful child but if such games continue from time to time, the children will become proficient in encouraging each other.

Probably at least one child will be in the classroom who wants to do a kindness for another person. That child may be enlisted to be a buddy for the revengeful child. If the adult can get some children to be a buddy at recess, at lunch or after school, it would help the revengeful child move toward cooperation and useful behavior.

As in power, natural consequences will work but logical consequences will seem punitive.

CORRECTING DISPLAYS OF INADEQUACY

The passive, withdrawn child is generally so discouraged that he/she cannot hope for any significance and expects only defeat and failure and stops trying. This provokes the adult into feeling equally helpless and to give up. Although the child's discouragement is contagious, the adult must not yield to this provocation. Huge amounts of encouragement are needed for the child and the adult must encourage him/herself.

These children need to learn that it is okay to make mistakes and that no one, not even the teacher or parent, is perfect. The child must learn to feel worthwhile; the teacher must keep a sincere conviction of not giving up and that this child, too, can be helped.

Preceding working on academics, an effective procedure is to play a simple game with the child during recess or after school so that the relationship between teacher and pupil can improve and become one of mutual respect and encouragement. Usually teachers feel that would take too much time but the expenditure of time doing the usual reminding or lecturing would be greater.

Structuring assignments into very small increments and checking them as soon as each is completed is an encouraging technique. Positive comments for each small attempt is necessary at first. Finding a buddy for the child could help him/her feel worthwhile. An encouraging technique is to have some classmates help with assignments.

Natural consequences will work but logical consequences must be carefully applied so that the child does not feel punished.

SUMMARY

As stated in this chapter, we must know the goal or purpose if we want to understand children's behavior and help them change from misbehavior to cooperation.

M

LEARNING THROUGH NATURAL AND LOGICAL CONSEQUENCES

PRELIMINARY NOTE

Since punishment and rewards are ineffective training techniques for children because of their autocratic nature, how can adults handle discipline and deal constructively with children's misbehavior? We can allow children to experience the consequences of their acts, which provide very real learning situations allowing them to make decisions and become responsible for their own behaviors.

This type of training can begin as early as infancy. For example, 23-month-old Mike, a poor eater, keeps parents and day-care teachers busy with him at meal time. He blows bubbles in his milk, dawdles, plays with the food in his plate. Getting him to eat seems to require constant attention and coaxing. Teachers and parents confer and decide to use a strategy to help Mike overcome this problem: When he does not eat properly, they will keep a friendly attitude, make no mention of his behavior, and remove his unfinished plate when everyone in the class or family is finished eating. The adults carried through the plan allowing him to experience the consequence of hunger by not giving him snacks before the next meal although he cried for something to eat. At the next meal when food was offered he dawdled again; the food was casually removed in silence. The adults did not look worried; they managed to wear a pleasant smile. After that Mike started to eat well. He quickly found out that if he doesn't eat, he gets hungry.

No matter how unhappy Mike may seem, the important point is for him to experience the natural consequence of not eating thus becoming hungry.

Adults must remind themselves that Mike will not be harmed by missing a meal or two and they must become genuinely unconcerned about whether he eats or not. Eating is his business and he can decide whether or not to do so. Adults should mind their own business and not the child's.

61

NATURAL AND LOGICAL CONSEQUENCES

Consequences of two kinds: natural and logical. *Natural consequences* occur out of the child's own actions, free of adult intervention. Mary, age two, touches Mother's hot coffee cup although she was told not to do so. The pain is a natural consequence. Tom forgot to bring his lunch money to school. Hunger is the natural consequence unless the staff feels sorry for him and lends him the money, thus preventing him from learning the valuable lesson of being responsible for remembering.

Logical Consequences involve adult intervention in planning a situation by which children learn through experience. Alan failed to get up on time despite having set his own alarm clock the night before. He must face the consequence of being 20 minutes tardy at school. When he arrived his teacher told him that he must make up the 20 minutes by staying after school. He accepted this as fair since his class formulated this consequence at the beginning of the semester. Schools need to have rules and then the staff must carry out such consequences so that children learn to become responsible for their own behaviors.

To establish order and discipline in the classroom the best procedure is to do it through classroom discussion at the beginning of the school year. However, such discussions can be done at any time. An example follows:

Mrs. Green, second grade teacher, is having a classroom discussion with her pupils.

Teacher: Who has to follow rules in the school?

Fred: The children.

Teacher: Do other people have to follow rules?

Susan: No.

Gary: I don't think so.

Teacher: Why not?

Bruce: Because rules are made for the kids.

Teacher: (Getting out her manual which she received last week.) Look at this manual. I'll read some things to you so you can see the kinds of rules I have to follow. (She reads aloud some of the regulations for staff.) What do you think might happen if I do not follow these regulations which are rules for teachers?

Susan: The principal could bawl you out.

Gregory: Maybe you would get fired.

Teacher: Yes, those are both possibilities. So, who has rules in the school?

Steve: I guess kids and teachers. Maybe the cooks and custodians too.

Teacher: Yes, we all have rules to follow in school. Are there other places that adults and children have to follow rules?

Sam: Yes. On TV I see adults who break rules and have to go to prison or to a judge.

Bruce: If you drive on the wrong side of the road you could get into a bad accident.

Teacher: So we have to follow laws and rules of the road. How would you like for us to plan together what our rules should be for this classroom so that we can know what to expect? How many of you would like to do that?

Class: All raise their hands.

Teacher: What should we do if someone comes to school and is tardy?

Alan: You could send him to the office and the principal could scold him.

Teacher: Why does the principal have to be responsible for that?

Sam: Maybe you should scold him.

Teacher: I would really not like to scold people. I have another idea. Have you heard of setting up consequences? It goes like this: We could make a rule that we must all be on time for class. Then if someone is tardy they would have a consequence. For example, a consequence could be that they must make up the time after school or during recess, something like that.

Alan: I think that would be better than being scolded. Then we could take care of it ourselves.

Teacher: How many of you would agree to that?

Class: All raise their hands.

Teacher: In one classroom if someone forgets their lunch money they go without lunch; no one lends them the money. What do you think of that?

Bruce: I wouldn't like to go hungry.

Teacher: If you forgot one time and had to go hungry, do you think you would remember after that?

Bruce: Yeah, I think I would remember then.

Teacher: How many of you think that is a good idea?

Class: All but two children raise their hands.

Teacher: Alice, what do you think?

Alice: I wouldn't like to go hungry.

Teacher: Okay. Bruce, what do you think?

Bruce: I wouldn't like to be hungry either.

Teacher: Do you think that you might learn to remember if you should forget and be hungry for one afternoon?

Alice: I don't know.

Bruce: I might learn to remember.

Teacher: Well, since there are only two of you who do not agree we could try it for a while and see how it goes. We'll have to send notes home to your parents to see if they will agree with that one. Some parents may not want their children to go without lunch should they forget their money.

The children will come up with their own ideas for consequences. In this manner rules for the semester can be established, allowing for such discussions again when situations arise. Additional examples of consequences devised and written by teachers are given at the end of this chapter.

To assist the reader in further understanding consequences Figures 61.1 and 61.2 are presented. They are from various writings of Rudolf Dreikurs, compiled by Ken Marlin, Practical Parenting, Columbia, Missouri. The authors appreciate being given permission to use them.

PUNISHMENT VERSUS CONSEQUENCES: DISTINGUISHING BETWEEN

Punishment	Consequences
1. Arbitrary—no relation to offense	1. Logically related to the misdeed
2. Variable	2. Consistent
3. Adult upset, emotionally involved, prestige at stake	3. Adult calm, objective, and uninvolved
4. Imposed in anger with desire to "get" the child, to make him pay	4. Adult feels he is providing an honest learning situation
5. Represents the power of adult	5. Represents the pressure of the social order, of reality
6. Adult's will at the moment	6. Mutual agreement made ahead of time
7. Child feels resentment toward authority	7. Child has no one to blame but himself/herself
8. Involves "talk"—(screaming, preaching, criticizing, "I told you so.")	8. Adult is quiet
9. Chaos	9. Group harmony
10. Adult may feel sorry, guilty, regretful afterwards	10. Adult feels that s/he helped the child learn, that the child has had a valuable experience
11. No choice for the child	11. Child has a choice
12. Adult is policeman, judge, jury, and jailer	12. Adult is teacher
13. Adult shows disrespect for child, lost dignity for adult.	13. Respect and dignity to all, mutual respect

Figure 61.1. Distinguishing between punishment and consequences.

PUNISHMENT VERSUS CONSEQUENCES: LONG RANGE EFFECTS

Punishment	Consequences
1. Child develops greater power of resistance, defiance, retaliation, rebellion, resentment, hostility, and aggression.	1. Child becomes cooperative.
2. Child's poor self image and negative goal of misbehavior are reinforced.	2. Child develops good self-concept.
3. Child learns to lie, hide feelings, or cheat to avoid punishment.	3. Child can be open, honest, and have the courage to be imperfect.
4. No long range success; when threat of punishment is removed, child is left with no incentive to behave. A high percentage of prisoners are repeaters; they have been punished and re-punished, but did not learn to "behave."	4. Child learns inner controls, becomes self-disciplined.
5. Child was denied the right to experience results of his actions and to take responsibility for them, thus has no sense of order.	5. Child learns to be responsible for self.
6. Child learns "might" makes right, becomes dominating, bossy, bullying. Power teaches power.	6. Child learns to consider needs of the situation, rights and freedom of others.
7. When child becomes adult may be submissive to authority out of fear, deny own needs, unable to stand up for own convictions, feel inferior.	7. Child will have self-confidence and courage.
8. Child may become power-drunk and tyrannical in interpersonal relations.	8. Child will be able to accept defeat, accept not always being 1st or best. Will know he is OK as is.
9. Child may lack creativity; conformity through fear.	9. Child wll feel free to try, to experiment, to make mistakes.
10. Child may withdraw, escape, live in a fantasy world, real world is too frightening and painful	10. Child will have realistic expectations and a healthy attitude towards himself and others.

Figure 61.2. Differences in long range effects between punishment and consequences.

Natural consequences always work. One must simply be sure that what follows the act represents the pressure of reality—that which would just naturally happen. The adult must not feel sorry for the child and simply allow the consequence to evolve.

Logical consequences, on the other hand, are structured and arranged by an adult but must be experienced as logical in nature by the child. For parents to deny TV if their son does not do his homework is not logical. To send a child to the principal's office if he/she misbehaves is not logical. The consequence must be logical and planned by the teacher and children. Consequences are very effective and in this way, reality replaces the authority of adults. They teach the child in a logical way, but the consequences are set up ahead of time with the child so that he/she understands that it is to help him to learn to remember or to learn a lesson in life. Although the consequence is pre-arranged, the child does have the choice to behave properly or experience the consequence of improper behavior. The teacher remains in a neutral attitude and the child sees that he/she cannot blame anyone but self for the consequence faced.

Having children make their own class rules along with consequences is a good way to establish logical consequences in the classroom so that children become responsible for their own choices and outcomes.

Logical consequences must be used cautiously. They cannot be used in a power struggle or they become punishment and make matters worse.

62

TEACHERS' EXAMPLES OF CONSEQUENCES

The following are classroom situations submitted by Dr. Painter's pupils enrolled in Adlerian classes for teacher training at Hawaii Pacific College. These situations are in two sections: (1) elementary school, and (2) intermediate and high school. They are further divided into natural consequences and logical consequences.

ELEMENTARY SCHOOL
NATURAL CONSEQUENCES

Situation 20
(Situations are consecutively numbered throughout the book)

A fourth grade girl had bed wetting problems. The child came to school with the same clothes all week, she had dirt in her hair, and smelled of urine. The teacher noticed this and informed the child that this was not proper hygiene. The mother was also notified. Still the child came to school the same way.

At first the children in the classroom wanted to know what the smell was and from where it came. Nobody knew but this girl and the teacher. The children eventually found out that it's the little girl who smelled and they started calling her "stinky." However, they still played with her at recess and in the classroom but finally they withdrew from her. They didn't want to play with her, and they didn't want to sit beside her. She heard the others talking about how dirty and smelly she was and stayed away from her. This upset the girl very much, so she wanted to change the situation. She asked the teacher how she can get some friends. The teacher instructed her as to how she can start by coming to school after taking a bath and putting on clean clothes. Losing her friends motivated her to want to change.

Situation 21

School and classroom safety were the topics of discussion at the beginning of the school year. We discussed the purpose of the signs posted on the walls outside, which read: NO RUNNING IN HALLWAYS AND CLASSROOMS. Railings on the stairs were to be used for holding on to, and not sliding or hanging on and jumping two-three steps up and down the stairs. Pointing out that the building was made out of concrete, we discussed the possibilities of injuries, that any fall could be painful and dangerous. One day, nine-year-old Kent, forgetting all that had been previously discussed, jumped from the stairs and tried to grab hold of the top of the iron gate, (like a monkey bar) and missed. He fell, and hurt his head. Painfully, he learned that rules are to be observed and discussions on safety are to be remembered.

Situation 22

I have a class of 27 kindergarten children. Our day starts with the class gathered together for our flag pledge, calendar work, and sharing time.

While one child was in front of the class telling us about his trip to the beach with his family, someone began to cry. Upon checking, the child who was crying said Elmer pinched her, that's why she was crying. "But she pinched me first!", said Elmer.

I think this is an example of a natural consequence. This was not the first time that this child had pinched someone. Now that she knows how it feels to be pinched, she has learned that if you pinch someone, the person will pinch you back.

Situation 23

The boys in my class love to play kickball at recess. The only problem was getting them to play far enough in the field so as not to kick the ball too close and hit the buildings. The boys knew where to play but continued to play near the buildings. One day while playing, the ball was kicked on to the school roof and it was several days before the custodian got the ball down. The boys were very upset to be without a ball to play kickball and now play out in the field.

Situation 24

Some of the children in my second grade class seemed to be in a hurry to get from one spot to another in the classroom. Instead of walking, they would dash across the room. We discussed safety in the classroom, and what could happen if everyone ran in the room. Most of the children understood that we could get hurt, so they would walk. A few needed reminders.

One day, Ned dashed across the room, fell, and skinned his elbow on the carpet. This incident showed the other children how easily one could get hurt by running in the room. Ned felt the physical pain, so he now walks in the classroom.

Situation 25

A frequent occurrence in school is to have children lose or forget their lunch money or token. As a second grade teacher, I find such action not a problem for the majority of the children but for one or two, it can be considered a chronic problem unless some action is taken.

If children lose or forget their lunch money, the natural consequence would be that they go without lunch.

In a home situation having a child go without lunch for whatever reason can be carried out with little difficulty. But in a school situation groundwork must be laid or serious repercussions can occur. One parent considered going without lunch cruel and something she would never do. She would spank her child rather than have him go without lunch. She was very closed-minded about this method of handling the problem. In this case I lent the child the money and phoned the mother to bring it to me. After several trips the mother decided to let him go without and become more responsible. He no longer forgot.

Situation 26

The kindergarten class was making their salt water solution to hatch and raise brine shrimp. Instructions were for each child to put only ½ scoop (1 tablespoon) of rock salt in 1 cup of water and stir. Shannon decided she would put a heaping scoop of salt in. She laughed as she stirred showing another child what she had done. I didn't scold her, but just said, "Let's see what happens." Of course, her solution was too concentrated and as a consequence, her brine shrimp eggs did not hatch. She was very disappointed because she had no cup of brine shrimp of her own to observe as her classmates thrillingly observed, counted, and compared theirs.

Situation 27

Our school is built on a hillside with convenient walkways but Steven, a very chubby first grader, is always seen running down the slopes. He has slipped, fallen, and tumbled several times. The teachers and vice-principal tell him that going down the slope is dangerous and he is reminded to walk on the sidewalk to no avail.

One day Steven misbehaved in his classroom. His teacher told him that he must eat his lunch in the classroom and stay there through the lunch period. The teacher sent Steven up to the cafeteria so he could buy his lunch and then bring it back to class. After Steven bought his lunch, he proceeded to walk down the hillside instead of using the sidewalk. He tripped over a rock and his food fell to the ground.

Steven looked like he was in shock. He knew that he had lost his lunch because he had not used the sidewalk. He would have to go without lunch that day.

ELEMENTARY SCHOOL
LOGICAL CONSEQUENCES

Situation 28

I was on yard duty for the third graders. The rule is that all children are to play outdoors, weather permitting. After the morning recess a group of boys who used the lavatory excitedly told me that there was paper "stuck in the toilet." Not only that, the floor was wet and papers were "stuck on the ceiling." After checking the lavatory I questioned the 3 boys who were missing during play period. None of them would admit they were responsible for the actions. Using the process of elimination I questioned them one by one. Finally the timid child of the group blurted out, "He told me to do it." Then they started to blame each other eventually admitting what happened. They not only threw wet toilet tissues onto the ceiling, but used the rest of the hand towels to plug up the toilets.

As a consequence the boys were told to clean the toilet bowls, scrub the swinging doors and wall, and mop up the floor. Instead of my checking to see whether they were doing the job properly, I sent 3 influential peer leaders to check up on them and to report to me periodically since I was busy with the class. After the boys were through with their cleanup chore we had a class-council and discussed behavioral objectives, sense of school pride, and good citizenship.

The consequences they experienced deterred them from further mischievous conduct.

Situation 29

Mary, a pupil in my third grade class, seemed to enjoy bringing all sorts of things that she bought or were given to her to show friends. Not just material objects but also assortments of "junk foods" in plastic bags. I had the impression that she always had a lot of everything.

One morning when I arrived in school, my third graders came running, to tell me that Mary stole money from their schoolbags after school. I could see that this was a peer action demonstration with those who were directly involved and peer sympathizers. Mary also exploited a couple of children to buy things for her with promises that she would repay them, which she didn't. These acts angered the children. When I questioned Mary she admitted she did all the things of which she was accused.

After conferring with the principal, we had a conference with her parents. They were obviously shocked and hurt by these incidents and they cooperated and openly discussed the matter. The ultimate decision was that Mary was to repay all that she owed with her weekly allowance. I didn't ask Mary, but found out from her friends that she repaid all her friends. I believe that the consequences she experienced will help her to be a better person.

Situation 30

Kevin comes to class and just sits. His reader isn't open and when he opens it, he turns to the wrong story. He is stubborn and does the opposite of what I say. He complains about not being able to find the page and someone finds it for him, but he doesn't follow along. He then complains because he wants to read, but when I call on him he's at the wrong place. He then very rudely shouts to the reader and says "I can't hear!," "Read more loudly!," or "You're reading too fast!" Then he starts giggling and distracts other children.

I'm then just about ready to blow my stack. At first, I did, only to find out it wouldn't work. I finally told him, "I realize you're not enjoying reading along with us. If you don't feel like it, you may find something else to do." Whenever he mimicked me or tried to distract the other children, I smiled, looked at him and reminded him very nicely, "Kevin, if you're not up to doing the work, let's find you something else to do." When I started this all the distracting behavior stopped. He either joined us or sat quietly. Usually, the day after he's really ready to work and he ends up staying during recess on his own because he actually hates being behind in his work.

Situation 31

I teach a third grade remedial reading program in which children come for reading help for 45 minutes a day. One of the rules is that you need a note excusing you for being late to class. Some of the children have a tendency to dawdle in the restroom and play near the drinking fountains. Two children came seven minutes late, which necessitated waiting for them when they were scheduled for a group lesson. The group was reminded of the rule regarding a note required for late entry to class.

The following day, everyone but Bennie and Casey were in class on time. The notes were requested but since they did not have them, they were asked to return to their respective teachers for a note. They each returned without a note and a similar message. "Teacher doesn't know why I was late so she is not going to write a note." When asked what they were going to do next, Casey suggested that they write me a note explaining why they were late. I accepted their notes, which took them about 15 minutes to compose, and we separately discussed their problems. They decided that they would no longer dawdle in the bathroom after recess. They did not enjoy writing the notes and I have had no problems with tardiness from either child or their fellow classmates from that time.

Situation 32

Before meeting with me for social studies, the children go to their cubbies, pick up a pencil case and a portfolio which they would be using. Then they meet in a circle in a designated area.

Tommy dilly dallies. He takes ten minutes before he joins us. The children have to open up the circle and with this movement are comments of "move," "Hey, quit pushing," "Sit here." I have had to repeat procedures relating to committee work, worksheets, and assignments.

To improve peer relationship, foster group cooperation and responsibility, I asked the group for their recommendations.

They suggested: (1) That each child have an assigned place in the circle; (2) When a child doesn't report on time, directions should not be repeated; (3) The child has to ask another classmate, not the teacher, for directions; (4) The child can pick up during recess material that was circulated earlier (an "inconvenient" time for the child since everyone looked forward to recess).

When Tommy reported late the next time, he missed out on map directions. During recess, he went to my desk, picked up a map worksheet and asked one of his classmates for the directions. He was unhappy in having missed recess.

The following week we saw Tommy gathering his supplies faster and walking over to the social studies area without dilly-dallying.

Situation 33

Kui and Moki were coming to school late more and more often. They walked to school together and played on the way.

Other fifth grade children seeing that nothing happened at this time began to be late also. Our first period is quite unstructured and used for class meeting, organizational discussions, study time, finishing art projects, and so forth. I brought up at a class meeting that some children might think first period was not as important as the rest of the day. The class decided that they would rather keep it than have a formal lesson or assignment at that time.

I then asked if some kind of consequence should occur for being late to school. They agreed that everyone should learn to be on time and that a consequence should occur if they were not.

After some discussion and several suggestions, they voted to require a child with an unexcused tardy to sit in the hall by the teacher's room at recess.

The next day Kui and Moki were late again and at recess they sat in the hall. They were not late again for some time but several weeks later they were, and again they sat in the hall at recess. Now they seem to have decided to arrive on time and the others are on time, too.

Situation 34

I have a niece, Alice, who is 6 years old and a son, Jay, who is 7 years old. When they were younger, our son was always taught that boys do not go around hitting girls and that he should respect others. We also have tried to teach him that vulgar language is neither polite nor necessary.

Presently, my niece spends time after school with me waiting for her parents. Alice began to take advantage of Jay through manipulative ways. She knew what we expected of Jay, therefore, she kept harassing Jay, knowing that he would not strike back. At this point, we explained to Jay how much to tolerate, when to turn the other cheek, and when to "fight back."

My niece kept up with her verbal and physical abuse for awhile longer. Meanwhile, I just kept an eye from afar. Finally, after a few days, Jay walked up to his cousin, gave a hard pinch on her cheek and said, "Are you going to keep on talking to me like that?" My niece had a good cry; however, she has since treated her cousin with a lot more respect.

Situation 35

At the beginning of the school year when we are discussing behavior in my kindergarten class I tell them, "If you are unable to sit and listen attentively without bothering others when we are sitting on the rug during story time, you will be sent back to your seat because it is unfair to the children who want to listen. I will continue to read the story but I will point to the child who isn't listening and then point to his seat; he will have to leave the circle and return to his seat. He can go back to the circle when ready to listen."

When I first started using the pointing system, the child usually stopped misbehaving but remained seated in the circle.

I then told him/her firmly but making very sure I have said it without any feelings of anger, "Please go to your seat until you are ready to sit and listen without disturbing others. You may return to our circle as soon as you're ready."

The class responded well to the pointing system and I seldom have to stop or interrupt whatever we're doing because the children behave well now.

Situation 36

Children in a class for the emotionally disturbed often have problems adjusting to the new class environment. They get in trouble with teachers, playground supervisors, and their peers. The classroom teacher tries to have children control themselves. If this doesn't work with teacher guidance, children are told that they will be sent home or taken home, whichever can be arranged with the parents. The teacher makes an agreement with the parents of each individual child. The next time the child acts up the teacher makes a phone call to the parents. The parent usually comes to pick up the child. Sometimes transportation is a problem for the parent and the teacher will take the child home. Usually children don't like to be sent home and they argue and even cry. But they are sent home anyway without any arguments or scoldings from the teacher. They may get sent home four or five times and they then learn more self control and do not have to be sent home again.

Situation 37

John is constantly rocking his chair in class. I discussed the situation with him after which I offered him the choice of sitting with all chair legs on the floor or giving up the use of his chair for the period. John felt that this was a reasonable consequence.

All went well for several days until once again John rocked in his chair. Upon noticing, I immediately signalled the removal of his chair, after which I returned to my ongoing task. John quietly removed his chair to the back of the room and returned to his desk to work. At the end of the period, he went back to get his chair and sat properly. At the end of the day, he came to me and said that he was glad to have his chair back. He sat properly after that.

Situation 38

When a child loses his/her lunch money at our school, he or she is loaned the money to buy lunch. Michelle, a second grader, lost her money four times during the first quarter. Michelle's mother was upset and wanted a conference with me to see how the problem could be solved.

During the conference with Michelle and her mother, I suggested that since the lunch money is Michelle's responsibility, the logical consequence would be for her to go without lunch when she lost the money. Michelle and her mother agreed to the consequence. The mother talked with the administrator and he agreed to let Michelle go without lunch when she lost her money.

Michelle lost her money once after the logical consequence was set. She understood the consequence and did not even bother to ask for a loan. She simply said, "Mrs. Johnson, I can't buy lunch today because I lost my money." She had the money after that.

Situation 39

George age 9, is in the third grade. George is playful, and has a short attention span. He had a habit of always being late for math class which was right after first recess. After being late on several occasions, George was told that we would not wait for him and that I would continue working with the rest of the class on the day's assignment. He was to be given the assignment instruction after the others had started their seat work. George was to complete his work in my class even after the others had left and the math period was over. George found himself (the only child from my math class) sitting among the rest of my regular homeroom class. Not being too happy about this situation, George remembered to come in right after recess to his math class.

Situation 40

We have talked with the children about proper recess rules. The rules are those suggested by the children with the safety of all in mind. Mark is an active and playful child. He does not keep still during class time and becomes rough on the playground. The children came into the room during recess and complained that Mark was throwing rocks at them and pushed some children into the bathroom. When making the rules the children also decided what was to happen to those who broke the rules. Because Mark did not follow the rules that day, the next day he became a "wallflower," a term used in our room to describe a child who has been removed from the group and must sit outside by the wall and not participate in recess. Although Mark wanted to join in the play and have a good time, he knew he had broken the rules and needed to take the consequences. He became less rough.

Situation 41

Math is the favorite subject of most of the second graders in my class, but a few would rather do other things. I would keep them in during recess to finish their work, but this didn't work out too well. The class discussed this problem and decided that if a child played during math, then he/she should do math during "play-time," if the child drew pictures, then he/she should do math during art, and so forth. We all agreed to this, so one day when Brian didn't finish his math because he was busy drawing pictures, I didn't keep him in during recess. That afternoon when we had art, I gave him his paper and said he could do his art project as soon as his math was done. His favorite subject is art so now he does his math when he should.

INTERMEDIATE AND HIGH SCHOOL NATURAL CONSEQUENCES

Situation 42

I am a home economics teacher. A day prior to the children's cooking lab, I demonstrate the food product they will make. The demonstration allows the children to visualize the ingredients, steps taken, and final product. If a child is not paying attention during my demonstration, I remind her *once* to please listen.

On our cooking lab day, some class members are lost and confused because they weren't listening. These children have encountered (1) cakes that boil to death (too much baking soda or baking power), (2) cookies that taste too salty or too sweet, and (3) breads that do not rise (yeast breads always require warm water). They learn from these natural consequences to listen to instructions.

Situations 43

The chairs I have in my 8th grade classroom are pretty good for rocking. At first I warned the children about rocking their chair, the dangers, and so forth. Then I said that if I had to warn them more than once in a period, they would have to stand for the entire period.

When I would warn someone, he/she would argue, "Well, you didn't catch so-and-so rocking." After a while the children were squealing on each other.

One day I decided to not do anything and a rocker fell off his chair. The result was a loud crash, and the whole class silently staring at him. This rocker learned his lesson about rocking. We seldom have rockers now.

Situation 44

As an auto mechanics teacher, at times some children do not listen to my instructions and demonstrations.

The day before the children are to work on a car's section, I demonstrate the jobs at hand. We go over the tools needed, the sequence and the final product.

When the time comes for them to work on the car, some class members are lost and confused because they were not paying attention. As a result of not listening, those members have encountered (1) engines that won't start, (2) engines that won't perform, and (3) dissatisfied "customers." These are natural consequences and they lead to paying attention.

Situation 45

Billy was the starting quarterback for his school's varsity football team. The school had one more game to win before they could go into the districts playoffs. On the last day of practice, the coach reminded the players as usual to have a good rest and be sure to eat a light meal about four hours before game time.

The next day, Billy had a good rest, but he did not follow his coach's advice about eating four hours before the game. Instead, he ate a heavy meal two hours before game time. He reported to the locker room feeling great, contented and ready to play football.

The game was only five minutes old when Billy made a spectacular quarterback sneak and ran the ball 85 yards for a touchdown. People were jumping and screaming with joy, but not Billy. He felt nauseated and dizzy. His breathing was extra heavy and his stomach began to cramp up until he finally could not take it anymore. He was escorted to the locker room and was out for the remainder of the game.

The back-up quarterback tried his best, but he could not pull the team through this one important game. When Billy heard the final score, he knew he let his team down. He knew he should have eaten a light meal four hours before game time, like he always had done before. He had another season of football remaining, Billy vowed that this mistake will never be repeated.

Situation 46

Before I really understood Rudolf Dreikurs' philosophy, I was a real nag in my high school English class. If the pupils weren't doing what I thought they should, they were told in no uncertain terms what they should be doing.

I started a new procedure last quarter by giving the children a real voice in their class, through a class council. We decided to eliminate the long tests and substitute a quiz format. They believed they would do much better since the quiz would be given immediately after covering material that was important to remember.

During a lecture introduction, recording, and discussion, one of my class members was totally absorbed in her senior memory book complete with pictures and autographs. Since she was one of the youngsters I had nagged on numerous occasions about similar behavior, I decided to let natural consequences be the outcome rather than reminding her to pay attention.

About fifteen minutes before the end of the period, I passed out quiz papers. She looked incredulously at the quiz when it was placed on her desk, but she did not say anything. When I returned to the front of the class she was scanning her fellow classmates. As she noticed that everyone was working on their quiz, she looked up at me and I silently mouthed the words, "Do your best." Slowly she returned my smile. At that point I think she fully realized she had not spent a very productive fifty minutes prior to the quiz. From her smile and our subsequent contact, I knew she doesn't harbor any resentment about her failing quiz grade, and I feel good because she learned something valuable and I didn't have to preach.

Situation 47

In the foods laboratory session, class members in each kitchen group are responsible for the planning, preparation, serving, and the clean-up of the meal or food product. Each member in the kitchen group is given specific responsibilities for the successful completion of the lab. In the case of cookie baking, one child is designated the chef and is responsible for watching the cookies while they're baking in the oven. Other group members can pitch in to help, if the need arises.

Sometimes, instead of watching the cookies and the baking time as they're taught, the chef and the rest of the kitchen group get distracted and forget to watch the time. As a result, that kitchen group ends up eating burnt cookies or having less cookies to divide and eat amongst themselves. Usually such an incident has to happen only once for the students to be more alert and take extra care the next time they have a foods lab.

Situation 48

Several factors contribute to the undesirability of having to teach an afternoon literature class in my situation: the young people had just finished their lunches, my classroom, a portable, becomes very warm in the afternoon, and class members are tired near the end of the day. These factors, together with classroom reading assignments which require a quiet classroom, often combine to produce sleeping children. I used to have to continually patrol the classroom and nudge these nappers back into consciousness, a procedure which would often disturb the concentration of those who stayed awake and their laughter at the expressions of their newly-awakened classmates would waste much valuable time.

At the beginning of the next semester I simply did not awaken anyone. When a class member slept through instructions, he/she would have to ask another class mate or me. This was embarrassing and I chose an inconvenient time for the sleeper to come in for instruction.

The use of this natural consequence was very effective. Not only do few children fall asleep now, but those who do are quickly awakened by their friends' quiet nudging and the situation of the sleeping children has all but disappeared.

Situation 49

In my pre-algebra class, the period usually begins with my discussing the classwork/homework assignments, answering any questions the children may have, introducing new concepts, and with the time remaining, they may start on their classwork/homework assignment. If a child is unable to finish the assignment in class, then it must be taken home and finished as homework. Whether they choose to do the assignment or turn it in at the next class meeting, is left up to each child.

Many children, after repeatedly not turning in their assignments, learn the hard way, that if they do not understand the material being covered, they have a difficult time doing their quiz and exam, and thereby experience the natural consequence of being lost, confused, and frustrated. After they have learned the hard way, they are more than happy to start doing their assignments, and their grades start to reflect this change of attitude. During this period of not turning in their assignments, I do not scold them, I let the natural consequence take its place.

Situation 50

In my typewriting class, children do their class work by units. Previous to taking the class, I've always set a deadline on each unit. When this was being enforced, the pressure to meet the deadline by class members was evident.

In the classroom some signs of resentment, and revenge existed—classroom copies of the typewriting books were being stolen even though I don't allow any class work to be done at home. The young people started approaching me for an extension of the deadline and I found myself saying "yes" to mostly everyone. Doing this made me feel uneasy because I felt doing so was unfair for other class members who worked diligently and handed in their assignments on time.

We held a class discussion and selected a consequence—no extensions of deadlines. I have found much success in the application of this consequence. I introduce each unit and give them a date on which they will be tested on the type of work in the unit. I tell them: "I will accept your assignment up to the week before the grading period ends; however, before the date of the test, be sure you know how to type".. . .(I go over the problems on which they will be tested.)

If children procrastinate, they will experience the consequence of their work not being accepted which lowers their grade. I do not apply any pressure.

Application of this philosophy, has made my class relaxed and very democratic. Class members go out of their way to find time to do their assignments. They enjoy being in class and typing. The quality of the work that is being turned in has improved much and no typing books have been stolen.

Situation 51

I find that the greatest difficulty in using natural consequences is in allowing them to occur. I supervise a high school hiking club.

During one of the pre-hike planning sessions some of the more experienced hikers began complaining about having to share their water with people who forgot to bring theirs. They were finding it necessary to carry two or three times their normal amount and frequently had to stop to get water for someone else out of their pack.

We held a meeting and they suggested we institute a "no water sharing" policy for the next hike. Well, that hike took place on a very hot day and, as expected, a few of the novices .forgot their water.

Everyone tried to stick to their guns, but as the day wore on it became more and more difficult. Finally a few gave in and quickly depleted their water supply. Now it became a matter of not sharing water with someone who had given all his water away, a task that not even the most stalwart of us could meet. Soon we were all sitting around, drinking each other's water and not finishing the hike. The lesson was well learned as no one has forgotten his/her water since.

Situation 52

Thomas was a seventh grader in my homeroom class. He was a very discouraged child and had difficulty in many of his classes because of it. However, we maintained a pleasant relationship and he considered me a friend. He stayed after school one afternoon to help me put up bulletin boards, so I drove him home afterward. I was surprised to find that he lived in field officer's military housing because he always came to school looking like something the cat dragged in.

I do not know who was responsible for Thomas' appearance. Perhaps clothing was a struggle at his house every morning, or perhaps his parents stayed out of the problem and gave Thomas responsibility for dressing himself. At any rate, I never mentioned his appearance because I felt it would damage our relationship. To me to say to a child what I would not say to an adult seemed rude.

One morning Thomas appeared in homeroom looking particularly bedraggled. He was wearing the same shirt and pants he had on the previous day. The knee of one pants leg was badly torn. His yellow shirt was covered with red dirt and his shirt tail was hanging. Seventh graders are notoriously blunt and as soon as he walked in, the attack began. "Look at Thomas!" "Don't you ever change your clothes?" "You wore that yesterday!" "How can you come to school looking like that?"

In my pre-Adlerian days I would have rushed to Thomas' defense and have given the class a lecture on manners. This morning I said nothing. I went back to my desk and began making out attendance forms. Thomas said little in his defense, but I could see that he was embarrassed. My heart ached for him, but I remained deaf.

That was the last time Thomas ever came to my class in that condition. Some days he was less than shiny and starched, but his appearance underwent a marked change. Criticism from his peers had accomplished what no amount of lectures from adults could have.

INTERMEDIATE AND HIGH SCHOOL LOGICAL CONSEQUENCES

Situation 53

As a physical education teacher on the secondary level, I am faced with the problem of convincing young people to take showers after activities, and once in the shower to control "horse-play." We have had our share of accidents in the shower area due to playfulness and disregard for safety.

At the start of the school year, all class members are reminded of the need for showers and encouraged to do so. Along with this encouragement goes out a reminder from time to time, for safe practices in the shower area. Despite these reminders for safety, I still find kids running and sliding in the showers.

I have pointed out the dangers of these practices and still find young people who choose to disregard my cautions. We talked about consequences in the various classes and the class members came up with "anyone engaging in horse-play or sliding in the shower areas will be excluded from gym for a week and will go to the study hall instead." The problem has diminished.

Situation 54

As a ceramics teacher I am faced with keeping the art room reasonably clean and well organized. A second concern is the school's requirement that class members report to class on time. Repeated tardiness is generally reported to the Dean for disciplinary action. I feel there is a better way to deal with tardiness and I have combined these two concerns into a logical consequence.

On the first day of class, the young people are given a course outline describing the projects, procedures, and responsibilities. Keeping the lab clean is their responsibility as well as being to class on time. We discuss both requirements. Each class member is allowed two unexcused tardies per semester (if they do not exceed a few minutes). However, after the third tardy the person must spend five minutes cleaning tools or doing other lab maintenance. Class members generally agree this procedure seems fair and that it benefits all the young people by having the lab operate smoothly.

On the third tardy I assign a small cleanup job. No one has ever refused because five minutes cleanup is a lot easier than going to the Dean. I always make it a point to thank them when they are finished and sometimes joke that I have a lot of dirty tools left for the next time. I like to get away from the idea that the person is being punished, the extra cleanup is simply the consequence of being tardy. The class members have been more responsible for being in class on time. If they are late, they bring tardy passes from another teacher, or call to let me know a problem exists.

Situation 55

I teach shorthand to high school juniors and seniors. Speed development is measured by tests which require that dictation be taken and transcribed with 95 percent accuracy. Most class members are very eager to pass these tests.

I have been announcing one day ahead to my classes that a test will be given the next day and in order to give each person a fair chance with no interruptions, doors will be locked during the dictation and no other test opportunity will occur until the following week.

RESULT: Two children who were continually late to class missed one test. Now all class members are really prompt to class and are very respectful and quiet when the various speed tests are given.

Situation 56

As registrar of a high school I have encountered one very frustrating experience—registration with complaints from kids that they do not get their preferred courses. We started a new system: Registration for the school year starts in January, with pre-registration. All the young people are reminded to complete the proper forms at pre-registration so that they may participate in the final scramble, consequently they are urged to pre-register on time so that their chances of getting their desired courses would be better. They are told, "If you do not complete your pre-registration, you may not participate in the scramble. If you do not participate in the scramble, you will have to wait until September. At this time many of the classes will be closed and you may not obtain your first choices—in some cases not even your alternate choices. You will just have to select from what is available."

Here each person has a choice to register on time and be able to pick classes or register late and choose only from what is available. The person would have to live with this schedule for a whole year because those who register late due to their own negligence are not permitted to make any changes.

Situation 57

My field is secondary special education, mentally retarded educables. Max is in the ninth grade and is functioning at a mental age of a third grader. He would habitually forget his lunch money. At first I lent him the lunch money and he would pay me back after several days of reminders. Finally, I called his mother and informed her of the situation. After speaking with Max and his mother about the responsibility and importance of keeping track of money, we all came to a decision that I wouldn't lend money to him if he should forget or lose it. His mother would leave lunch money on the table every morning. If he should forget or lose his money, he would have to go without lunch for the day. Very soon Max began to have his lunch money with him.

Situation 58

Daryl, a senior in my ceramics class, and I were in a power contest. Before each new project I would demonstrate the proper construction process, as well as point out various procedures not to use because they would cause the pot to collapse. When the class members started working I noticed Daryl often used the exact techniques I told the class not to use. At first I though he had misunderstood the instructions or was having difficulty in handling the clay, so I gave him extra help. However, after I corrected his mistakes and left him to work on his own, he would go right back to using the wrong methods, and would again ask for help. By this time, I realized Daryl was very capable of understanding and completing projects, and that he was using the wrong techniques to show he could do whatever he wanted and not listen to me.

After the second project was demonstrated, Daryl once again used the exact techniques I had just told the class not to use. This time when he asked for help, I told him that I could not help unless he used the correct methods. He replied that he wanted to do it "this way." I said nothing and left him alone to work. After two class meetings his pot was hopelessly misshapen and on the verge of collapsing. Daryl on his own initiative destroyed the piece, and started over using the proper techniques, with much greater success. I said nothing of the incident and later volunteered my aid and complemented him on how well the pot was working out.

Situation 59

I teach special education children in the high school. This year we decided to take a large group to the State Special Olympics to be held in May. Many deadlines have to be met and a lot of forms have to be filled out. During each class, I discussed the importance of meeting all the deadlines for their physical examinations, parental permission forms, and other requirements. Everyone was excited and we began to plan for the preliminary regional meet.

I passed out the parental permission/physical examination form and spoke to each child personally to see if he or she was truly interested in participating as an athlete. I explained the form to each child and marked the places where their parents and physicians were to sign. They had three weeks to turn in the forms or not be able to participate if they did not meet the deadline. They understood that no exceptions would be made.

Thereafter I simply made a small poster that remained on the bulletin board until the due date. Most class members turned in their forms on time. A few sheepishly brought their forms in late and were informed without harsh scoldings, that the due date had come and gone and I had already turned in the forms to administrators and under these circumstances the child could not participate. I did not have too many arguments, but I got excuses that ran the gamut. I told each negligent child that the Olympic form was old news and assured them that we would be participating next year. Amazingly!! No hassles!! In years previous, we (as a team of special education teachers) ran around to the last minute screaming for those forms. We were even driving kids on our own time to the doctors. We now use this procedure for all field trips and school programs—our arrangements are much more effective and less work for us.

Situation 60

In schools around the state "fighting" was occurring. I don't mean black and blue, knock down fights . . . I mean "pencil-fighting." It became such a big thing at my school that our principal put memos in the daily announcements discouraging the activity. Besides the mess of pencil bits, the wasted classroom time, and the useless scoldings, the biggest problem is class members coming to class saying they can't do any work because they have no pencil (they lost a pencil-fight in the previous class).

I refused to lend my pencils and children with pencils refused, too. I expect all assignments by the end of the period. We had a class discussion and one pencil fighter suggested that he would do the assignment on the spare blackboard, the class agreed. They found that standing the whole period, raising an arm for a long time, having to fumble with chalk, and being the last one to finish in the class was *very* uncomfortable. I soon found my class with pencils, invariably.

Situation 61

I teach secondary special education (mentally retarded educable). Ben is in the eleventh grade and is functioning at a fourth grade mental age. He never completes the work assigned to him over a one week period. Therefore, his assignments were cut from weekly to daily. I discussed a logical consequence with Ben stating that if he didn't complete three-fourths of his daily assignments, he would receive no points for the day, which meant failure for that week. After seeing an "F" for the first week on his new contract, he started finishing his assignments from that day on to the present. Ben is still on a short range objective contract and it seems to be working out just fine.

Situation 62

One of the irritating problems of teaching high school kids is their lack of consideration for property and its placement in the classroom. They often fail to return materials to their proper places at the conclusion of a class period. Books are left either on or under their seats when they leave.

I tried to deal with this problem in a variety of ways and finally talked about it with my classes which were learning the principles of logical consequences. In one class the agreement was that those class members whose materials were found on chairs or the floor at the end of a class session would forfeit the use of such materials during the subsequent class session. Instead of being able to do their assignments during their regular class time, they would have to return after school to use their materials.

After the first enforcement of this logical consequence, I found that almost miraculously, all materials were being faithfully returned. Not only did the use of this logical consequence solve an irritating practice, but none of the class members who were subjected to it complained because it was their decision. In time all my classes chose this solution.

Situation 63

One day in my algebra class, we were having an informal discussion. Anthony came up with an idea of giving a consequence to pupils who failed to do their classwork/homework assignments. The other kids were all in agreement. So the class began to list alternative consequences and agreed to the following: Children who fail to do their classwork/homework assignment will (1) not be able to make up the assignment, and (2) have one point taken off their average for each non-returned assignment. Children are allowed to miss two assignments before the points will be deducted.

All the children were asked to vote since it did affect them directly, and they all agreed to this consequence. Since this was set up, no one has argued or questioned why a point was taken off for their assignment, or why their grade was lowered. This logical consequence, developed and agreed upon by the class members, has worked wonders in the class.

Situation 64

I am currently teaching home economics at the intermediate level. My specific area is teaching clothing to both boys and girls at the eighth grade level.

Teaching class members how to use the sewing machine properly and safely has been the most difficult part of their nine week course. In the beginning of each quarter, I emphasize the importance of safety within the classroom and while using the sewing machine. Because many of them have either never worked with a sewing machine before or at the most just sat in front of one, class members are almost always likely to view the machine as a brand new toy. To many of them, its operation is similar to a car. The harder you press on the foot pedal the faster the machine will sew. They get their kicks listening to the motor run at top speed.

Before the kids even get to sit in front of the machine, I discuss the money value of the machine, the cost of repair per machine, and the time and inconvenience involved when a machine is not in order. Class members are amazed at the number of dollars allotted each year for the maintenance of sewing machines.

Class members and I discussed and set rules to follow when using the machines: If class members purposely try to abuse or improperly use the machine, they will be asked to leave the machine and sit at their desk for a total of forty-five minutes. This time continues to the next day until they sit for a total of forty-five minutes. I would then approach class members at their desk to discuss the reason they cannot use the machine that day. They are allowed to use the machine again the next day. If they continue to misuse the machine, they will sit at their desk for two periods of ninety minutes. If it still continues, they will sit another day longer. By this time they have learned because they would obviously be behind in their sewing project.

This happened about four times in all of my six classes. Now, none of the children misuse the machines.

Situation 65

Two high school sophomore girls enrolled to work in the counseling office as aides. The primary responsibilities of an office aide are to deliver "call" slips to kids wanting to see the counselor, to deliver messages to the staff, to greet visitors, and to do other clerical duties such as filing, cataloging, and so forth.

During the first semester of school, both girls did satisfactory work and their attendance was good. However, their attendance became quite irregular during the second half of the year. During this time, a conference was held with both girls regarding their attendance problem (mostly class cuts). They related that they were having personal problems—boy/girl relations. As weeks passed, we held periodic conferences to talk about their concerns. But their attendance remained spotty.

At this point a written contract (with their permission) was drawn stipulating conditions for them to remain enrolled as aides. The agreement stipulated that should they be absent (unexcused) for more than two more days they would be assigned to a study hall class for the rest of the year.

Within a month's time, they had exceeded their allotted days of absences and thereby, transferred to the study hall class. The two girls and I learned from this situation. The girls learned about keeping commitments. I learned that a necessity is to have a detailed contract before the work begins.

Situation 66

I teach typing to an active and very vocal group of eighth graders. They have 5 minutes of passing time which is adequate since our school grounds are centralized, but the problem seems to be chattering and visiting friends in the classroom well after the tardy bell.

To gain the class' attention used to be a problem. I tried speaking louder than necessary and gradually lowering my voice to almost a whisper, but doing this five times a day was not going to solve the problem. My main problem was getting the class to settle down after the tardy bell had rung. Several times I have stood up in front of the class and in a normal tone say, "I have some work to do at my desk, so when you are ready to begin class, will someone tell me." Then the usual was heard, "Aye, you guys, shut up!" The group quieted themselves down, and a brave soul would approach my desk with the message that I can begin class. This was still not satisfactory until I came upon your class discussion and logical consequences. The class decided that when the class is not quiet I would pull out my stop watch, raise my hand and start the time. When the room became absolutely quiet I would stop the watch, write the time on the board, and begin the lesson. When the bell to go to lunch rang, instead of excusing the class, I pulled out the stop watch and began the time. The class made up during lunch hour the few minutes it took for them to settle down at the beginning of the period.

After a few days with the stop watch, the class settled down quietly without my having to say anything. About staying in a few minutes either after school, recess, or lunch for the time lost at the beginning of the period, I have not had a single complaint. The class has respect for my friend the stop watch since they participated in the decision.

Situation 67

I teach band in my school. At the beginning of each year, the band members and I set rules for the class. We decided this year that in order for them to be able to perform in the annual spring concert they (1) must be able to play up to a certain number in their method book before receiving the concert music, (2) must be able to play all concert pieces, and (3) must attend all morning and noon rehearsals. Some band members will be disappointed if they do not complete one or more of the requirements and have to experience the consequence of not being able to perform in the concert.

Situation 68

At the beginning of the school year locks and lockers are issued to every boy in my class. Each boy is then responsible for the lock and his personal belongings. Locking the lockers would prevent any type of vandalism in the locker room. Signs are posted to remind them about locking their lockers.

Even with all the reminders many children would still be careless and forget to lock their lockers. Consequently their valuables and locks would be missing.

Whenever the lock is lost, the child is supposed to pay the office for the lock. Most of the time the locks were not paid for. This loss comes under our department budget.

After losing too many locks, we had a class meeting and decided that each child should bring his own lock, be responsible for his personal belongings, and lock his locker. If a child should lose or misplace the lock he would either do without a lock or bring another from home.

This consequence has proven to be very successful. Fewer complaints have occurred and most of the children are being responsible for their own locks and lockers.

Situation 69

At the beginning of the track season, the boys on my track team meet with me to decide on the training rules for the season. We also decide on the logical consequences for any infractions of these rules and repeated infractions.

This season the boys decided that consequences should fit the degree of the offense. For breaking a major rule, such as those concerning smoking and drinking, the decision was that the boy would be immediately dropped from the team. For minor infractions such as unexcused absences from daily practice or more than three unexcused tardinesses, the boy would have to run the one hundred yard wind sprints after the daily practice. The consequences became more severe as infractions reoccurred.

Because the boys helped determine the rules, understood and agreed to the reasons we had set them, infractions were quite infrequent. Since the boys also had set the logical consequences for rule infractions, they called each others' attention to rule infractions and reminded each other of the logical consequences they had agreed to as a team. It was unnecessary for me to enforce rules.

Situation 70

A long standing rule in my ceramics class is "Anyone who fails to clean their wheel after throwing doesn't get to use it for an undesignated period of time." The time period was never established because doing so was a very personal matter determined by the child who was in the dog house. The rule was very rarely broken, and to my knowledge, never broken twice.

Situation 71

In my art class, we discussed how we might overcome the difficulty of getting everybody to bring in the "textures," rolling pins, plastics bags, cloths, and so forth necessary for a rather ambitious hand-building project in clay. The class members decided with me on the rules: "Anyone who did not bring their things would be unable to work in clay, but could work in another medium so as not to distract the others." No animosity occurred when the rules were enforced. Most of those who had forgotten got their act together and/or worked out partnerships to share so that we established a studio atmosphere. and turned out some good pieces.

Situation 72

An annual event for all mentally retarded children is the Hawaii Special Olympics. The contest allows the mentally handicapped to participate in track and field events as well as swimming and softball throw competitions.

The kids I coached were very enthusiastic about the whole affair because they had had a chance to take part in the contest when they attended intermediate school. To gain everyone's cooperation we all sat together and made rules for our practice sessions. Each participant understood and agreed upon each rule. The decision that a class member would be given only one warning for breaking a rule and then he/she would be removed from the team.

When the practice sessions began, Helen began to act up. She ran around and talked to another child while everyone was gathered for instructions. I gave Helen her first warning saying, "Helen, you have broken two of our rules so I am giving you your first warning. Please settle down and listen for instructions."

Helen settled down for a while, then refused to take her laps around the field. At that point I asked Helen to leave the field and go back to her class. I also reminded her that she would not be allowed to participate in the Special Olympics.

I was surprised to see how fast the other children took their laps and returned to the group for further instructions.

Situation 73

For every food product that is made, the class members must write a plan sheet. Another task that must be completed is copying the recipe from the board. I give the class one class period to complete these tasks. The agreement was that no group may cook, until both jobs are completed. They may finish these tasks as homework but they must be done before we cook. I've had class members who fool around during class time, and forget to do it for homework. The day we're supposed to cook, they're scrambling about trying to complete their tasks. But its too late. I don't allow them to cook. As a result, they get zero grade for the day, but worst of all, they starve while the others eat.

Situation 74

Susan, a high school freshman, had been 30 minutes tardy at first period math class almost every day. When she would arrive I'd be half through my lecture. Since she missed so much she had a difficult time understanding the work and therefore couldn't do some of the homework problems. She asked for special help and the explanation on material she had missed during class.

She was told to come in after school for any extra help that she needed because it wasn't fair for the rest of the class members if I gave her extra help during class. After a couple of days, Susan started coming to class on time and hasn't been tardy since.

Situation 75

Early second semester I was having definite problems in my 7th grade, co-educational P.E. class.

The problems as I saw them were unsportsmanlike conduct (especially swearing), and unsafe performance of flag football for those children who were just learning the game.

I held a class meeting to see if we could resolve some of these problems. I opened the meeting by saying that I felt we had definite problems during P.E. class. I did not say what I felt the problems were, instead I said, "What suggestions can you give me to help me become a better referee?"

In the course of the discussion those whom I considered the core of the problems spoke freely. They really gave me outstanding suggestions for refereeing the game. The ideas they came up with convinced me that by following them to the letter, the P.E. class would become a safer and more enjoyable one for everyone.

The problem of swearing was brought out by one of the girls. One of the captains volunteered to monitor this for his team. The captain of the other team followed suit. The consequence they came up with for swearing was "first offense, warning; second offense, out of the game for that class period."

I felt really good about this meeting because the class members not only recognized the problems, but came up with logical consequences for them.

Situation 76

I apply logical consequences in all my craft classes. At the beginning of each course, I go over a list of thirty basic safety rules with the class. We cover each rule one at a time. I ask the class members why they think the rule is necessary, what they think of it, and what should be the consequences of breaking the rules. Some rules are modified according to the response. Then they copy the rules and study them. The basic reason for all the rules is safety. Ignoring or breaking a rule may cause injury to that person or to someone else. The following are examples of safety rules and their logical consequences as determined by the class members.

Rule: Shoes must be worn at all times in any shop.

Reason: Shoes can prevent injury to the foot.

Consequence: No shoes, no work.

Rule: Horseplay is not permitted in any shop.

Reason: Horseplay is unnecessary action which may cause accidents.

Consequence: First offense, warning. Second offense, the child must leave the shop area.

Rule: Before starting a project in the shop, the class member must pass the general safety test with 100% accuracy.

Reason: Failure to know even one rule may cause an accident.

Consequence: If class members don't pass the test with 100% accuracy, they may not work in the shop. (The test may be retaken after two days.)

I have very little trouble with persons working in the shop because they feel the rules and consequences are fair and that they apply to everyone, including teachers.

N

CENTERING

THE RELAXATION RESPONSE

PRELIMINARY NOTE

Ideas found in this chapter are compatible with but not actually found in Adlerian theory and practice. However, the authors believe that incorporating effective, new ideas in addition to the traditional ones is necessary and helpful.

Dr. Painter has found a national, if not international malaise prevalent among most people—high stress, a symptom of our fast lane, high-tech mode of life. Most of us find that we must live a fast pace in order to manage all that is necessary for our daily survival, our achievement in work, our social and family obligations. With or without our realization we live in a stressful manner as evidenced by present levels of heart disease, hyper-tension, ulcers, headaches, and other stress related ailments.

In her psychological private practice Dr. Painter has found that many people do not know how to relax in order to bring down their stress level. Upon arrival at home after a hectic day at work, the hectic evening of food preparation and family matters is overwhelming. If they live alone, the stress of loneliness may be severe. They may suffer from sleeplessness or their dreams may be disturbing. Even in recreational activities they put themselves under pressure through competition to win at all costs. She finds it effective to teach her clients centering, the Relaxation Response, a procedure to quiet the body and mind. Children are often showing evidence of high stress levels. For this reason, she has added centering to her work with children and to this book.

63

NEW CLASSROOM DIMENSIONS

The findings on hemispheric specialization tell us that our education system and modern society generally, with its very heavy emphasis on communication and on early training in the three R's, discriminates against one whole half of the brain. I refer, of course, to the nonverbal, non-mathematical, minor hemisphere, which we find has its own perceptual, mechanical, and spatial mode of apprehension and reasoning. In our present school system, the minor [right] hemisphere of the brain gets only the barest minimum of formal training, essentially nothing compared to the things that we do to train the left hemisphere.

Roger Speery

Education in the past has mainly stressed learning to read, write, compute, discuss, debate, and analyze—primarily intellectual and logical pursuits. On the other hand, modern educators are now becoming concerned with new psychological perspectives—the teacher/child relationship, the distinction between knowledge and wisdom, and the purpose of life.

A strong controversy occurs regarding whether teachers' tasks should be only intellectual instruction or if they should now be expected to help children in their general adjustment by including the new psychological perspectives.

TEACHER-STUDENT RELATIONSHIP

Today teachers are often incapable of imparting knowledge because of the increasing number of reluctant learners. As a result test scores are down, illiteracy is up and the drop-out rate is soaring. If teachers are unable to influence the motivation of young people, they are unable to teach effectively. A very important aspect is to improve teachers' relationship with their class members in order to influence them.

We often hear puzzled teachers and parents say, "But, I went to a similar school and I learned just fine!" Children are definitely not like they used to be and we should rejoice. Our world is not like it used to be and our children are preparing themselves differently for life than we had in the past. In an autocratic society where children had to conform, whether they liked it or not, all the teacher had to do was teach subject matter and the children learned it. Today, the children decide whether or not they want to learn what is presented and teachers need a new perspective and training in techniques to inspire the motivation to learn. Such training does not imply a greater burden on teachers. On the contrary it can make teaching assignments not only more effective but also more enjoyable.

At the present, teachers learn little about what to do with children who do not want to learn, to study, or to behave properly in the classroom. The time required for such training is minimal in contrast to the benefits it provides and many teachers who are now enrolled in seminars and workshops as well as reading newer materials are finding this to be true. Many books, such as this one, are available which propose more democratic methods for the teacher and parent. These improve the adult/child relationship so that learning can take place.

In recent years, as a result of the breakdown in our educational system across the country, a bombardment of alternative systems have been suggested which served mainly as bandaids being applied to an old system. For the most part these changes did not work well and the back to basics movement became a demand. This is a good situation since our children do need to learn the basic tools. However, they need to be inspired and motivated to want to learn what the school wishes to teach them.

DISTINCTION BETWEEN
KNOWLEDGE AND WISDOM

Most schools would like their young persons to be attentive, relaxed, creative, and imaginative while receiving knowledge—learning the basics. However, the usual educational procedures—reading, writing, computing, discussing, and analyzing do not generally lead to relaxation, imagination, creativity, and intuition. True education provides for an environment in which childrens self-regulated learning process can unfold naturally. The word, "education" comes from the Latin word, "educare"—to lead out from within. Enlightened educators are increasingly interested in teaching pupils how to lead out from within, enabling the expression of the self—the highest qualities of each child's unique essence.

In recent years business management firms and other organizations are increasingly interested in having middle management and higher ranks learn techniques of leading out from within to allow individuals to get in touch with their intuition in order to increase productivity. In an article, "Trying to Bend Managers' Minds," *Fortune*, Nov. 23, 1987, was stated, "Human Potential Groups all have a common aim: to alter people—or corporations—radically by unleashing energies that purportedly remain unused in most of us." This article mentions corporations such as Dow Chemical, General Motors, Allstate, Sears, General Dynamics, the Federal Aviation Administration, IBM, Boeing Aerospace, Lockheed, and others participating in the new kinds of education.

By getting in touch with our essence from within, we can find our intuition, the source of our wisdom, and become truly creative, finding new solutions for many situations. Our inner self or "center" of individual consciousness enables us to perceive clearly that which is occurring in our physical body, emotions, and mind.

Our center also receives guidance, often felt as an inner yearning which is the source of our wisdom, creativity, and imagination. Our center guides us to become aware of our life purpose, the contribution through work that we need to manifest during our lifetime. This is the fundamental meaning of self-actualization. We cannot get in touch with these phenomena through down to basics education alone. It is apparent that we need to offer both the basics (knowledge) and the self-actualizing perspectives (wisdom) in our classrooms—a holistic approach to education.

64

CENTERING PROCESS

Imagination is more important than knowledge. For knowledge is limited, whereas imagination embraces the entire world, stimulating progress, giving birth to evolution.

Albert Einstein

Schools generally impart knowledge. Of course, obtaining knowledge is important. However, to prepare youngsters for today's challenges of complicated technology they must be inspired to use their imagination as suggested in the statement by Albert Einstein. They must be able to take the knowledge which they acquire and extend it to fit into new situations through using the creative forces of imagination and intuition. Centering exercises, often called "The Relaxation Response," are the internal processes associated with the unconscious. They are techniques which inspire the creativity deep within each of us. One's intuition and awareness of a higher self, creativity, new insights, thoughts, and sense of purpose, are revealed to the child in the centering process.

Children are placed under many stressful conditions— learning to read and write, having to perform, worrying about not doing well enough, being criticized by teachers and parents, feeling hassled by contradictory ideas, undue demands on their time, too much homework, worrying over being socially acceptable. Such stress can be alleviated by the relaxation found in centering, a necessary part of education for today's young people.

In centering we learn to contact our inner wisdom by quieting our bodies, feelings, and thoughts. Only when we quiet these can our *real self* emerge. At such time we become very clear so that the answers come easily to questions we ask of ourselves. We feel an inner peace and sense of certainty. This gives us a sense of fulfillment and life takes on deeper meaning. The earlier we introduce children to this adventure in self-discovery the greater the advantage. Centering activities can be started with children of kindergarten age, initially for only a few minutes. No upper age limit exists since these activities are suitable for adults.

People of all ages appreciate the time spent in centering exercises and they report: "I like it a lot because it makes me feel relaxed." "I want to stay longer because no one is hassling me there." "I have more friends now and get along better with some that I didn't before." "I get along better with my parents now." In addition to the benefits to the children, teachers doing this work usually feel that the teachers are the primary learners since they are the ones who gain so much insight from the children's participation. Two excellent books on this topic are as follows

Harmin, M. & Sax, S. (1977). *A peaceable classroom: Activities to calm and free student energies.* Minneapolis: Winston Press.

Hendricks, G. & Wills, R. (1976). *The centering book.* Englewood Cliffs, N.J.: Prentice-Hall.

PREPARATION FOR CENTERING EXERCISES

To prepare class members for centering a necessary procedure is to create an environment of support and trust. Suggestions are provided in chapter 43, Guidelines for Classroom Discussions, which will help develop this environment. Exercises found in the book *100 Ways to Enhance Self-Concept in the Classroom* by Jack Canfield and Harold Wells and published in Englewood Cliffs, N.J., by Prentice Hall, in 1976 are very useful for preparation.

The authors are grateful for permission to use the many ideas in this chapter taken from various papers by Jack Canfield and Paula Klimek. To obtain a catalogue of Jack Canfield's books and tapes write to Self-Esteem Seminars, 17156 Palisades Circle, Pacific Palisades, CA. 90272.

Canfield and Klimek wrote that the first difficulty may be getting the children to close their eyes. They stated that the media are providing the tools: for example, ask, "What's this thing called 'the force' in *Star Wars*? How does Luke communicate with it? How does it help him?" And the ask, "Would you like to have this kind of experience?" Always the response is an overwhelming, "Yes!" Then you give the ground rules including closing the eyes. The children are more than ready.

CLASSROOM ATMOSPHERE

Safe Space

1. Protected environment: quiet room where children can feel relaxed and not criticized or judged for performance

2. Sign on door: "Do Not Disturb"; "Concentration Training"

3. Intercom turned off or down . . . office alerted

4. Do not do when expecting a bell to ring

5. Temperature regulated for comfort if possible

6. Lights dimmed, shades drawn but not totally dark; night light on if needed

7. Allow time; do not do immediately before a break, lunch, end of day, immediately following a meal since there is a tendency to fall asleep

8. If your room is in a noisy area, you can use white noise to block out much of the sound: air conditioner, fan, recording of seashore or rain

9. You can use relaxing music

Positions

The floor is best, sitting with back straight or lying on floor; loosen tight clothing

Rules

1. Keep eyes closed (okay to keep eyes open if anyone strongly objects to closing); remove contact lenses

2. No talking

3. No leaving the room

4. No touching another class member

5. Okay to fall asleep but it is better to choose not to; snoring is not okay; gently tap or shake anyone snoring

6. Raise hand if need assistance

7. No grades are given on centering processes

8. Do not compare, judge, or analyze other people's images

9. No pressure is exerted to share one's images

10. If an interruption occurs from the loudspeaker, just pretend that it is like a TV commercial. Remember the information if it is personally relevant; forget it if it isn't.

65

EXERCISES IN CENTERING

Exercise 1

One way to start centering is to sit or lie in a comfortable position on the floor with the back straight and relaxed. The teacher says, "Close your eyes. We are going to relax the entire body, one part at a time. Tense your right foot. Relax it. Tense the left foot. Relax it. Tense the right calf. Relax it. Tense the left calf. Relax it. Tense the right thigh, Relax it. Tense the left thigh. Relax it. Tense the right buttocks. Relax it. Tense the left buttocks. Relax it. Tense the stomach. Relax it. Tense the chest. Relax it. Tense the right hand. Relax it. Tense the left hand. Relax it. Tense the right forearm. Relax it. Tense the left forearm. Relax it. Tense the right upper arm. Relax it. Tense the left upper arm. Relax it. Tense the right shoulder. Relax it. Tense the left shoulder. Relax it. Tense the back. Relax it. Tense the neck. Relax it. Tense the face. Relax it. Tense the head. Relax it."

"Now take a very deep breath, hold it for a moment and slowly let it out. All the tensions leave your body as you feel limp and relaxed. Take another deep breath and slowly let it out. Take another deep breath and slowly let it out. You now feel relaxed and your body is still."

"Now that you are quiet, notice your breath as it comes into your body and makes you even more relaxed. Just breathe naturally. You do not have to breathe deeply now. Continue to breathe naturally." (Teacher wait for a few breaths in silence.)

Read the following slowly in an enthusiastic, spontaneous voice. Your voice should not be loud but it also should not be too soft or too relaxed or you will lose your audience.

"You are now at a beautiful lake. It is a nice summer day, not too hot, just right. You are slowly walking on the grass and enjoying just looking at the beauty of the lake. See the trees and the flowers. Bend down and smell some of the flowers. You are getting a little tired so you lie down to rest under a large tree. There is a gentle breeze; feel it on your skin. You feel wonderful. You are looking up through the green leaves on the tree and see the sky above you. The pattern of the green leaves against the blue sky is very beautiful. You feel so peaceful that you fall asleep and take a little nap." (Wait in silence for one or two minutes.) "You awaken from the nap feeling refreshed. You get up and walk over to the shore of the lake. You are feeling happy and you sing a favorite song very softly, just because you are happy. There are some pebbles on the ground. You bend down to get a pebble. The lake is so smooth and you decide to throw the pebble into it. You enjoy seeing the circles in the water that the pebble creates. You throw in another pebble and then another."

"The water looks inviting so you take off your shoes and socks and wade into the water. Feel how cool it is on your warm feet. You stay in the lake for a few minutes and realize that it is now time for you to go home. You walk out of the lake over to your shoes. You wait a few moments until your feet are quite dry and you put on your shoes. You had a very happy, quiet experience and you are feeling very good. You bid goodbye to the beautiful lake and start walking back to your home."

"In just a moment, I'm going to ask you to open your eyes and come back to this room. You will be fully awake and energetic. There is no hurry; you can take as long as you need. Now, open your eyes slowly and come back to this room. Wiggle your fingers and toes and stretch your arms and legs."

"Who would like to share what this experience was like for you?" Have several children share with the entire class. Or, have the class share in groups of three. Canfield also suggested drawing pictures, writing prose or poetry of their experiences before sharing.

Share.

Exercise 2

Start as in Exercise 1 with deep breaths and relaxing the body.

"You are in a beautiful forest. The trees are very tall and beautiful. You find a narrow path and start walking on it. A light rain just finished. As you look above, you see a beautiful rainbow. You stop for a while to watch the rainbow. The colors get even more beautiful as you watch it. You notice some billowy white clouds drifting by slowly. Watch them for a while. You continue walking on the path and you get to a place with five steps going upward. You walk up the steps and continue on the path. Look to your left. See the small waterfall. You stop to watch the water running downward. You are wearing a bathing suit under your clothes so you remove your outer clothing and run under the waterfall. The water feels so good on your body. It is all so beautiful that you feel very happy to be there. You feel refreshed from the water and you continue to walk on the path. Now you come to seven steps going upward. You walk up those steps and continue on the path. You see two tree stumps a little way down the path and you walk up to them and sit down on one to rest for a while. It is so nice and quiet and you are enjoying just sitting there. Feel the warmth and peace going through your body."

"Soon you see a person in the distance walking toward you. At first you cannot tell whether the person is a man or a woman. As the person gets closer you see that it is a man. He is quite old and looks very kind. He smiles as he gets close to you and he asks if you would mind if he would sit on the other tree stump. You tell him that would be all right with you. You now realize that he is a very nice old man and he looks very wise. He tells you that you can ask him for an answer to some question that you were wondering about. You think for a while." (Teacher wait for a few moments.) "You now ask him a question. The wise old man thinks for a few moments as you both sit quietly. He finally tells you the answer to the question you were wondering about. You feel very good to have that answer and you thank him. He walks away and you think about the answer to your question." (Teacher wait for a few moments.) "Now, you will slowly come back to this room and open your eyes, feeling wide awake, and relaxed. Take as long as you like. Wiggle your fingers and toes."

Share experiences.

Exercise 3

"Close your eyes. Take five very deep breaths. Let your breathing be slow and peaceful."

"We're going to build a quiet place inside our minds. This quiet place, built in your imagination, can be your very own retreat where you can go to get away from worries and pressures or to think about something on which you need to work. This will be a quiet center to which you can go whenever you need rest and peace. You can build it either indoors or outdoors, whichever you would enjoy and wherever you would be more comfortable."

"Picture in your mind's eye the shape of the area or room. Is it the shape of a circle? Or, a square or a rectangle? What does the floor look like? Is it a thick carpet, or grass, or sand? What color is the floor? Let your imagination flow freely, creating your special place as a center of restful beauty, just as you want it to be. Have a place for you to sit or lie down—a chair, couch, perhaps a mat on the ground or carpet on the floor. You might want to put in a work area which has a desk, computer, automatic typewriter, magic blackboard, encyclopedias, reference books. You can use this area for study. You can even have a magic elevator or escalator to bring anyone you want to be with you. Put in the finishing touches: drapes, pictures if it is indoors or trees, plants, flowers if it is outdoors. Perhaps you wish to add a stereo to bring soft music. When your place is complete, let your body and mind enjoy the peace, rest, the deep relaxation that it provides for you. Stay there in your space and find your own inner silence. Let your breath be soft and slow. Relax your jaws, keeping your teeth apart. Relax . . . relax . . ." (Pause a few minutes; for older or quieter persons wait for 10 minutes).

"Now in your imagination, let your eyes drift slowly about your quiet place. See the restful beauty that you have created. Tell yourself that you are leaving for a time but the place will always be there for your return whenever you wish. You could build a special entry that only lets you enter. This is your own space for peace, quiet and deep relaxation, or to work on some thoughts. Know that you can go there whenever you wish."

"Very slowly get ready to open your eyes and come back to now. You will be wide awake. Move your body and touch the floor."

Share.

Exercise 4

With each of the following exercises assist the class members in getting ready: sitting or lying with back straight, close eyes, help them relax, and so forth.

"It is a beautiful day and we are going to take a walk through the woods. See the back of your own hand. Notice the fine hairs, the skin texture, the nails, the knuckles. Now picture your hand resting on the bark of some tree trunk. Notice the color of the bark, the patterns in the bark, the size of the tree."

"Look around and notice other trees. Many of them are very tall. Notice how the pattern of the bark is different on each tree trunk. Notice how good the air feels. Feel the breeze sighing and rustling through the leaves overhead. There are birds singing rather close to you and some are in the distance. You can catch a glimpse of blue sky and also an occasional fluffy cloud."

"We're going to take a walk in the woods along the path that is nearby. It is so beautiful here, so quiet and peaceful, so restful. You are happy and comfortable, very relaxed. You feel at one with nature and in harmony with all that surrounds you. Feel the deep, cool, soft moss carpeting on the forest floor. It is a rather warm day and your feet welcome the coolness of the soft moss. Do you hear the sound of the brook that is near you? It is a peaceful sound. If you turn your head to the left you can see the brook. The path is leading you through a thicket of trees. You go through them. Pretty soon you see a small, quiet lake. It is so peaceful and beautiful here. Sit down on the shore of the lake. Not a breath of wind is stirring here. The lake reminds you of a smooth mirror. Enjoy the warm sunshine on your body. It comforts and relaxes you. Look into the surface of this small lake. What you see reflected is the highest that you can become. It is what you are becoming. Look at the reflection and make it your highest ideal for you. See all that you can become. It is reflected as you look in to the surface of this small lake. Rest here a while in this lovely silent place." (Teacher wait a few moments.) "When you are ready come back to the room and slowly open your eyes. You will be wide awake. Take the time you need. Let your hands touch the floor around you."

Share.

Exercise 5

Imagine yourself on a wide deserted beach. The sand is soft and white. You are stretched out for a sun bath. As the sun warms your body, you close your eyes. You feel the sun's rays penetrating every part of your body and you let go of every tight muscle and sink into the soft sand." (Pause) "As your mind becomes still you hear the waves rolling gently on to the shore. It is low tide and the waves make only a gentle sound as they curl across the wet sand and sink back into the ocean. Your breath becomes slow and regular and seems to flow in and out to the rhythm of the sea. The warmth of the sun blankets your whole body and you become more and more relaxed. The warmth reaches every spot on your body and relaxes your neck, jaws, shoulders, back, arms, and hands and seem to say, 'Let go-Let go'."

"You are now one with the sand, the sea, the sun. Let the sand hold you; feel the soft cooling breeze playing across your body as you sink into the silence of your own deep relaxation." (Pause for two to ten minutes depending on the age and quietness of the group.) "Slowly open your eyes and be wide awake; feel the energy flowing through your body—the energy you absorbed from the sun, the energy source of our world."

Share.

Exercise 6

"Find yourself in a beautiful garden. The sun is shining and the sky is a beautiful clear blue. The air is soft, balmy and very clear. The garden is large and has many lovely paths winding through the many different flower beds. You marvel at the many different kinds of gorgeous flowers and you notice the colors seem unusually bright and varied. As you slowly drift along the garden paths, you notice the delicate blending of the many scents from the various kinds of blossoms. Soon you come to a bed of your favorite flowers. You are very happy to discover them and you lean nearer to the blossoms to get a close look at the lovely petal formations. You smile with joy. You carefully pick one blossom and hold it close to your nose. You gently sniff and feel the scent penetrate your nostrils. Your nose is filled with the scent. As you inhale that delicate scent you can feel it going to every cell in your body. You are feeling wonderfully alive and relaxed. Stay with that good feeling for a few moments." (Pause) "When you are ready slowly open your eyes. You will be wide awake. You may take as much time as you need. Move your body and feel the floor beneath you."

Share.

66

LIFE
PURPOSE
FANTASY

Paula Klimek and Jack Canfield developed this fantasy which is taken from their paper: "Discovering Your Radiant Self: A Transpersonal Approach to Expressing Your Potential," *Elementary School Guidance and Counseling*, December, 1979. They stated that they have used it effectively with sixth grade children and with adults as well, and that it is a very powerful experience which can help persons become aware of their essential nature, their highest potential, their unique gift to the world, and their life purpose. As young people enter adolescence, they often become confused and are usually unable to get clear answers from parents or teachers about many basic questions of life: Who am I? What difference does my life make? What do I really want to do? Will I and do I make a difference? When these questions are addressed from within oneself, from inner wisdom, remarkable awareness and transformation occurs.

These activities must not be sprung on the class members without preparation. You must first create an environment of increased trust and mutual support among the persons through classroom discussions and after doing many of the preceding centering exercises.

Before conducting this guided fantasy, a class discussion must be conducted on what is meant by the term "Life Purpose." Just have the class brainstorm what the concept means to them. The class member pre-session comments are usually very career-related; the post-session comments are much different. The latter statements are more in depth; the process helps persons become intuitively aware of their unique gifts with which they could make a contribution and be in service to others.

After you are satisfied that the class members have an adequate understanding of the concept, ask them to find a comfortable position, sitting or lying down with backs straight and eyes closed. Help them relax, then begin the fantasy. Wait a few moments between sections for the children to process their thoughts.

"We are about to review your life. You will begin to experience yourself going backwards in time. Begin by thinking about this day. Go back to when you woke up this morning . . . What have you done all day? . . . Now look back at the past week . . . the past month . . . the past year . . . Review the significant events of this time . . . What did you look like? . . . Who was with you? . . . Where have you been? . . . Try not to get caught up in any particular event or to be judgmental. Allow your life to pass by as if you were watching a movie . . . Now go back to your previous grade . . . To your elementary grades . . . To the primary grades . . . To the time you first entered school . . . To being a young child . . . A two-year old . . . A baby . . . And now go back in time as far as your fantasy will take you. You are about to meet a special guide, your own special guide. A guide whom you may ask what the purpose of your life is . . . Meet this guide and pose your question . . . Feel your guide's unconditional love and strength and beauty . . . Let whatever happens happen . . . Communicate with your guide in whatever way possible . . . Listen to your guide for a gift to represent your purpose, your essence, your unique gifts, your genius . . . Now you must begin your journey back. Say farewell to your guide knowing you may visit your guide at any time . . . Begin to make your journey back bringing with you both your life purpose and the gift from your experience. Make your journey through time, through your birth, your infancy, your childhood, and finally to the present moment in this room . . . When you are ready, open your eyes; you will be fully alert and awake, feeling refreshed and rested. Remain silent and draw and write about your experience. We will share our journey after a few minutes." You can allow five minutes to draw, five minutes to write, and ten minutes to share in groups of three.

The responses to this work have covered a wide range of expression. The drawings have contained many moving archetypal symbols, such as light, rainbows, the sun, flowing robes, mountains, meadows, flowers, animals, and so forth. The writing has been poetic, creative, beautifully simplistic and yet full and rich, as in the following responses: " I felt like I was very special." "Everything was very clear." "I could relate to my guide quite well."

Our task as educators is to help pupils find their special gifts, their potential. The artistic expression can be a very deep experience. Klimek and Canfield caution teachers to not take these ideas simply as recipes in a cookbook and suggest instead that teachers use their own creative self to improvise, to experiment, and to have fun. And, at the very least teachers will have regular periods of silence in the classroom, and in these days of stress and burnout, that's a nice thing to look forward to.

SUMMARY

This chapter offers a new perspective in education in which a holistic approach is suggested. In the past schools only offered intellectual procedures—reading, writing, computing, debating, analyzing, and so forth. Most schools have not been going beyond the intellectual and into the intuitive and creative processes.

With the challenges of complicated technology, children must be inspired to use their creativity and imagination for future work. Now and in the future a great need exists to be able to take present knowledge and extend it creatively and intuitively to fit new and complicated situations. The use of centering exercises at an early age can be one of the most useful tools offered in our school. They not only can assist future generations to tap into problems of high technology with their intuition and creativity but the relaxation and ability to get in touch with one's inner resources are also instruments for improving human relationships. Thus, the improved cooperation between teacher and child can help alleviate our frequent classroom rebellions.

What becomes apparent is that we need to offer both the basics of knowledge and self-actualizing perspectives of wisdom in our classrooms—a holist approach.

NOTE: Material used with permission. To obtain a catalog of Jack Canfield's books and tapes on Self-Esteem, write to Self-Esteem Seminars, 17156 Palisades Circle, Pacific Palisades, CA 90272.

O

CORSINI
4R SCHOOLS

PRELIMINARY NOTE

Adlerians use the verb *discipline* to describe a process of making a person a *disciple,* and so *to discipline a person* is to train, educate, develop, instruct, teach, or edify someone to think, feel and act as you do. Consequently, in this section *to discipline a child in school* means to deal with children so that they will accept the values and copy the behavior of their teachers. We do not mean scolding, threatening, demeaning, embarrassing, spanking or other psychologically or physically painful methods, that Adlerians reject as useless and harmful, even thought they may appear to work for a short time in some cases. Punishment of any kind in schools can break the spirit of children, make them into sneaks and liars, get them to hate school, and can generate attitudes that will later harm both them and others. We believe that teachers use such ineffective and inefficient methods reluctantly and out of desperation, simply because they don't know what else to use.

Adlerian disciplinary methods are intended to achieve the goals of immediate good behavior as well as long-term good behavior by means that are always based on mutual respect employing logical and natural consequences as their vehicle of transfer of information.

67

THE C4R
SYSTEM

HISTORY OF
ADLERIAN SCHOOLING METHODS

Alfred Adler, soon after World War I, began to counsel
parents and teachers about dealing effectively with children,
and as part of his procedures he did public demonstrations of
his methods, which showed that even very difficult children
could be turned about from useless to useful behavior. Two of
Alfred Adler's associates, Oskar Spiel and Ferdinand Birnbaum,
after working with Adler for years, decided to start their own
school based on Adlerian principles which they ran from 1931
until 1934, when due to "the resurgence of authoritarian
regimes which looked unfavorably upon educational experi-
ments" (Lewis Way, 1962, p. 14), the school was closed as a
result of Nazi influence in Austria.

Essentially, this experimental school (Spiel, 1947, Seidler
1930, 1936) was primarily concerned with handling difficult
and disadvantaged children. The faculty attempted to understand children, encourage them, and give them loving support.
In the various readings one sees the general Adlerian concept of
trying to be firm and fair, operating according to principles of
mutual respect.

Rudolf Dreikurs in his educational efforts expressed in his book *Psychology in the Classroom* (1957), and later in his co-authored book with Bronia Grunwald and Floy Pepper, *Maintaining Sanity in the Classroom* (1971) his interest in helping teachers to understand and deal effectively with difficult children.

Adler, Speil and Dreikurs concentrated on how teachers and parents could best handle individual children. They took what is known as the *ideographic position,* trying to understand and to deal with individual children. This point of view is discussed elsewhere in this book.

THE CORSINI 4-R SCHOOL SYSTEM

In contrast to the point of views of Spiel and of Dreikurs, et. al, who were concerned with how individual teachers could handle situations with children, Raymond Corsini was concerned primarily with the prevention of problems in schools. He assumed the so-called nomothetic position, not having particular concern with individual children but rather with the general relationships between four classes of people in schools: Parents—teachers—administrators—children.

He concluded that schools themselves were often the primary cause of certain problems that children demonstrated, and that it was wrong to attempt to blame children for behavior problems if the school was the cause of the problems. For this reason he attempted to devise a whole school system which would develop a generation of children who would be disciplined by the nature of the treatment they would receive so that they would be unlikely to become disciplinary problems either in the school or in life after school.

Corsini argued that the traditional school system was philosophically and theoretically undemocratic with children sentenced to attend an institution in which they had no choice of teachers, rooms, subjects levels of study. The right thing to do was to start a new kind of school in which children would be treated with respect, and therefore would be expected to no longer rebel or to behave in useless manners.

In traditional schools, children are treated no differently than dogs sent to obedience schools: forced to obey and never to ask the reason why, just do what they were told.

Corsini concluded that children should be given: (1) primary responsibility for their own education, (2) opportunities to receive advice from self-selected faculty members, and (3) opportunity to learn the academic basics and also useful skills in the area of work and society to best prepare them for the real world of work and play. Schools were to be child-centered with adults serving them, rather than the other way around. Corsini argued for the basic wisdom of children, that they knew best what, when, and how to learn. Teachers were to offer children an education but not force them or coerce them to learn. Children had a right to learn or to not learn whatever they wanted.

This point of view relative to children is similar to milieu therapy for persons generally considered incompetent to make good decisions. Joshua Bierer (1951), an English Adlerian psychiatrist, has organized social clubs within mental hospitals to be run by the inmates, independently of staff.

Adults in C4R schools act as providers and children act as customers. In a C4R school there is equality which extends to every aspect. But what about discipline in the narrow sense of dealing with misbehaving children, those who do not adjust, or cooperate? We shall discuss this in a later section of this chapter.

Some Aspects of the C4R System of Schooling

Perhaps we can best summarize the C4R system by making a number of short statements. Almost every one of these points differs from conventional traditional schooling methods, and the reader is invited to consider the logic of each of these against the logic of methods ordinarily used by traditional schools.

1. Admission to a school is based on an understanding and an acceptance of how the school works, with

parents and children having veto power regarding admission.

2. Children compete with themselves, not with others.

3. Studying and homework are up to the children.

4. Children can learn when, how and what they want.

5. Feedback information about learning is given as soon as possible.

6. Every child has a faculty advisor of own choice.

7. A few fair rules are impartially enforced.

8. Children have opportunities to develop special talents.

9. Faculty can teach special creative subjects.

10. Children can learn special creative subjects.

11. Learning is a privilege and not an obligation.

12. Teachers have academic freedom regarding how to teach assigned subjects.

13. Teachers have the right to keep out or remove children from their classrooms.

14. A C4R school teaches academics, creative subjects and socialization skills.

15. Children have freedom to not learn what they don't want.

16. Evaluations are objective.

17. Teachers can establish unique classroom rules.

18. Peer teaching is encouraged.

19. Academic progress reports go to children rather than to parents.

20. Individualized pacing of learning is possible.

21. Teachers are responsible for teaching, children for learning.

22. Emphasis is on the development of a successful child in terms of society, family, work.

23. Community resources are used.

24. Children are advised to study at the growing edge of their abilities.

25. Faculty has three functions: Academic teaching, Creative teaching and Socialization training.

26. Children are encouraged to have independent class councils.

27. There are never rewards, honors, or extraneous motivators.

28. There are never criticisms, warnings or other forms of punishment.

29. The school operates on the basis of natural and logical consequences.

30. The goals of the school are the development of the four Rs of Responsibility, Respect, Resourcefulness and Responsiveness (social interest).

Each of these thirty points call for considerable amount of explanation available in a number of sources. (See Corsini, 1977, 1979; Manaster & Corsini, 1982; Simpkins, 1985.)

How a C4R School Works

Below might be a simplified statement given to parents or children about how the C4R system works as a whole:

You have the right not to enter this school, but first you should know how it works. Essentially, every parent is expected to take a free of charge parenting course we will give to help you understand how to deal with your children in the home and in relation to the school. In our school children will be given a variety of tests and basic information about how the school works, and will be advised relative to what levels on the academic ladder they should study—in terms of their aptitudes and abilities. Children will have the freedom to select a teacher-advisor of their own choice. They will have to be in a homeroom the first period of the day but after that they have freedom to choose where they would want to be and choices always include the library, the study hall and classes. Academic subjects are taught in weekly units, and testing is objectively done. Reports of tests passed are given to children weekly. In addition to the usual academic subjects, there are two other programs: one called Socialization and the other Creative teaching. Children will have all kinds of choices where to go and what to do.

We have a specific disciplinary program which contains only three rules and four consequences for violations. Some children have been in one of our schools for eight years and have never had a violation.

The Specific Disciplinary Program

A C4R school has only three school rules but many classroom rules. Violations of any classroom rule leads to the use of School Rule 3. Violations of school rules leads to one of four consequences.

To make this a bit clearer: every teacher can establish idisyncratic classroom rules. Say one teacher wants no gum chewing, another wants no whispering, another wants no loud talking, and so forth. Should any child violate one of the teacher's rules, there is only one consequence if the teacher wishes to use the consequence—the GO! signal, which happens to be rule 3 of the school rules.

So, let us begin with the three school rules which are so simple that normal 4 year old children understand them.

1. Never do anything that could be dangerous or damaging.

2. Always be in a supervised place or en route to such a place.

3. If a teacher gives you the GO signal, leave the room instantly and silently.

Now, a bit of discussion about the whole matter of specific discipline in a C4R school.

First, it is important to realize that no child ever has to go to any classroom, or to the library or to the study hall, but enters such rooms voluntarily. Equally important is to know that every child once in any of these rooms can leave without asking permission. So entering a room or leaving a room is completely up to a child. No child is ever imprisoned in a room in a C4R school.

Second, it is important to know that every teacher has the right to keep any child from entering any room she is in charge of and the right to send any child out of the room.

These two rights of children to try to enter or to leave and of teachers to prevent children from entering their rooms or sending them out means that at any time every single child is in that particular room on the basis of mutual decision: the child's and the teachers.

Now, this is a most important matter, because every child is free to decide which room to try to enter and is free to leave at any time, THERE IS ABSOLUTELY NO REASON EVER TO MISBEHAVE IN A CLASSROOM, THE LIBRARY OR THE STUDY HALL.

And if a child does not want to enter any of these rooms, he or she can go to the office and just wait there in silence or if he or she does not like the shcool, can ask to be taken out of the school, and this request is to be granted immediately without question.

Now, one may ask: Why might a teacher either prevent a child from entering her room or send a child out? And the answer is simple: because the teacher does not want that particular child to enter her room or wants the child to leave the room. Let us give some examples:

Mrs. Hutch, a teacher, has had nothing but trouble with Jim. He has constantly been a source of annoyance to her. On the particular day once again, he is whispering and giggling, interfering with the learning of other children around him and bothering her. What can she do?

In a C4R school, the only one thing the teacher can do is to point her hand at the child and then at the door. *This is Rule 3—the GO signal.* It means: *Leave this room immediately and in silence.* Say the teacher is prohibited from telling Jim to stop, or telling him he must sit somewhere else, etc. The only thing he/she can do, if the decision is to take action, is to get Jim's attention, and then point his/her hand to him in silence. He must now leave the room without saying a word. That is the end of the incident. Frequently other children are not even aware of the use of the GO signal.

Jim, now outside of the room, what can he do, where can he go? His options are: (1) try to return to the classroom or (2) go somewhere else.

Say that he decides to return. As soon as he closes the door behind him, he reenters the room. Now, the teacher has two options: (1) to let him in, in which case he/she does nothing or (2) to refuse to let him in, in which case the teacher again points to him, this meaning: "I don't want you in my class this period." Jim must find another place to go to. Where can he go?

He has several options: (1) the library, which is always open during classes, (2) the study hall, or (3) any other classroom. So, let us follow Jim to see what might happen. He goes to the library, but sees a sign on the door: LIBRARY FULL. DO NOT ENTER. "Rats," he says, and goes to the study hall. As he opens the door, the teacher in charge, points her hand at him, which informs him that he can not enter the study hall. Barred from three rooms, he goes to a classroom, looks at the schedule posted outside of the door and he sees that the subject being taught is mathematics 15. Since he is studying mathematics at level 83, he goes to the next room, checks the schedule, see the subject is science 188. He is at science 72, but he figures he might as well go into this room. He opens the door, the teacher looks at him, but says nothing, whereupon Jim who has now found a safe harbor, takes a seat.

What is important to understand is that the rights of everyone have been upheld: the original teacher, Mary, as well as the rest of the class by Jim being sent out of the room. When Jim tried to come back into the room, the teacher did not want to give him another chance. The librarian had decided that the number of students in the library had reached the saturation point and so had put a FULL sign on the door. And the teacher in charge of the study hall, knowing Jim to be a persistent trouble maker, refused to let him in. So, some adults had protected their turf, exiling Jim either because of his misbehavior or their perception of him as a trouble maker. Finally, he did find a teacher who allowed him to enter her room.

But suppose no teacher would let him in (this has actually happened)—what then? He can now go to the office, where he can remain the rest of the period. At the bell, he can go wherever he wishes.

Consequences of Violations

Suppose in the first instance, when the teacher pointed Jim out because he was bothering Mary, Jim on seeing a finger pointed at him, exclaimed "Why?" This "Why?" would be a violation of Rule 3. Now, the teacher must write out a violation report and give it to Jim to take to the office. At the office, the clerk asks Jim whether he did in fact violate Rule 3. (About 95% of children admit violations.) If the answer is YES, then a note is put on the child's disciplinary card and the chid is free to go wherever he wishes. If the answer is NO, the child is kept in the office so that the principal (or whoever handles disciplinary problems in the school) can meet with the child and the complaining teacher, to hear both sides. Then the principal decides whether or not to let the disciplinary mark remain on the child's record.

If in any academic year a child has three disciplinary violations, a conference is arranged with the principal, the TA, and the child to find out if possible, the cause of the repeated violations, and what can be done about stopping them. Should there be a sixth violation, another conference is called and this time the parents attend for the same reasons as before. There is never any suggestion of any punishment, the issue is solving the disciplinary problem that Jim presents.

At the sixth violation meeting, the principal asks Jim and his parents whether they would want to transfer to another school, on the argument that perhaps this is not the right kind of school for Jim. Usually, they want to remain in the school. A seventh and an eighth violation are handled in the usual fashion. But at the ninth, tenth, and eleventh violations, there are one-day suspensions. Should a twelfth violation occur within the academic year, the principal generates a committee of three faculty members to study the situation, interviewing anyone they wish: Jim, his TA, the parents, other children, etc., and then they prepare a report to the principal recommending either expulsion or giving Jim another chance.

The principal makes the final decision. He/she may decide that this is not the right kind of school for Jim, in which case, the child is expelled, which ordinarily means transferring him to another school. Should the principal give him another chance, then should Jim have an additional violation that year, once again a new committee is established and again a recommendation goes to the principal.

This system has a considerable number of advantages over either a disciplinary program that does not have specific rules or a disciplinary program with dozens of rules. These three rules are simple enough for three year old children to understand, and broad enough to cover most violations. In the first year of a C4R school, up to five per cent of children will be transferred to other schools, but as time goes on the percentage drops to about one per cent.

An important final point: say Jim transfers from the Lincoln school to the Hoover school, the principal of the Hoover school now has the right to refer any child from that school to the Lincoln school. This exchange of "bad apples" can be of value to both children and both schools. We have found that some children who do not get along in a C4R school will do well in a traditional school, and vice versa. So, both principals will be happy that troublemakers have been reduced.

RESULTS

In 1986 nine principals of C4R schools were asked to rate their schools on a scale of one to 10 on six aspects: Learning, Discipline, School Spirit, Parent Attitudes, Faculty Attitudes, Children Attitudes.

Ratings of Principals on Seven Areas

(Principals)	1	2	3	4	5	6	7	8	9
Learning	7	8	5	7	7	8	8	7	8
Discipline	9	9	10	8	9	10	9	8	10
School Spirit	9	9	5	9	8	9	9	8	10
Parent Attitude	8	8	5	9	7	8	8	6	10
Faculty Attitude	9	9	8	9	9	10	10	8	10
Student Attitude	9	8	9	9	10	9	8	9	9
Overall Gain	9	9	7	9	9	8	8	8	9

Summary of Results

Ratings could run from 1 to 10. Doing just as well as a traditional school would get a rating of 5. Ratings below a 5 meant that the C4R school did not do as well as the traditional school. Ratings above 5 meant that in the principal's opinion the C4R school did better than the traditional school. Thus, a rating of 10 might mean a 100% improvement.

1. Learning: In the judgment of the principals, except for one who rated learning the same in both schools, children learn more in the C4R System than in the traditional system.

2. Discipline: The ratings indicate a high degree of satisfaction with discipline, an aspect which is very important to both teachers and parents.

3. School Spirit: With the exception of one who rated this aspect the same as the traditional school the principals rated this aspect high (from 8 to 10).

4. Parent's attitudes: Only one principal rated this aspect a 5. The other principals thought that parents liked and approved of this system to a greater degree than the traditional school.

5. Faculty Attitude: This was the highest rating obtained. Notice that principal No. 3 who gave a rating of 5 for learning and for parent attitudes, gave a rating of 8 for faculty attitude. The others also rated this high, from 8 to 10.

6. Childrens Attitude: This aspect was given high rating, from 8 to 10.

It is most gratifying to the children, staff and parents that children and teachers enjoy being in school, the discipline and school spirit are excellent and in general the children are learning more than in the traditional school.

BIBLIOGRAPHY

Adler, A. (1927). *Understanding human nature.* New York: Greenberg.

Adler, A. (1930). *Guiding the child.* New York: Greenberg.

Adler, A. (1938). *Social interest: A challenge to mankind.* London: Faber and Faber.

Albert, L. (1982). *Coping with kids.* New York: E.P. Dutton.

Ansbacher, H.L., & Ansbacher, R.R., (Eds.). (1956). *The individual psychology of Alfred Adler.* New York: Harper & Row.

Asselin, C., Nelson, T., & Platt, J. (1975). *Teacher study group leader's manual.* Chicago, IL: Alfred Adler Institute.

Bayard, R.T., & Bayard, J. (1981). *How to deal with your acting-up teenager: Practical self-help for desperate parents.* New York: M. Evans.

Beecher, W., & Beecher, M. (1955). *Parents on the run.* New York: Julian Press.

Benson, H. (1975). *The relaxation response.* New York: William Morrow.

Benson, H. (1984). *Beyond the relaxation response.* New York: New York Times Book.

Bierer, J. (1951). *The day hospital, an experiment in social-psychiatry and syntho-analytic psychotherapy.* London: H.K. Lewis.

Borba, M., & Borba, C. (1978). *Self-esteem: A classroom affair (101) Ways to help children like themselves.* Minneapolis, MN: Winston Press.

Borba, M., & Borba, C. (1978 & 1982). *Self-esteem: A classroom affair, Vols. 1 and 2.* Minneapolis: Winston Press.

Branden, N. (1983). *If you could hear what I cannot say.* New York: Bantam Books.

Brassington, R. (1982, December). The changing family constellation in single parent families. *Individual Psychology, 38,* No. 4. 369-379.

Burt, M.S., & Burt, R. (1983). *What's special about our stepfamily?* New York: Doubleday.

Canfield, J., & Wells, H. (1976). *100 ways to enhance self-concept in the classroom.* Englewood Cliffs, NJ: Prentice-Hall.

Carkhuff, R.R., Berenson, D.H., & Pierce, R.M. (1977). *The skills of teaching: Interpersonal skills.* Amherst, MA: Human Resource Development Press.

Carlson, J. (1978). *The basics of discipline.* Coral Springs, FL: CMTI Press.

Cater, M. (1990). *An Action Guide for Effective Discipline in the Home and School.* Muncie, IN: Accelerated Development.

Cihak, M.K., & Heron, B.J. (1980). *Games children should play.* Glenview, IL: Scott-Foresman.

Clarke, J.I. (1978). *Self-esteem: A Family affair.* Minneapolis, MN: Winston Press.

Clemes, H., & Bean, R. (1981). *Self-esteem: The key to your child's well-being.* New York: Putnam.

Corsini, R.J. (1977). Individual education. *Journal of Individual Psychology, 33* (22), 295-349.

Corsini, R.J. (1979). Individual education. In E. Ignas and R.J. Corsini (Eds), *Alternative education systems.* Itasca, IL: F.E. Peacock.

Davis, C.M. (1928). *American Journal of Disease of Children,* pp. 36, 651-79.

Dewey, E.A., (1978). *Basic applications of Adlerian Psychology.* Coral Springs, FL: CMTI Press.

Dinkmeyer, D. (1970 & 1973). *Developing understanding of self and others, DUSO-1, DUSO-2.* Circle Pines, MN: American Guidance Service.

Dinkmeyer, D. (1977). *The basics of self-acceptance.* Coral Springs, FL: CMTI Press.

Dinkmeyer, D., & Dreikurs, R. (1979). *Encouraging children to learn: The encouragement process.* NY: Elsevier-Dutton.

Dinkmeyer, D., & Losoncy, L. (1980). *The encouragement book.* Englewood Cliffs, NJ: Prentice-Hall.

Dinkmeyer, D., & Losoncy, L. (1980). *The encouragement book: Becoming a positive person.* Englewood Cliffs, NJ: Prentice-Hall.

Dinkmeyer, D., & McKay, G. (1973). *Raising a responsible child.* New York: Simon and Schuster.

Dinkmeyer, D., & McKay, G. (1976). *Systematic training for effective parenting.* Circle Pines, MN: American Guidance Services.

Dinkmeyer, D., & McKay, G. (1982). *Systematic training for effective parenting: The parent's handbook, rev. ed.* Circle Pines, MN: American Guidance Service.

Dinkmeyer, D., & McKay, G. (1983). *Systematic training for effective parenting of teens: The parent's guide.* Circle Pines, MN: American guidance Service.

Dinkmeyer, D., McKay, G., & Dinkmeyer, D., Jr. (1980). *Systematic training for effective teaching. Teacher's resource book.* Circle Pines, MN: American Guidance Service.

Dinkmeyer, D., McKay, G.D., Dinkmeyer, D., Jr., Dinkmeyer, J.S., & McKay, J.L. (1987). *The effective parent.* Circle Pines, MN: American Guidance Service.

Dinkmeyer, D., McKay, G.D., Dinkmeyer, D., Jr., Dinkmeyer, J.S., & McKay, J.L. (1987). *The next step: Effective parenting through problem solving.* Circle Pines, MN: American Guidance Service.

Dreikurs, R. (1935). *An introduction to individual psychology.* London: Kegan Paul.

Dreikurs, R. (1950). *Fundamentals of Adlerian Psychology.* New York: Greenberg.

Dreikurs, R. (1957). *Psychology in the classroom.* New York: Harper-Row.

Dreikurs, R. (1958). *The challenge of parenthood, rev. ed.* New York: Duell, Sloan & Pearce.

Dreikurs, R. (1968). *Psychology in the classroom: A manual for teachers, 2nd ed.* New York: Harper & Row.

Dreikurs, R. (1971). *Social equality: The challenge of today.* Chicago, IL: Henry Regnery.

Dreikurs, R., & Cassel, P. (1972). *Discipline without tears.* Ontario, Canada: The Alfred Adler Institute.

Dreikurs, R., Corsini, R.J., Lowe, R., & Sonstegard, M. (1959). *Adlerian family counseling.* Eugene, OR: University of Oregon Press.

Dreikurs, R., Gould, S., & Corsini, R.J. (1974). *Family council.* Chicago, IL: Regnery.

Dreikurs, R., & Grey, L. (1968). *Logical consequences: A new approach to discipline.* New York: Hawthorn Books.

Drekurs, R., & Grey, L. (1970). *A parent's guide to child discipline.* New York: Hawthorn Books.

Dreikurs, R., Grunwald, B., & Pepper, F. (1971). *Maintaining sanity in the classroom.* New York: Harper & Row.

Dreikurs, R., Grunwald, B., & Pepper, F. (1980). *Maintaining sanity in the classroom, 2nd ed.* New York: Harper & Row.

Dreikurs, R., & Soltz, V. (1964). *Children: The challenge.* New York: Hawthorn Books.

Dreyer, S.S. (1977, Vol. 1; 1980, Vol. 2). *The bookfinder: A guide to children's literature about the needs and problems of youth aged 2-15*. Circle Pines, MN: American Guidance Service.

Druckman, P. (1984). Cited in Erna, Paris. *Stepfamilies: making them work*. New York: Avon.

Einstein, E. (1982). *The stepfamily: Living, loving, and learning*. New York: Macmillan.

Feshbach, N.D., Feshbach, S., Fauvre, M., & Ballard-Campbell, M. (1983). *Learning to care*. Glenview, IL: Scott-Foresman.

Fluegelman, A. (Ed.). (1976). *The new games book*. New York: Doubleday/ Dolphin.

Gaither, G., & Dobson, S. (1983). *Let's make a memory*. Waco, TX: Word Books.

Ginott, H. (1965). *Between parent and child*. New York: Macmillan.

Glasser, W. (1969). *Schools without failure*. New York: Harper & Row.

Gnagey, W.J. (1965). *Controlling classroom misbehavior*. Washington, DC: National Education Association.

Gordon, T. (1970). *Parent effectiveness training*. New York: Peter H. Wyden.

Gordon, T. (1974). *Teacher effectiveness training*. New York: Peter H. Wyden.

Gould, S. (1977). *Teenagers: The continuing challenge*. New York: Hawthorn Books.

Grey, L. (1972). *Discipline without tyranny*. New York: Hawthorn Books.

Grunwald, B.B., & McAbee, H.B. (1985). *Guiding the family: Practical counseling techniques*. Muncie, IN: Accelerated Development.

Hendricks, G., & Roberts, T.B. (1977). *The second centering book*. Englewood Cliffs, NJ: Prentice-Hall.

Hendricks, G., & Wills, R. (1975). *The centering book*. Englewood Cliffs, NJ: Prentice-Hall.

Klimek, P., & Canfield, J. (1979, December). Discovering your radiant self: A transpersonal approach to expressing your potential. *Elementary School Guidance and Counseling*.

LaPointe, V., & Overtoom, C.G. (1979). *Socio-teleo analysis: Stories for classroom discussion*. Glendale, AZ: Socio-Teleoanalysis.

Losoncy, L. (1977). *Turning people on*. Englewood Cliffs, NJ: Prentice-Hall.

Losoncy, L. (1980). *You can do it: How to encourage yourself.* Englewood Cliffs, NJ: Prentice-Hall.

Manaster, G.J. (1977). *Adolescent development and the life tasks.* Boston: Allyn and Bacon.

Manaster, G., & Corsini, R.J. (1982). *Individual psychology.* Itasca, IL: F.E. Peacock.

McKay, G. (1976). *The basics of encouragement.* Coral Springs, FL: CMTI Press.

Mulac, M. (1956). *Fun and games.* New York: Harper & Row.

Muro, J., & Dinkmeyer, D. (1977). *Counseling in the elementary and middle schools: A pragmatic approach.* Dubuque, IA: Wm. C. Brown.

Neisser, E.G. (1951). *Brothers and sisters.* New York: Harper & Row.

Painter, G. (1971, 1982). *Teach your baby.* New York: Cornerstone Library/ Simon and Schuster.

Popkin, M. (1983). *Active parenting: Teaching courage, cooperation and responsibility.* Atlanta, GA: Active parenting.

Purkey, W. (1970). *Self-concept and school achievement.* Englewood Cliffs, NJ: Prentice-Hall.

Rigney, K., & Corsini, R. (1970). *The family council* (pamphlet). Chicago: Rudolf Dreikurs Unit of the Family Education Association.

Satir, V. (1975). *Self-esteem.* Millbrae, CA: Celestial Arts.

Seidler, R. (1930). The vienna child guidance clinics. In A. Adler Associates, *Guiding the child.* London: Allen and Goodwin.

Seidler, R. (1936). School guidance clinics in vienna. *International Journal of Individual Psychology, 2* (4), 75-78.

Shaftel, F., & Shaftel, G. (1967). *Role playing for social values.* Englewood Cliffs, NJ: Prentice-Hall.

Simon, S.B. (1975). *I am lovable and capable.* Niles, IL: Argus.

Simpkins, A. (1985). Introduction (to individual education). *Individual Psychology, 41,* 3-7.

Spiel, O. (1947). *Discipline without punishment.* Vienna: Verlag für Jugend und Volk.

Spiel, O. (1962). *Discipline without punishment.* London: Faber and Faber.

Way, L. (1962). Introduction. In O. Spiel, *Discipline without punishment rev. ed.* London: Faber and Faber.

Weinstein, M., & Goodman, J. (1980). *Playfair.* San Luis Obispo, CA: Impact Publishers,

Wood, P., & Wood, M. (1979). *Living with teens and surviving.* Toronto: Alfred Adler Institute of Ontario.

CHILDREN'S STORIES

Andersen, H.C. (1945). *The emperor's new clothes.* New York: Oxford University Press.

Andersen, H.C. (1955). *The Princess and the pea.* New York: Oxford University Press.

Andersen, H.C. (1955). *The Ugly Duckling.* New York: Oxford University Press.

Elkin, B. (1954). *The loudest noise in the world.* New York: Viking Press.

Geisel, T.S. (1954). *Horton hatches the egg.* New York: Random House.

Geisel, T.S. (1954). *Horton hears a who.* New York: Random House.

Geisel, T.S. (1958). *Thidwick, the big-hearted moose.* New York: Random House.

Gudrum, T. (1926). *The giant who had no heart in his body. A book of giant stories.* New York: Dodd, Mead.

LaPointe, G.V., & Overtoom, C.G. (1979). *Socio-Teleoanalysis: Stories for classroom discussion.* Published Privately. To obtain a copy, send $5.95 and $1.00 postage to: Socio-Teleoanalysis, P.O. Box 460, Glendale, AZ 85311.

Moore, L. (1952). *The terrible Mr. Twitmeyer.* Eau Claire, WI: E.M. Hale,

Steptoe, J. (1969). *Stevie.* New York: Harper & Row.

Zolotow, C. (1963). *The quarreling book.* New York: Harper & Row.

GUIDED IMAGERY AND MEDIATATION

Demille, R. (1973). *Put your mother on the ceiling: Children's imagination games.* New York: Viking Compass.

Eberle, R.F. (1971). *SCAMPER: Games for imagination and development.* Buffalo, NY: DOK Publishers.

Harmin, M., & Sax, S. (1977). *A peaceable classroom: Activities to calm and free student energies.* Minneapolis, MN: Winston Press.

Hills, C., & Rozman, D. (1978). *Exploring inner space.* Boulder Creek, CA: University of the Trees Press.

Journal of Mental Imagery. Bronx, NY: Brandon House.

Lionni, L. (1967). *Frederick.* New York: Random House.

Lorrayne, H., & Lucas, J. (1974). *The memory book.* New York: Ballantine Books.

Rozman, D. (1975). *Meditating with children.* Boulder Creek, CA: University of the Trees Press.

Samuels, M., & Samuels, N. (1975). *Seeing with the mind's eye: The history, techniques and uses of visualization.* New York: Random House/Bookworks.

Sherman, H. (1978). *How to picture what you want.* New York: Fawcett Goldmedal.

RELAXATION

Davis, M., Eshelman, E.R, & McKay, M. (1980). *The relaxation and stress reduction workbook.* Richmond, VA: Harbinger Publications.

Mason, L.J. (1980). *Guide to stress reduction.* Culver City, CA: Peace Press.

Walker, C. (1975). *Learn to relax.* Englewood Cliffs, NJ: Prentice-Hall.

White, J., & Fadiman, J. (Ed.). (1976). *Relax.* New York: Dell.

ENERGIZERS

Fleugelman, A. (Ed.). (1976). *The new games book.* Garden City, NY: Doubleday, Dolphin.

Ichazo, O. (1976). *Africa psychocalisthenics.* New York: Simon and Schuster.

Weinstein, M., & Goodman, J. (1980). *Playfair.* San Luis Obispo, CA: Impact Publishers.

INDEX

Interaction
  problems 149-84
Interest
  social 12
Involving mother 193-4

J

Judgemental 236

K

Klimek, P. 421, 430, 452
Knowledge 417-8

L

Labeling 280
LaPointe, G.V. 454
LaPointe, V. 313, 452
Late for the show 190
Late to school 51-2
Leader
  democratic, *Figure* 285
Leadership styles
  autocratic 284-5, *Figure* 285
  democratic 284-5, *Figure* 285
Leaving dirty dishes 121-2
Lending money to children 144-5
Life purpose fantasy 430-3
Lionni, L. 455
Listener
  active 237
Listening
  effective 236-7
Living
  problems 45-90
  routine 45-90
Lorrayne, H. 455
Losoncy, L. 450, 452, 453
Love
  unconditional 263
Lowe, R. 451
Lucas, J. 455
Lying
  discussion 225
  examples 226-30
  solution 225-6

M

Manaster, G.J. 453
Marlin, K. 330, 377
Mason, L.J. 455
Masturbator, chronic 206
Mate
  uncooperative 42-3
McAbee, H.B. 452
McKay, G. 314, 450, 451, 453
McKay, J.L. 451
McKay, M. 455
Meat eaten 67-8
Messages
  I will 236
  implementing positive 236
  nonverbal 236
  you should 236
Messiness/clutter 115-24
Messy children 122-4
Methods
  autocratic 279-80
Misbehaving in a restaurant 167
Misbehavior
  goals 355-60
Money and property 134-47
  application 138-40
  discussion 135
  examples 140-5
  problem 134-5
  solution 135-7
Moore, L. 454
Morality 224-31
  discussion 225
  examples 226-30
  lying 224-31
  problem 224-31
  solution 225-6
  stealing 224-31
Moralizing 280
Mulac, M. 453
Muro, J. 453

N

Nap time 90
National Geographic 78
Neisser, E.G. 453
Nelson, T. 449

Genevieve Painter, Ed.D., is a clinical psychologist in Honolulu, maintaining a private practice specializing in cooperative family and classroom relationships. In addition to her doctor of education degree from the University of Illinois she holds a certificate in psychotherapy from the Alfred Adler Institute, Chicago, where she worked with their Community Child Guidance Centers from 1945 to 1960. These centers, directed by the late Dr. Rudolf Dreikurs pioneered in the field of preventive community mental health programs, using group counseling as a major technique for families and schools. Dr. Painter extended these methods of community mental health when, in 1968, she founded the Family Education Association of Champaign County, Illinois, which she directed until 1973, when she moved to Honolulu.

Her pioneering research in infant and early childhood education resulted in her best seller, *Teach Your Baby*, of which Buckminster Fuller stated, "I am confident that this book can make an important breakthrough to human evolution for this critical moment of human existence."

Dr. Painter is listed in the National Registry of Health Providers in Psychology, in *Who's Who in Frontier Science and Technology*, in *Who's Who in American Women*, and in *The World's Who's Who of Women*. She is the mother of two adult sons.

Raymond J. Corsini, Ph.D., received the MS in Education from the City College of New York in 1941. He taught high school French and was an elementary school psychologist before becoming a correctional psychologist in New York, California, and Wisconsin. While working for the Ph.D. at the University of Chicago, he studied parenting counseling with Drs. Rudolf Dreikurs and Harold Mosak at the Alfred Adler Clinic in Chicago. After his degree, he went into private practice as a consulting industrial psychologist.

At age 50, he had a career change and became a professor at the Illinois Institute of Technology and then at the University of California (Berkeley) before moving to Hawaii in 1964, where he started a private practice, and established the Family Education Centers of Hawaii. This is a voluntary organization where he has served as a senior counselor for the past 25 years.

Corsini has written or edited twenty-five books including the best-selling text, *Current Psychotherapies*, and the award-winning, four-volume, *Encyclopedia of Psychology*. He has developed the Corsini Four-R System of Individual Education in use in schools in the United States, Canada, Holland, and Israel.